Meet Carl Ciarfalio
Author of
Stars, Stunts, and Stories
A Hollywood Stuntman's Fall to Fame

I've known Carl for over thirty years now. He's doubled me in several TV episodes and feature films. Carl is a fantastic person, stuntman and actor as well! Glad he makes me look like a star with his great athletic look and glad he makes audiences enjoy me in my dangerous action scenes! I always felt safe. In fact, his knowledge and experience have helped a lot of major actors stay safe and injury-free in dangerous situations. Good luck with your book!

—Lou Ferrigno

I've worked with Carl a number of times, in fight scenes on *Renegade* and also *Falcon Crest*, as well as on a few of my films. As a martial artist, I was always impressed at how graceful he is for a man his size. He moves smoothly and effortlessly in complicated fight choreography as if he's been doing it all his life. One particular stunt on *Falcon Crest* wasn't a fight scene, but a complicated and dangerous rescue scene. It was amazing to watch Carl scale a fire truck ladder up two stories, put Margaret Ladd over his shoulder and haul ass right back down without stopping. All while surrounded by flames. Really impressed the hell outta me.

—Lorenzo Lamas

There isn't enough that I can say about Carl Ciarfalio. Fantastic actor, stuntman, and all-around good guy. He has the ability to move even the Toughest Man Alive to tears when I hear his velvety baritone voice crack jokes at my expense. I always know that he is in my corner, and I'll forever be in his.

—"Judo" Gene LeBell
Stuntman, Martial Artist, "The Godfather of Grappling"

From a past president of the Stuntmen's Association of Motion Pictures, to one of the finest actors on screen, Carl Ciarfalio has seen and done it all! Like watching the great action films he's done, sit back in your seat, hold on to this book and enjoy the ride!

—**Peewee Piemonte**
Director, Two-Time Emmy Winning Stunt Coordinator

In a movie-making career spanning four decades and much of the world, I have met many funny, kind, professional and talented people. Carl Ciarfalio is not one of these things, he is all of them. Carl is an extremely talented raconteur, and his stories are always very entertaining. I am very much looking forward to reading this book. I also hope that by me giving such a glowing reference to my friend's character, any embarrassing or derogatory things said about me in the book will be deleted.

—**Andy Armstrong**
Stunt Coordinator and Action Director

When I think about what it means to me to be a professional stuntman there are some high standards to meet. The first is to have the natural physical talent to perform. The second is developing the mental discipline to train hard to be your personal best. The third is to respect and have the back of your fellow stunt person. And the fourth is to mentor or teach others through your knowledge and experience. Since the day I met him, Carl has always met all of these requirements.

I consider Carl a true friend and a true professional in the stunt business. With this book, he shares his knowledge and experiences with you. Learn and enjoy this opportunity to know the man and what it takes to survive the hard knocks of being a professional stuntman. I happily give this endorsement with lots of laughs and respect.

—**James Lew**
Stuntman, Stunt Coordinator, Fight Choreographer

So you want to REALLY know about the behind the scenes of the film/television industry? Well, you have hit the jackpot with *Stars, Stunts and Stories* by Carl

Ciarfalio! This actor/stuntman/stunt coordinator has literally done and seen it all! What a terrific opportunity to get a real taste of movie making . . . from the hugely hysterical to the remarkably engaging and those moments it's do or die. I dare you film lovers to put this book down without a sweaty palm!

—Julie Michaels
Actress—*Road House*

I feel that *Against All Odds* was a great launch for Carl's career, even though it could have ended it even faster. He did exactly what was asked of him and scared the shit out of all of us. It certainly gave the stunt community a great excuse to bounce his name around. GREAT JOB on the book and good luck my friend!!!

—Gary Davis
Stunt Coordinator, Stuntman

What a treat to read this! The first-chapter story of you being, quite literally, thrown in at the deep end is exactly why a book like this should be a massive success. I bloody loved it and can't wait to read the whole thing. Thank you so much for giving me a glimpse inside what I can safely say will be a winner. My thanks and continued admiration go to you, sir.

—Jon Auty
Owner & Publisher, *Behind The Stunts*

Wouldn't you love to hear the stories of a man with over thirty-five years of experience in the Stunt Industry? Carl Ciarfalio has many to tell. He's an accomplished stuntman, actor and stunt coordinator. He's the "big guy" doing stunts who could act and take a really hard hit. Carl is also the gentleman who helped get stunt men and women recognized by working with Red Bull to start and sponsor the Taurus Stunt Awards. Enjoy this book as I've enjoyed working with Carl through these many years.

—Jeff Imada
Stuntman, Stunt Coordinator, 2nd Unit Director
Stunts Unlimited

I've known Carl for about thirty years, and we became close friends because we were both big stuntmen—at the time there weren't many of us who were both big and athletic. We also had acting ability which increased our potential for getting work. When I wasn't available for a job, I would recommend Carl to the Stunt Coordinator.

When I started Stunt Coordinating myself, I hired Carl on many different films, and he always came through. If it was a stunt that Carl wasn't sure about, we would talk about it. I always liked his honesty. In our business, you have to be honest about what you're doing. You can't let your ego get in the way, and I always appreciated how Carl understood that.

Carl has a great attitude and we would have a lot of laughs on the set, especially when I would sing the Oldies but Goodies. In closing, I would like to say that Carl is a good friend of mine and he takes his job seriously—and that's important in our occupation. He's never let me down on the job, period. Thanks for the many memories, Carl.

—**Allan Graf**
Stunt Coordinator, Stuntman, Actor

Carl and I have been friends for many, many years. I have had the pleasure to work with him and hire him. On *Montana Amazon,* a feature I coordinated, they were looking for someone to not only do the stunt (getting hit by a car and then being plastered to the hood while driving all around Las Vegas) but also to play the acting job of a down-and-out gambler. I recommended Carl, and he did an amazing job. The director, the whole company and I could not have been happier. I am looking forward to reading his book and remembering all the other wonderful stunts he has done.

—**Sandy Gimpel**
Stunt Coordinator, Stuntwoman

Carl and I have been friends and have worked together for over forty years. He has been a great influence on me and so many other stuntmen. Enjoy the book: it is the fascinating journey of one of the most talented stuntmen/actors in the business. Love you, my friend.

—John Casino
Stuntman

I remember the first day I met Carl Ciarfalio. It was over forty years ago when I was in charge of the stuntmen at Knott's Berry Farm. I was called to the office because there was someone who wanted to apply for a job. I walked into the office, and there was Carl standing in front of me wearing a baseball cap that I think said "Caterpillar" on it. He stood there and said, "I want to be a stuntman." The rest is the history written in this book. Congratulations, Carl.

—Gary R. Salisbury
President, Salisbury Productions

I can't think of anyone who exemplifies the action actor/stuntman more than Carl Ciarfalio! Outside of being an amazing stuntman, his human spirit and kindness have never gone unnoticed in our world of showbiz. Carl was the perfect choice to represent the Stunt Peer Group/EMMY at the Academy of Television Arts & Sciences because of his knowledge, experience, and political savvy—all were so needed to be effective within such a prestigious organization. For me, Carl has always been a star, and I hope "Stars, Stunts, and Stories: A Hollywood Stuntman's Fall to Fame" will Rise to Fame!

—Spice Williams-Crosby
Actress, Stuntwoman

Few men earn the title of Journeyman Stuntman in Hollywood, but Carl has, because he never, ever, ever gave up his dream of being a Hollywood stuntman. In fact, in an industry that sucks people in, uses them up, and spits them out into the trash heap of history, Carl is still standing and still working. Thank you for this book, Carl. It documents the golden age of Hollywood's Stunt Business, which I believe was our generation. All the best, buddy, you are one tough cookie!

—Lane Leavitt
President, Leavittation, Inc.

Carl is not only a tremendous stuntman, but an equally skilled actor. I had the pleasure to coach Carl for several years at my studio and was just floored by his comedy chops, creativity, and his consummate professionalism. Carl nails the bad guys roles and the family man, sensitive roles. He also has amazing timing for sitcoms, dramady and romantic comedy roles. Carl is a pleasure to be around. He always lifts the spirits of those with him on a set or in the classroom. He's just simply a great guy with talent and guts out the wazoo!!! I was honored to work with Carl.

—**Deke Anderson**
Next Level Acting Studios
"The Art of Booking the Role"

Carl has gone above and beyond for me as a friend and a mentor, and I would be completely lost in this business without him! I couldn't have been more fortunate than to have received his generous guidance, advice, support and encouragement from the beginning of my career until now. I am thrilled that so many others will now be able to benefit from his knowledge and experiences through this book!

—**Vaia Zaganas**
Stuntwoman

Carl Ciarfalio was the first real stuntman I ever met, and he made the mistake of giving me his number if I ever had any questions. First boss I ever had in stunts, first call I make whenever I have a job or question, first person to calm me down when I think a gag is going to kill me, and best friend in the business. I made Carl my mentor over a decade ago, and I won't ever let him out of that job. More than a mentor only when the cameras roll, he is a compass for my life.

—**Brian Munce**
Stuntman

I've known and worked beside Carl for over twenty-five years. A list of a hundred colorful adjectives would not do him justice. The poster child of the "consummate professional," Carl would stand out above his peers in any industry. He has garnered the respect and admiration of scores of Hollywood's elite "A" listers. He moves easily from dramatic to comedic work, while doing what most stuntmen can't—he can speak! He throws out dialog as good as many actors, and can just as easily throw a John Wayne haymaker or take one on the chin.

Stunt work is a blend of many sciences and is yet also an art. Carl has perfected it all. I've trusted him with my life and personal career many times. He's always been there, and stood the charge.

On one particular occasion, Carl performed what we in the business call a "car hit." He should have died, but as I've intimated, he is one tough guy. He crashed into the windshield and sailed over the car, higher and longer than any before. You'll read about it in the book, but I want you to know that it stands out in my mind as equal to the chariot race in *Ben Hur* or Yakima Canutt's drag under the stagecoach, doubling John Wayne. I'm sure he must have felt as though he were riding a bull for eight seconds, blindfolded, and then tossed into a cement mixer. He survived, and I'm thankful he did so he could hang around to write this book. I'm sure you'll enjoy it.

—**Randy "Fife"**
Forty-Year Veteran of the Stunt Profession
Frisco TX

STARS, STUNTS, AND STORIES

A HOLLYWOOD STUNTMAN'S FALL TO FAME

CARL CIARFALIO
with TERI RYAN

Stars, Stunts, and Stories: A Hollywood Stuntman's Fall to Fame
www.StarsStuntsAndStories.com

The events, locations and conversations in this book, while true, are re-created from the author's memory. The essence of the story and the feelings and emotions are intended to be accurate representations. In certain instances, names, persons, organizations and places have been changed to protect an individual's privacy.

Except where otherwise indicated, photographs are from the author's collection. All efforts have been made to accurately acknowledge the source of images. If any errors have occurred, they are inadvertent and the author can be reached at www.ryanpublishinggroup.com.

For information about this title or to order other books and/or electronic media, contact the publisher:
Ryan Publishing Group
www.ryanpublishinggroup.com
ryanpublishinggroup@gmail.com

An application to register this book for cataloging has been submitted to the Library of Congress.

Printed in the United States
Cover and Interior design: 1106Design.com

Publisher's Cataloging-In-Publication Data
Ciarfalio, Carl.
　　Stars , Stunts and Stories : A Hollywood Stuntman's Fall to Fame / Carl Ciarfalio ; with Teri Ryan.
　　p. cm.
　　ISBN 978-0-9861552-7-7
　　Includes index.
1. Ciarfalio, Carl. 2. Stunt performers—United States—Biography. 3. Actors—United States—Biography.
I. Ryan, Teri. II. Title.
PN1995.9.S7 C53 2015
791.4302/8092 –dc23

In loving memory.

Lucille Menotti Ciarfalio and
Nick Carlo Ciarfalio

CONTENTS

Meet Carl Ciarfalio i

Dedication. xi

Acknowledgments xvii

Prologue xix

CHAPTER 1: Against All Odds 1

ACT 1: Carl Becomes a Stuntman

CHAPTER 2: My Wonder Years 11

CHAPTER 3: The Stunt Pup 15

CHAPTER 4: Knott's Berry Farm 18

CHAPTER 5: Universal Studios Live Show 23

CHAPTER 6: Stunt Training 30

CHAPTER 7: Hustling Stunts 35

ACT 2: Carl on Television

CHAPTER 8: Television Action Explodes. 49

CHAPTER 9: BJ and The Bear. 51

CHAPTER 10: Scarecrow and Mrs. King. 53

CHAPTER 11: Wild, Wicked Ratchet Rides. 56

CHAPTER 12: Fair Game 62

CHAPTER 13: Trauma Center. 68

CHAPTER 14: In The Heat of The Night 79

CHAPTER 15: Rescue 911 85

CHAPTER 16: Walker, Texas Ranger. 92

CHAPTER 17: Trekkies & Fivers 97

CHAPTER 18: Days of Our Lives. 99

CHAPTER 19: 24 102

CHAPTER 20: Heroes 104

CHAPTER 21: Stunts and the Emmys 106

ACT 3: Carl In the Movies

CHAPTER 22: Getting My SAG Card. 123

CHAPTER 23: Black Moon Rising. 126

CHAPTER 24: Extreme Prejudice 130

CHAPTER 25: Halloween 4: The Return of Michael Myers 138

CHAPTER 26: Glory 142

CHAPTER 27: Direct Hit. 148

CHAPTER 28: The Fantastic Four. 151

CHAPTER 29: Casino. 157

CHAPTER 30: Far and Away. 164

CHAPTER 31: Natural Born Killers 175

CHAPTER 32: Stallone: The Specialist, Tango & Cash, Lock Up. 178

CHAPTER 33: Bonds. James Bonds.. 185

CHAPTER 34: Mallrats. 190

CHAPTER 35: Batman and Robin 198

CHAPTER 36: John Carpenter's Vampires 200

CHAPTER 37: Fight Club 208

CHAPTER 38: The Taurus World Stunt Awards 211

CHAPTER 39: The Whole Ten Yards 218

CHAPTER 40: Mission: Impossible III 222

CHAPTER 41: The Book of Eli 227

CHAPTER 42: Channeling 229

CHAPTER 43: Out Of The Furnace 233

CHAPTER 44: Mentors, Maniacs and Me 239

Epilogue 267

Appendix: Kickstarter Contributors 269

Index 273

ACKNOWLEDGMENTS

n the year 2000, I had several stunt friends visit me while I was convalescing at home—a pretty common experience in my world. After days of listening to the stories fly, my wife suggested I turn them into a book. I thought she was nuts. Me? Write a book?! That's just crazy.

But once the idea was planted, it just had to grow, and here we are today. I couldn't be more grateful. Creating this book has afforded me an extremely enjoyable limp down memory lane. It has also allowed me to create a lasting record of my career for my family. Writing this book has even helped me further define what my future will hold.

Not unlike making movies, writing this book has been a creative process that required the collaboration of many generous and talented individuals.

I'd like to thank Diane Waida, Janey Dutton, Beverly Gray, Ron Sarchian and Steve Hart for their patience and invaluable feedback when reading early drafts of this book.

Thanks and kudos to Mary Karcz, a fine up-and-coming stuntwoman who put her editing skills to work as our proofreader.

Big thanks go to Michele DeFilippo and her gang at 1106Design.com for translating my words and pictures into the beautiful book you're now reading.

I also give tremendous love and thanks to my sister-in-law-turned-sister, Mary Caldarone, for her sense of humor and unfailing support through every step of the writing process.

I am humbled to offer my grateful thanks to my Kickstarter contributors. This wonderful group of individuals stepped forward with support that helped me take this book to the finish line. Please take a moment to view their names in the appendix and know that were it not for them, you and I would not be meeting on these pages.

My friends at Eddie Brandt's Saturday Matinee in North Hollywood, California—ebsmvideo.com—were indispensable in helping me step through my years of work. They have tens of thousands of titles in stock, and are always willing to share their deep knowledge of films, television shows and documentaries.

I would also like to thank all the entertainment professionals I've worked with over these many years. I am privileged to be in your company. In particular, I thank and recognize my brothers and sisters in the stunt community. As you read on, you'll find me repeatedly using phrases like "my good friend." I did that for a reason. I am honored to consider these brave, talented and dedicated men and women my friends.

Finally, to my beloved wife and partner, Teri Ryan: thank you, my love, for your loyalty, generosity, hard work and most importantly on this project—your immense talent and creativity as a writer and editor. You made it possible for me to get my stories on the page.

PROLOGUE

I was laid out on a stone slab high atop the ruins of the El Castillo pyramid in Chichen Itza. Actor Jeff Bridges was about to make my dead body disappear into the Mayan rainforest. I felt his strong push, and I began to roll.

With the first turn, I could hear the shale and pebbles grinding underneath me. Then I felt their razor-sharp edges cutting through to my skin. The next revolution sent me into a free-fall off the cliff.

At that last second, I took a deep breath, closed my eyes and made my body still. I wanted to scream all right—but from pure joy, because here I was, a boy from West Covina, California, performing in my first Hollywood blockbuster.

Instead, I did my job. Which was to have no reaction at all as I hurtled through the dense jungle air to my target sixty-five feet below—an impossibly small, murky, green sinkhole known as the Sacred Well of Sacrifice.

MY NAME IS CARL CIARFALIO, AND I AM A STUNTMAN.

When this particular stunt took place, I was a fledgling stuntman doing his very first big film gag. Prior to this point, I had done a few movies that had fights and falls in them. I had also worked on several TV shows where I was able to show off some of my motorcycle skills and do some young bad-guy acting. I had also been performing in the Wild West Stunt Show at Universal Studios Tour, and before that, in the live-action stunt show at Knott's Berry Farm.

I already thought I was living the dream.

This stunt, however, in a big-budget Hollywood feature film titled *Against All Odds*, was my first big gag in the majors. I was young, strong, indestructible, and ready for my close-up—figuratively speaking, because my face would never be seen. Even so, I knew that this was the kind of stunt in the kind of movie that would get my name around town.

This job meant I had made it to the show. And through hard work, good fortune and the grace of the universe, I've been there ever since.

During my career, I have beaten Tom Cruise to a pulp, manhandled Brad Pitt's ass and been shot at point-blank range by Kiefer Sutherland. Clint Eastwood choked me until my eyes about popped out; Steven Seagal pinned me to a wall with a cleaver; Robocop blew me away; Chuck Norris used his lethal martial arts skills to bring me to my knees on many, many occasions; Jennifer Garner once kicked the hell out of me; Olympia Dukakis got in the game—she ran me over in the Nevada desert; and Joe Pesci called me a mother-effing effer as he crushed my head in a vise while Martin Scorsese stood nearby screaming "Blood! More effing blood!"

But don't be surprised if you've never heard of me.

Because that's the thing about stunt people: we're "those guys" in your favorite action films and television shows. We're the men and women who support the villain and protect the hero. Stunt people play the henchmen, goons, hit men, thugs, assassins, soldiers, cops and even innocent bystanders. We also appear in comedies, romances, and pretty much all genres, handling anything physical. We are there to engage in whatever heinous attack or hilarious pratfall that comes our way.

In essence, stuntmen and stuntwomen do our very best to bring to life whatever creative action has been dreamt up by producers, directors, writers, and stunt coordinators.

Thanks to the imagination of these excellent storytellers, I've killed and been killed, beaten and been beaten, fallen off buildings and cliffs, rappelled from helicopters, been set on fire, tumbled down stairways, been run into, run over, and kicked in the . . . well, you know.

I've played a *Star Trek* alien, a classic comic book hero, a prisoner and prison guard, a clown, cop, security guard, special forces team member, spy, alien, Vatican guard, and a hottie in a sexy red halter dress. (Ok. Maybe 'hottie' is a stretch.)

I have enjoyed—and am still enjoying—an exciting career in television and film filled with adventures I never imagined while growing up in a conventional Los Angeles suburb in the 1950s and 1960s.

Now, at this time in my career and life, with two beautiful daughters and a loving and supportive wife and partner, the time seems right to reflect back and share some of those experiences with all of you.

So to all the film and television lovers out there, to my beloved family and friends, to my stunt community brothers and sisters, to all of the filmmaking professionals I've worked with all of these years, and to the young people who dream of their own career in pictures, here is my story—in bite-size chapters you can jump into and out of whenever you have a few spare minutes. I hope you'll enjoy this inside look at my experiences in film and television.

MY ORIGINAL FALL TO FAME IN *AGAINST ALL ODDS*. AFTER PUSHING ME OVER THE
CLIFF, ACTOR JEFF BRIDGES WATCHES FROM ABOVE.

CHAPTER 1
AGAINST ALL ODDS

Courage is being scared to death but saddling up anyway.

JOHN WAYNE

L et's start off by finishing up the story I teased at the opening of the book about my work on the movie *Against All Odds*.

As I mentioned, I worked at the Universal Studios Tour, entertaining park visitors in live stunt shows that ran throughout each day. During my few minutes off between each show, I would race down to the back lot of Universal Studios to hustle work on any and all filming that was going on. Hustling work meant I would find the stunt coordinator on each set, introduce myself with a polite hello, drop off my picture and resume, and get right back out of their way. Quick. Clean. Professional.

And there was a lot of work to hustle! Cable television transformed TV in the 1980s, bringing a huge demand for entertainment. This meant there was more work than ever for stunt performers. There were always several television shows and at least a few features shooting inside Universal's massive sound stages and throughout its huge collection of backlot locations.

After my day of performing and hustling new work was done, I'd spend more than a little bit of time with my fellow twenty-something buddies at a restaurant and bar located at the entrance to Universal—a place called "Whomphoppers."

That name alone should give you an idea of the kind of fun we had there!

On what turned out to be one of my most memorable days, I joined my pals after our last live show for a cocktail or five. I knew most of the folks in there, and those I didn't know were mainly tourists who recognized us from the show. Whenever one of them would come over and ask us to pose for a photo, it created even more reason for all of us to celebrate.

Not that we needed much encouragement.

On this particular day, somewhere between my second and third drink . . . or was it my fourth and fifth? . . . a wonderful young stuntman named Shane Dixon (a good man who was taken from us far too soon) came up to me and said, "Hey, I just talked to Gary Davis (a big-time stunt coordinator), and he's looking for someone to go to the Yucatan and double Alex Karras falling off a cliff into water. You could double him. You ought to give Gary a call. Here's his home number." And back he went to dinner with his friends.

Here's what went through my head.

First, *Alex Karras*! I had idolized Alex Karras since my high school days. Ever since I read George Plimpton's *Paper Lion*. As a young athlete, I particularly identified with Alex's attitude about playing hard but hating to practice. We were close to the same size. And we played the same positions. Plus, he was an All-Pro, and I wanted to be an All-Pro. In fact, when I made my high school varsity team, I chose number 71, Alex's number. I had always wanted to meet him. But to actually double him? OHMYGOD!

Next I thought "*Yucatan*." What a great opportunity to go to a place I'd never been before! In fact, at that time, I hadn't been *any* place before. So let's see—far away, tropical, exotic. Yep—count me in!

Then, duh, I realized the most important thing of all to an up-and-coming stuntman. I had in my possession the home phone number of a big-time stunt coordinator. Yeah, Baby!!

I ran (stumbled, actually, thanks to my happy hour activities) to the pay phone booth (way before cell phones) and dialed away.

"Hello, Gary? Thish is Carl Ciarfalio. I underschadt you're looking for someone to double Alex Karras. Yeah, I'm available for those dates. Sixty or sixty five feet into water? Yeah, that sounds fine. You don't know how I'm getting off the cliff? Shur, we can figure it out when we get there. That sounds great. Okay, sshee you then. And thank you. I really apprecshiate the opportunity."

I was as high as a kite when I got back to the table and told my friends the news. We whooped and hollered and drank and celebrated my good fortune for the rest of the evening.

The next week found me on a plane to Mexico where I met Gary for the first time. He seemed like a great guy. Tall, blonde, handsome with an infectious smile just this side of devilish. There was another stuntman on board, too. Hubie Kerns Jr., a fine second-generation stuntman who was excellent in the water and was there to be my "safety diver." Cool.

The plane took off and reached an altitude safe enough to move around the cabin. I stayed put, dreaming of what was in store for me; sun, fun, margaritas, senoritas, and a whole week-and-a-half of work.

Suddenly I realized Gary was standing next to my seat. I looked up, startled as a kid getting caught playing pup tent. And all I could see were those pearly whites, smiling down at me. Then he broke into a chuckle. So I said in all my naiveté, "Hey, how ya' doin'?" And without breaking the smile on his face he says to me, "Do you know how many people turned this job down?"

"What?? Yeah, but . . . huh? What do you mean 'turned it down'?"

"I couldn't find anybody that wanted to do this gag," he said, still with the same big smile. "Yep, they all told me I'd have to find somebody crazier than they were to do this." And with that he slapped me on the shoulder, shook his head, and moved on through the plane.

The reality of saying "yes" to this job hit me square in the gut. I broke into a huge sweat—something I'd get used to over the next ten days.

The big plane dropped us in Mexico City to pick up the small plane that would take us to the most remote third-world place I could ever imagine. It was in the middle of the jungle. Where the Mayans once ruled the earth. And not much had changed in the centuries since.

Our cabbie drove us two hours from the airport on roads that were mostly paved and dropped us at one of the two hotels in Chichen Itza. The hotel room had a bed and a dresser and a bathroom, and the windows had shutters but no glass. Different. Exotic. Hot. Boy, I was already sweating my ass off.

We weren't working the next day, so I joined a few other members of the crew for a tour of the Mayan ruins with a liaison who had been hired by the production company. He was a wonderful man who spoke perfect English and loved his Mayan heritage. We spent hours at the ruins, exploring areas tourists didn't usually get to see. It was the perfect beginning to my first out-of-the-country location experience.

We all got back to the hotel in time for drinks and a swim. I was just starting to enjoy myself when I looked up and saw that now-familiar megawatt smile coming at me. "Tomorrow we'll go out and scout the location for the gag," Gary said.

"Um, sure . . . that sounds great." I uttered with false bravado. And the sweats rained down.

The next day we went deep into the jungle, into a dark underworld looking for just the right cenoté. This was what the Mayans called deep sinkholes filled with salt-water from the ocean and fresh water from the jungle. The light was dim, the air was thick and musty, and tree roots hung around us like stalactites, reaching down for the water. When we finally reached our first cenoté, we discovered that the water gave off an other-worldly blue-green glow. When I looked at the cliffs up above, I saw the light piercing down through absolutely massive trees. Right about then, someone in the group shared the fun fact that these wells were probably filled with skeletons because cenotés are where the ancient Mayans made human sacrifices to their gods. Nice.

The first cenoté we found was too difficult to film at. The next one was too shallow. And the cliff above the third one we scouted was too high. For four days, we crawled to the edges of cliffs to see if we could throw, launch or push a body off and into the water below. My body. And every day as I looked over yet another ledge, it became clearer and clearer just how far sixty-five feet was. It's freakin' six stories. And every day Gary would just look at me . . . and smile.

We finally found the perfect cenoté, topped by a cliff of about sixty-five feet. The director, camera operator and Gary asked me what I thought about the spot. I took one quick look at it, and as I walked away, said if it worked for them then it was good for me.

They asked me to come take a second look to make sure. I did and repeated it was ok by me, but then said I didn't want to look over the edge anymore. Sixty-five feet was beginning to more like a hundred.

The location was set. Reality was sneaking up on me.

Other than location scouting, I worked one day that week. Gary and I, doubling for Jeff and Alex, worked with the actors on the setup to the fall. The shot called for Jeff to carry Alex to the edge of the cliff and lay his body down so he could push him over the side, thus hiding the fact that he had been murdered. This meant we had to capture footage of Gary carrying my dead body through the jungle as well as to the top of the cliff surrounding the cenoté.

While I waited for "that" day to happen, I had all kinds of terrific experiences in Chichen Itza. I enjoyed the gorgeous ruins. I swam in a nearby underground pool with the locals. I also did my extremely sweaty laundry at the "other" hotel—because that's where the town's three washing machines were.

On the ninth day of the trip, Gary came to me and for the first time he wasn't smiling. He informed me that it was time. We had an early call the next morning. Everyone would trek out to the chosen cenoté to get set up, and we'd shoot it around midday. My heart jumped, my butt puckered, the sweat poured off my face. "Great!" I said, in a screech that rivaled that of any twelve-year-old boy.

So this was fear. Hmm, didn't know if I liked it or not. So I spent some time with myself that evening, gathering my thoughts and confidence . . . and sweating.

The next morning, the hour-and-a-half ride to location reminded me of traveling on the bus to a championship wrestling match in college. After greetings all around, nobody said a word. I remember thinking that I had signed on for this job and that I would do whatever I could to give it 100 percent. I even chuckled to myself about the adage, "*What doesn't kill you, only makes you stronger.*"

Our director was the great Taylor Hackford, who had just completed *An Officer and a Gentleman*. He and Gary had decided the best and most realistic way to get a body off a cliff was to push it. Since Gary was needed at the bottom to get me out of the water (however this came out), Jeff Bridges would do the pushing.

Hackford was definitely on a mission. He wanted to make sure I would stay still so there would be no question that this body going over the cliff and dropping about sixty-five feet into the water was a "dead guy." I assured him and Gary that I wouldn't move. That however Jeff Bridges pushed me off is how I would go over. No shifting or correcting myself in the air.

Yep, I promised that.

So with this on my mind, I retired to my air-conditioned honey wagon room—these are mobile trailers of various sizes used for dressing rooms—and let my nerves put me to sleep until duty called. I think it was the first shot after lunch, but I certainly didn't eat. Just drank and drank and drank to replenish the sweat.

Then came that knock at my door. It was an assistant director telling me we were about thirty minutes away. So I put on my three-quarter 2-mil wetsuit and my all-important cup and pulled my wardrobe on over it.

Gary, Jeff, a camera operator, and I walked to the spot where I was to start the scene. Hubie was in his position in the water down below and relayed the info that the water was at least 15 feet deep. At one end of the cenoté was a small sandy island. Production had built a contraption there that would lift me back up to the top after Hubie fished me out of the water. It looked like it came straight out of an episode of *Gilligan's Island*.

Gary asked me if I was ready, and after I told him yes, he headed down to the bottom. Meanwhile, I looked at Jeff. Poor Jeff. He was fully concentrated and in the moment, but he looked like a deer in the headlights. Was he really going to be the guy to push another guy off a cliff? I said, "Jeff, you can do this. Just roll me off straight. I don't want to do a helicopter act in the air." He nodded and assured me that he would do his best. That's all anyone can ask for.

Cameras were rolling, and the Assistant Director called "Action!" I looked at Jeff and said "see ya when it's over, just push me even." I noticed that he was sweating, too.

I felt his strong push. I heard the shale and pebbles scraping underneath me as I rolled, took one last deep breath, and closed my eyes. And as my body slipped off the edge of that sixty-five-foot cliff, I made time stand still for me . . . mostly because I was playing dead, but also because by closing my eyes, I wouldn't react to the ground disappearing beneath me, or the turning in air, or the water below.

The next thing I remember was a soft voice mumbling something to me. I opened my eyes and saw the most beautiful light. And in the light I saw people, looking at me, waving at me, but from very far away. I heard birds singing, and the voice comforting me, and the warmth of the light on my chest. I thought, "How beautiful this is. I feel like I'm floating on air. And those people up there in the light, I must know them. Hey, I think I'm in heaven. Wow, it's all so good."

And then I started to come around. The voice belonged to Hubie. His was the soothing voice of the man who turned my body upright in the water so I wouldn't drown. "I got ya. You're okay now. Just breathe and relax. I got ya."

And the light from heaven above? That was the sun shining down on me. The people in the light were the movie crew, looking over the edge of the cliff to see if I was alive. I thought "Oh yeah! I just did . . . what the hell did I do? What am I doing here? Am I dreaming this? Am I dead?"

It took a few minutes for it to all sink in. The fact that I was in the middle of the jungle and just did a stunt for a movie. "Oh, riiight. I got it now. But I can't quite feel anything yet. Ah, there's a leg, and another, and an arm. Okay, I'm back."

Hubie got me to the small island from where I would be hoisted up to the top, and Gary was there waiting with open arms and that big ol' smile. I took two steps toward him . . . and he had to catch me before I fell on my face. I kind of remember the ride back to the top. I definitely remember a local doctor waiting for me with a full syringe. I must have said yes because he stuck that thing in my arm, and it worked fast. I don't remember any pain after that.

The next few hours are a little cloudy. Gary released the helicopter; turns out he had told production that he wouldn't do the shot without a rescue copter standing by. I got changed, was tucked into a car by production, and went back to my hotel, where someone had packed up my things for me. And off to the airport we went. Gary, Hubie, a few more of the crew and me—because when they're done with you, they pretty much get you off the clock and out of town.

I remember being helped through the airport and onto the plane by Gary and Hubie. I think it's there that Hubie told me I hit the water so flat that I only went down four or five feet. I also remember looking into a mirror and noticing that my usual olive Italian skin color was nowhere to be found. I was as gray as a ghost.

Gary kept a close eye on me on the plane back home. But I'm guessing whatever "Dr. Grande Needle" shot me with was working fine. I just stared ahead and blinked every once in a while.

When we finally landed in L.A., I was a darker shade of pale and starting to feel alive again. I could tell because the pain set in. Only the imprint of my wetsuit sleeve broke up the purple and yellow bruising on the entire left side of my body.

That was in May of 1982. Twenty years later I went to the Taurus™ World Stunt Awards, something I'm proud to have helped establish. The program included a montage of action clips from various movies, and there it was. My fall from *Against All Odds*. I was thrilled to see it and proud afterwards when so many of my friends mentioned it to me.

It really is against all odds that I have a career in the movies, and that moment in that film is one of the great memories I have from my many years living . . . and dying . . . as a Hollywood stuntman.

ACT 1:
CARL BECOMES
A STUNTMAN

CHAPTER 2
MY WONDER YEARS

Your work is to discover your world and then with all your heart give yourself to it.

BUDDHA

M y parents were first-generation Italians, both of whom grew up in Chicago's west-side city of Cicero.

My dad's dad Carlo was a shop welder, a trade he counted on when he emigrated from Bari, Italy, in 1911. His wife Mary joined him a couple of years later, and they settled in Illinois. My dad Nick carried on his father's tradition throughout the 1960s and 1970s by helping to form the skyline of downtown Los Angeles with his high-rise ironwork.

My mom's dad Giuseppe—or Joe as he was called in the neighborhood—was a shopkeeper and bar owner who catered to Chicago "businessmen" and policemen of the 1920s and 1930s. From what I understand, he also ran "errands" for some of the city's more well-known, um, bosses, if you know what I mean.

My mom Lucille was a real looker, and she was also a pistol. When she was only around ten or so—a time when prohibition was still going strong—she stood guard at the Chicago apartment where our family made its illicit booze. She also beat up boys who were mean to her little brother, earning her the nickname "Butch."

Nick and Lu raised me in West Covina, California, where they moved when I was about a year-and-a-half old. There were over thirty kids on our block, and you'd better believe we played pretty much every game and sport there was. I was the ultimate boy, up for any and all physical activity that came my way. Though I was never a thrill seeker, I always enjoyed overcoming physical and psychological obstacles.

Doing stunts, however, was an unlikely future for me, since I wasn't from a stunt or circus family, as the majority of stuntmen were at that time. I had no personal connection to Hollywood. I was just a regular kid from a working-class family.

I spent the best seven years of my life at Edgewood High in West Covina. Okay, old joke, but my high school years were so enjoyable that I said 'no thank you' when it turned out I had earned enough credits to graduate a semester early.

High school was a thrilling new world to me. There were beautiful girls, guys who shaved, and most appealing to me, upperclassmen who wore these really bitchin' letterman jackets. They were green and gold with a really cool "E" on the chest. I immediately began a quest to have the best letterman's jacket ever! My road to earning that classic high school symbol was paved with grades good enough to play team sports. This included football, wrestling, and one season of baseball followed by three years of track and field.

I played football on the junior varsity squad my freshman and sophomore years, and we were pretty much a squad of tackling dummies for the varsity team. I played hard and learned as much as I could, even working as the varsity team's water boy just to absorb more of the game. I also fell in love with the weight room during football. After the season ended, I went out for wrestling just so I could continue my strength training. Turned out I fell in love with that, too, and I made the JV team there as well. It was the perfect way to keep my athletic momentum going.

When I started wrestling, I was big and getting stronger every day, but I didn't know a thing about the sport—except for what I learned watching Big Time Wrestling on TV with my grandpa. Haystacks Calhoun, Bobo Brazil, Gorilla Monsoon and

"Nature Boy" Buddy Rogers were the stars in those days. I had all their best moves down—which turned out to have nothing to do with real high school wrestling.

I learned a lot that year and the next wrestling on the JV team, and was so proud when we wound up winning League Titles both of those years.

During the spring season of my freshman year, I moved on to baseball. I had a cannon for an arm, could stop almost anything on the infield and could pull a hit down the left-field line. But what I didn't realize at sign-up was that while I had developed my skills playing softball, the boys I'd now be competing with had been playing baseball since the second grade. That training gave them an advantage I just couldn't match. So I stuck out the season, playing catcher at every practice, but that marked the end of my high school baseball career. Beginning my sophomore year, I dedicated my spring season to track and field. Not surprisingly, my strong, young self took to the shot put and discus.

Beginning my junior year, I played on the varsity football team, starting at offensive tackle and defensive nose guard/tackle. I was elected co-captain of the football team my senior year, which was quite a surprise since the head coach and I never got along. I remember feeling honored to be held in such regard by my peers. I could have done better as a captain and as a leader, but it was all a learning and growing process.

Each of those last two years, I jumped from the gridiron to the mats with great excitement. I won the starting spot as the varsity heavyweight my junior year, and our team ended up winning the League Championship. Although I was seeded number one during finals, a wrestler I had beaten earlier in the season managed to best me, so he took the gold. I can tell you that I didn't much care for second place.

My senior year I was elected co-captain by the wrestling team. What an honor it was to captain a returning championship team! We went into the last dual meet of the season tied with Los Altos High; at stake was a spot in the League Championship.

I remember there were thirteen weight classes, and the score was tied after the twelfth match. This was a place of pressure for me . . . it was the first time I took a real look at what it meant to be on top, to be first, to be a winner and help my team be a winner.

I wanted that triumph.

I was wrestling a worthy opponent who was strong, quick and knowledgeable. The stands were packed, marking the beginning of what I would soon long for . . . an audience. My mom was in the stands, and she was loud—so much so that when I looked up at her between periods, she had cleared the seats around her.

"Come on, Chip!" she yelled. "You can do it!"

Well, my blood was boiling, and I showed this opponent of mine no mercy. Our yearbook has a photo of me burying his head into the mat with my elbow. When the final buzzer went off, and the ref raised my hand in victory, the stands erupted, as did my team, my coach, and the cheerleaders.

I went on to avenge my championship loss from the year before and became an All-League Wrestler for my second year in a row. This time my dad was in the stands. When I won the last of my three matches—thus securing championships for me and our team—Nick came bounding down from the stands and gave me the biggest, longest, warmest hug ever. It lasts with me to this day.

Once I graduated that May, I had a simple plan in my mind: go to college, be a jock, graduate, and become a jock's coach.

I chose to enroll at the two-year Mt. San Antonio College in Walnut, California. My first order of business was heading to the gym to find Fred Burri, the wrestling coach. He was a big, thick-necked Swiss with a Neanderthal brow and a booming baritone voice. If you're ever standing in line at Disneyland's Matterhorn, you can hear it yourself. That guy yodeling is Coach Burri.

That first year at Mt. SAC was amazing. I became the wrestling team's starting heavyweight. And I met so many new and interesting people! Guys and gals who raced motocross, surfed, rodeo'd and rock climbed. I was like a kid in an athletic candy store.

My last year at Mt. SAC was more of the same, culminating with a Team Conference Championship. But after wrestling season ended, classes quickly fell to the bottom of my priority list. Instead, I was out constantly, trying new sports and activities with all of my new friends and teammates. One in particular, Mic Rodgers, was the most fun.

CHAPTER 3
THE STUNT PUP

I couldn't wait for success, so I went ahead without it.

JONATHAN WINTERS

Mic—Michael Glen Rodgers—is a leading stunt coordinator and second unit director who came up through the ranks of Stunts Unlimited, one of Hollywood's leading groups of stunt performers. He's a guy who calls "A list" actors by their first name . . . like Mel, Drew, Cameron, Brad and Angelina.

But back in our college days, he was just Mic, a wild, energetic kid with a wiry body who liked to race motocross and ride street bikes. He also did a really good John Wayne impression. His style of living was all too wonderful for me to pass up, so I began skipping classes and lying to my folks about where I was and what I was doing.

Mic and I went through the next several years as best of friends.

Although I had scooted around a bit in high school, it was Mic who taught me how to ride a motorcycle. While he was doing it, he always talked about wanting to become a stuntman. Stunts this and stunts that. I thought it sounded kind of cool, but at that point all I really wanted to do was get on the bikes and go fast.

Our weekends were a blast. Mic introduced me to Indian Dunes, an off-road motorcycle playground located out in the boonies outside of Los Angeles, past Magic Mountain. *On Any Sunday*, Steve McQueen's 1971 motorcycle documentary, was shot there as were such classic TV series as *Dukes of Hazzard* and *Black Sheep Squadron*.

The Dunes had a boatload of trails to ride, but I wanted to be with the guys who raced on its two motocross tracks. These were guys who had been riding since they were five. Guys who were already doing stunts in big movies and were coordinating action for big stars like Jack Nicholson and Burt Reynolds. The bug finally bit me. I wanted to be in that club!

After a couple of trips out there, I geared myself up for action: boots, helmet, gloves, a mouth guard, and a brand new, off-the-floor, shiny red Honda XL 500cc motorcycle. It was big and beautiful and powerful and sounded amazing. More to the point, it was the same bike a couple of stuntmen were riding around the Dunes. They were smaller than me but could throw that big turd around like it weighed nothing.

"Yep," I decided, "that's the bike for me!"

My next trip to the Dunes I was all decked out and knowing my place, let the pros go in front of me. But I wasn't worried. I'd been watching. And I had my new bike. I figured I'd catch them around the third or fourth turn.

Well, I didn't catch them at all that weekend . . . or the following one . . . or the one after that. What the hell was I doing wrong? Aha! It must be the bike! So I putted on over to a very nice gentleman who also happened to have a 500 Honda. But his was different somehow. So I said to this guy—who was named Alan and was clearly a leader on that track—"what did you do to get such great speed and handling on your bike?"

He was more than gracious in explaining it to me, and he even told me where he had gotten the work done.

Come to find out this was Alan Gibbs, the hottest stuntman around. *Smokey and the Bandit. Cannonball Run II. Crocodile Dundee. Scarface.* Alan Gibbs is an icon. There wasn't a stunt he hadn't done, and he knew how to set up and coordinate any gag you could throw at him. Alan left us at much too young of an age, a victim of cancer. When you're around stunt people and the stories start to fly, Alan's name will come up with lots of "ooohs" and "aaahs."

The next day, I was off like a shot to the legendary White Brothers motorcycle shop—experts in the modification of stock suspension components. They concurred that if I wanted my bike to handle better and go faster, they were the ones who could do it—for just around 500 bucks. "Well, hell," I told them, "if it works for a guy like Alan Gibbs, it'll work for me. Do what you need to do!"

I spent money that I didn't really have, and my bike *was* a little lighter feeling and *did* go faster, and Alan thought that the White Brothers did a fine job on it.

"*Finally,*" I thought, "*I'm gonna' kick some ass on the track.*"

But it turned out that the only ass I kicked was my own. Thanks to my souped-up bike, I ended up with bigger "get-offs" and got launched further and more times than anyone on the track.

And let me tell you, those get-offs were worthy of any *Jackass* movie ever made. They actually provided me with my first and most important stunt lesson: Humble Up.

Just because you think you're the biggest, baddest, strongest, fastest dude around, doesn't mean you are. Someone will come along—and probably several will come along—who will easily put you in your place. I learned the hard way that you couldn't just walk onto a track and expect to be Mr. Motocross. Just like you can't walk onto a movie set and expect to be Mr. Stuntman.

There's so much to learn throughout life. This experience taught me that if you put your ego in check, you'll be way ahead of the game.

C H A P T E R 4
KNOTT'S
BERRY FARM

Life is not about how fast you run or how high you climb, but how well you bounce.

VIVIAN KOMORI

n June of 1973, after a couple of years hanging out around stunt guys, Mic called to tell me he had landed a job at Knott's as a cowboy/stuntman. He also shared the news that they were still hiring. They were looking for someone who was larger than average, could be physical and funny and knew stage fighting. He suggested we get together and work out a routine for the audition, which was in a couple of days.

So it was that Mic taught me my first fight routine. It was going to be worked into a little show called "The Count Five" that the cowboys were already performing on the streets of Knott's Berry Farm.

I was in a fun mood the day of the audition, and just a little nervous—like before a wrestling match or that first snap of the ball in a football game.

The audition went well!

Everybody gasped and laughed where they should have, and everything went according to plan—except that I wanted to give them a little extra. At the last minute, I decided it would be funny to run into the tree we were auditioning under and act as if I banged my head on it.

So in the middle of this little street play, I turned to the tree, took a couple of steps to get into position, and bang! A branch hit me right across the bridge of my nose. I hit it pretty good and scraped my face to the point that blood was oozing. But no matter, I finished the skit to applause.

And so it began, this thing I did that turned into a career.

Knott's Berry Farm, the Berry Patch, the Place Down from Disneyland—that's where I got my start in the entertainment business.

Picture this: a big kid getting paid to play cowboy, get into shootouts, rob stagecoaches and hang out with saloon girls. What could possibly top this?

Certainly not the jobs I'd held to this point. Between semesters at Mt. SAC, I worked the graveyard shift at the "San Gabriel Tribune" stacking piles of newspapers and *TV Guides* and loading them onto trucks for delivery. I also—get this—worked as a "ring attendant" at dog shows. Picking up some of the worst and biggest piles of dog crap I have ever seen or smelled.

I didn't really like working at the newspaper. And picking up dog poop isn't all it's cracked up to be. So I definitely thought this Knott's thing would be the best option for my summer job. After that, I was all set with a scholarship offer from Cal State Fullerton to wrestle on their team. The plan was to attend a four-year university, graduate, and coach.

Well, we all know what they say about making plans.

At Knott's, we cut our teeth performing for a live, up-close audience. We put on street skits for the crowds, robbing the stagecoach as we developed our talents and public personalities. We also almost immediately started working on the new *Wild West Stunt Show* they wanted to present at the end of summer.

As I worked through that summer of my twentieth year, I remember being so very excited about my job. I still lived at home, and since Mic's house was only about five miles from mine, we would trade off driving to work. We were always laughing, singing, joking around . . . 'cuz we was going to go play stuntman for the day.

Gary Salisbury, who wrote and directed the stunt show, was a staple at Knott's. He was a gunfighter on the streets long before I was hired and stayed in their employ for many years after I had left. He had worked his way up to a manager in the Entertainment Department, and was responsible for the shows, which were rapidly growing in popularity. He was also the man who hired me and changed my life's path, which was a very good thing. Although changes have since been made, that same stunt show is still running as of this writing. It is possibly the longest-running live show at an amusement park in history.

My character was actually introduced to the audience as a Hollywood stuntman brought in by Knott's to do the show in place of an injured comrade. (How prophetic is that?!) Although we started with all the basics in place, we worked as a team to perfect the show by finding the spots that would become "golden."

I don't recall what my character's name was in the original script, but it doesn't matter, because while we were still in rehearsals, the star of the show asked my character what his name was. I blurted out something like, "Well, I'm the Beaumont Bear! But you can call me Mr. Bear."

It stuck.

That's how I became the first Beaumont Bear the "Wagon Camp Wild West Stunt Show" ever had. I'm proud of being known that way in very small circles. OK. Perhaps the better term here is "minute" circles.

So there I was. On stage, gun on my hip, cowboy hat perched on my head. People laughing, people applauding and a lot of pretty, smiling girls.

"*College can wait*," I thought to myself. "*I could stay here a couple of years. I can always go back to school . . . I . . .*" and blah, blah, blah.

Who was I kidding? Stunts? Cowboys? Girls? I was hooked! Ultimately I spent three years working the Knott's Live Show. What a blast we had!

Working at Knott's really gave me a base from which to move forward. I learned fights and falls, but more importantly I got to learn showmanship, timing, and teamwork. These important fundamentals would help advance in my career.

Throughout this time, my parents kept after me to go back to school or get a trade. They wanted me to get a steady job and maybe do this "stunt thing" on the weekends. They only wanted the best for their Carlo, and they certainly didn't understand the business. They only knew what they heard—smarmy tales of Hollywood corruption and sly deals in secret and luxurious back rooms.

At one point during those years, I succumbed to their parental pressure and left "The Farm." I figured my dad was right. I had to find a real job that had some security and benefits.

I found work as a furniture mover. Hated it!

I steam-cleaned carpets. Really hated it!

I sold discount products to newlyweds. Hated that even more!

I clerked at a deli. Yep, sucked!

I dug ditches for a plumber. Really effin sucked!!

Bounced at a nightclub. What was I thinking?

Unloaded freight from trucks at Long Beach Harbor. What do you think I thought about that one?

These were wonderful jobs for some, but there was no way any of them would work for me. I needed to perform. I needed to create.

So one day—when I was either cleaning a carpet or digging a ditch, can't recall for sure—I got a call from my buddy John Casino. John started working on the Knott's stunt team a year after me. Handsome, strong, and talented, he would become Kurt Russell's stunt double, a job he has held for years. You can see John's work in *Tango and Cash*, *Backdraft*, and *Stargate* as well as a slew of others. He told me that the Universal Studios Tour was holding auditions for their live-action western stunt show.

Back I went to performing.

We grabbed another friend from Knott's, Bob Elmore, to put together an audition piece. Bob would go on to become John Candy's stunt double. He also played the original killer in *Texas Chainsaw Massacre*, and he had roles in such classics as *Casino* and *Pirates of the Caribbean: Curse of the Black Pearl*.

The three of us created a little show, complete with fights, falls and—of course—comedy.

The audition got us a callback to perform the routine at a final audition.

We kicked ass!

There were two spots open, and John and I were hired to be on the new Universal Stunt Team.

Audience. Action. Comedy. Paycheck. No turning back. I had finally found the place where I belonged.

CHAPTER 5
UNIVERSAL STUDIOS LIVE SHOW

Acting is the perfect idiot's profession.

KATHARINE HEPBURN

T he transition to Universal Studios Tour was awesome for me. I was now working at the largest movie studio in the world. Hollywood was booming, the studio lots were hustling and bustling, people were buying homes right and left, buying new cars and boats, and stuffing hundreds of thousands of dollars up their nose!

Once John and I started rehearsals, some of the veterans who knew their stuff when it came to live performances taught us the intricacies of the show. The beats, the timing, the laughter, the attitude of the characters—all things that John and I had been absorbing at Knott's, but on a bigger scale. This was a huge step forward in the career I was building for myself.

Lance Rimmer, who had worked alongside the likes of Red Skelton, was the show captain. He had a booming voice, a Gable-like presence, and some very good physical talent. He also understood what it meant to be 'in character' and how to keep the audience with you throughout each fifteen-minute show.

Lance, who rarely broke character, was always a true professional. He was proud to have helped grow the Universal live stunt show from little more than a stunt demonstration to the highest-rated live show in the biggest movie studio in the world, at the time.

Did you notice I said that Lance "rarely" broke character? Can you imagine why? You probably guessed it. I made it my mission to make that man break—and I'll tell you more about that in a minute.

John and I worked together as two-thirds of a three-man team, alternating with several other stuntmen in the third spot. We mostly worked with Ron Kelly and Bill Oliver, both very talented. John would play one of the two "heavies" in the show, one 'good' and one 'bad.'

I had the pleasure of playing the comic, a role I had prepped for during the hundreds of shows I did at Knott's. I played a "sissy-type" cowboy in blue and yellow flowered shirts with a floppy hat that was turned up in the front. He was a bumbling sidekick with half-a-brain and a loaded gun.

By this time, I had learned I could make most people laugh just by making a funny face. I had also learned how to play with the audience by making a physical move or doing a "double-take" at a situation. So it was inevitable that I would use these talents to have some fun with my co-stars.

Ron Kelly, a very fine actor who worked for many years on TV and in film, was particularly susceptible to my comedy. When we worked together, his strategy was to avoid looking me in the eye. But that only meant I had to change my game. From that point forward, when he would stare at my forehead or over my shoulder, I'd look around, and then look back at him, and make a face like "what the hell are *you* lookin' at?"

He was so easy to get to laugh. Love that guy.

Then there was the day we had to scramble because we were short a man, and I ended up playing the bad guy. After years of being the comic relief, I got to be a badass doing a fistfight, ax-handle fight, and whip fight with my best bud, John.

I'll never forget that first show. I jumped down from a roof to a ramp, and then to the stage floor where John met me with swift punches to the body and head. I reacted, blocked his next punch and threw my own right, sending him reeling back.

John punched me again, sending me sprawling to the mat. I got up, turned to him and made eye contact to signal I was ready for his next move, which was to throw a punch at my head. Remember, this was a performance, so in reality, we used angles to our advantage. While his punch, together with my reaction, would look like a solid impact to the audience, in truth, his fist would never make contact with my noggin. Except it didn't work that way that day. I looked at him; he looked at me; here comes a left punch (his power hand); and smack! Sudden impact, square in the forehead.

All things stopped for a second or two. He looked at me, I looked—or tried to look—at him, we started laughing—unsuccessfully trying to stay in character—then went on with the show.

Afterwards, as we broke it down to see where we went wrong, John started laughing all over again. He pointed me to a mirror, and there they were. John's knuckle prints, swelling on my head. We howled even more!

John and I have been best of friends since we met in the mid-seventies. Love my brother.

Okay, back to Lance. I got to work with him and his team whenever their comic would get a job in television or on a film. It was a treat because it kind of shook things up for me and made me pay a little more attention to the show.

It was also my opportunity to mess with Lance.

There was a part in the show where Lance's character exits a saloon and holds the flapping doors open as he steps out onto the boardwalk to face the audience. He then barks, "Where is he?" That was my cue to step up behind him and into the center of the doorway. Sure enough, he'd let go of the doors, and they'd swing back into my face.

The live action trick to protect my ugly mug was a block of wood concealed in my ham hands. (Yes, they are unusually large.) I'd toss the block aside as I snapped my head back in reaction to getting hit. I'd then stumble out onto the boardwalk while Lance reacted to what just happened. Next I'd take a pose above a tin bucket and proceed to spit white beans out of my mouth, plinking them in the bucket as if they were my teeth. I was able to hold a whole bunch of beans in my mouth, and I milked spitting them into the bucket. The audience ate it up.

After expressing his disgust, Lance led me on search for the bad guy.

Well, I soon discovered that I could keep a few of the beans in my mouth while Lance and I moved around the set. With that, I knew I had him.

The next time Lance boomed orders at my hapless character, I took it for a moment, then spit out a bean. That's all it took. Lance's stone-like face cracked into a huge smile and his bushy eyebrows rose, shooting his hat up a good couple of inches. That made the audience crack up, which destroyed Lance even further. His shoulders would start to shake; he'd work as hard as he could to gather himself; and yes, at that point, I'd let another bean trickle out.

Lance had my number then. The next time we performed together, he looked at my forehead and over my shoulder—anything to avoid my cracking him up. Well, we all know what happened then, don't we? The next time he focused over my shoulder instead of directly at me, I did my quick over-the-shoulder, "what're-*you*-looking at!" take, and he'd crack all over again. Ah, the simple pleasures in life.

I have to say that for all the fun I had, this was also an important time of growth and maturity for me. Just in time, too, because just when I was at the end of my run at Universal, just when I really began to make my mark in the world of television and film, the universe handed me an unexpected gift. One that turned out to be the best and most important experience of my life to that point.

I became a single dad.

The challenge of jumping into the stunt industry with both feet paled in comparison to being a full-time single dad to a thirteen-year-old girl. It was a duty and a privilege that I loved.

You see, my high school girlfriend and I briefly reunited after our first year in college. She then decided she didn't want to rekindle the relationship after all, so we once again went our separate ways. But about two months later, she contacted me with the news that nature had taken its course. After talking everything through, I wanted to be married, but was out-voted by her and all four parents. They ultimately decided it would be best for her and her family to raise our baby without me or my family participating, other than some initial financial support. Months later I was informed that our daughter was born and what she had been named. After that, all went silent, as planned.

It was a very different time, and both sets of loving parents wanted only to do right by their grandchild and us. Yes, they were old-school in their thinking, but their hearts were in the right place.

But I am cringing as I write these words.

The solution that everyone thought was best was most definitely not best. All of us suffered consequences from this well-meaning decision. I can trace its impact through all of my subsequent life and relationships. I won't go into all of that because this book is about sharing my high points, but I will say that back then, the complete truth was that I isolated myself. I quit college, gained twenty-five pounds, worked on my car, worked at a Baskin Robbins® restaurant, and basically tried to avoid feeling the pain, emptiness, loss and the deep awareness that things were not right.

I rejoined life a year later and kept watch from a distance, as my former girlfriend fell in love, married and had three more children. I basically resigned myself to the fact that I'd have to wait until—or if—my daughter ever decided she wanted to meet me.

Cut to her thirteenth year when my mom called out of the blue saying she'd been contacted with the news that my daughter was now living with her maternal grandparents. She said that all these years my little girl had been told that the person her mother married was her dad, and that she only found out about me on the day she fled his home.

Fled?

You can't imagine the blinding tsunami of horror and white hot rage that engulfed me the moment I heard that word. That one word was all it took for me to understand. To see it all. To formulate an immediate and brutally primitive plan for justice. I remember being astonished to simultaneously experience an even stronger compulsion to keep my head. I knew I had to be around to forever more give my daughter the love and protection she needed and deserved.

The awful details continued. Most of which I won't share. I will say that mom told me her granddaughter had bravely run to a neighbor's home, told them about years of violation, and asked for their help. They called the authorities, and Carlene soon found herself surrounded by uniformed adults.

After repeating her story to first one, then another and yet another officer, one of them finally said, "O.k., now tell me about your dad." It was too much. Overcome with emotion she cried out, "I've been telling you about him!" The officer responded, "No, I'm talking about your real dad."

That shocking, world-changing reality instantly gave this overwhelmed little girl a beacon of light that would guide her out of a nightmare darkness.

I went to be with her the very next morning, arriving at her grandparents' home about the time school let out. I waited as her school bus pulled up to the stop. I found myself holding my breath as I searched the sea of little faces through the bus windows, wondering if I would recognize my child, when finally, about halfway back, there she was.

I needn't have worried; I would have known her anywhere. She was a beautiful little female version of me. I saw my mom, my dad, my grandparents and me in her light-dark Italian eyes, her olive skin, and thick brown hair.

My eyes stayed glued as she stood up and made her way out of the bus. She paused at the top step and our eyes locked. Then she stepped down, walked up to me, and with a heartbreakingly quiet grace said, "Are you my daddy?"

Every parent reading this will understand when I say our bond was instant. Even though we had never spent a minute together, we knew we were father and daughter—me and this beautiful young girl, who, in spite of everything, was full of life and wonder.

The next day I got myself a lawyer, set a court date and quickly won full custody.

For the next several years, it was pretty much just us—Carlene and me, with a couple of dogs and a few lovebirds to round things out. I was so grateful and proud to be her dad as together we made sense out of the unthinkable, and built her a new, safe and secure life. We saw doctors and therapists, and we sat together in our backyard, talking about the past. A lot. Endlessly, really. About the horrible whats, the inexplicable whys, and the heartbreaking why nots. I was humbled by her courage and her spirit. Elated as she slowly and steadily healed. Ultimately we both came to learn that it wasn't healthy or helpful to live in the past, and we truly began to create a future.

Sure it was work. It was the most wonderful kind of effort, because it was us and we were together and so very grateful. We learned together, we cried together, we laughed together, and we continue to do so to this day.

Make no mistake, some forty years later I still have deep regrets, but what overshadows everything is the gift of my relationship with my girl.

Carlene has grown into a beautiful woman with the most magnificent soul. She is an exceptional daughter, sister, wife, stepmother, and teacher of children with special needs. She is also a brave and giving woman who shares her experience with groups of young people, so they may be better able to recognize predators in their midst and better understand how to help themselves.

My daughter is the best, most loyal friend anyone could want. I've learned so much from her. I'm endlessly grateful for her. And I'm so very proud of her. She's a very special and wonderful human, and I love her beyond all measure.

CHAPTER 6
STUNT TRAINING

There is nothing like a challenge to bring out the best in man.

SEAN CONNERY

W hile my young stunt-pup self was working to refine my performance skills at the Universal Live Shows, I also kept working to improve my stunt skills. Somehow I was lucky enough to hook up with a very talented and charismatic individual by the name of Buck McDancer.

Is that a perfect name for a Hollywood stuntman or what!

Buck has amassed a huge range of credits over his forty-plus years in show business. During my pup years, he took a liking to me, and one day volunteered to take me "out driving" whenever I wanted to go. What a great offer! A guy who actually works as a stunt driver wants to take me out and teach me a few things. This was and still is the dream of every up-and-coming stuntman.

I was about to learn all about tire pressure, power, inertia, weight shifting and much, much more.

We set a day to rent a car and find a spot to practice things like 90s and 180s, reverse 180s and power slides. These are "authentic stuntisms" we use to describe whipping a car in a half and full circle, backward and forward and sideways, in order to hit a pre-determined mark. Other lingo we use includes "gag" (a stunt), "dead man" (your body coming to an abrupt stop after reaching the end of a tethered line), "suicide" (a type of high fall), "cannon roll" (flipping over a car by exploding a short telephone pole out of the bottom of the vehicle), "running W" (getting pitched forward off a horse whose legs have buckled while running), and my all-time favorite, "jerk off." More about that later.

Buck brought cones to the car rental office, and I don't mean ice cream cones. I mean bright orange roadwork cones. This guy was ready! He chose a full-size sedan, explaining it was the same size used for most cop cars on TV and in film. He wanted me to get the feel of the kind of car I would most likely be driving most of the time.

Buck explained to my eager young self, for example, how to make an abrupt right turn while barreling forward. You'd stomp on the emergency brake, turn the wheel to the right, then correct your over-turn by letting the rear end fishtail around the corner. Finally, you steer out of the turn, all the while keeping control of the car. Do this, and *voila*, you have created a 90-degree turn.

OK, I got it. Bring it on!

So away we went with our orange cones and cups of 7-11 coffee (before Starbucks) to a place far, far away, called Valencia. Today Valencia, California, is an affluent, beautifully-landscaped city brimming with gated communities, office parks and luxury shopping malls. But back then, it was a bunch of dirt in the scrub desert about twenty miles north of Los Angeles that was being cleared for new housing developments. It was basically an empty space on the back road to Vegas.

Most importantly, Valencia was filled with newly-paved streets that were empty. Looping and stretching around random cement foundations. Which meant we could race the car to the end of a cul-de-sac and not be worried about a kid running out after a ball or a car backing from a driveway. I was as happy as a kid in an amusement park with keys to all the great rides.

Buck set up the cones, then proceeded to teach me how to set up the car for spins. Tire pressure, e-brake, steering wheel position. It may sound a little ho-hum, but these are the little specifics, the tricks of the trade, that make the gag work. And practice, practice, practice was the game of the day.

We drove the tires square on that car, and I did okay for a stunt pup. Admittedly I crunched a cone or two, but it was better than slamming against a parked car or into a wall.

Late that afternoon, we headed back to the car rental office. As we drove into town, I noticed that the car seemed to be "limping" just a bit. Buck shrugged it off, telling me this was a typical symptom of stunt driving. The tires can only slide sideways so much before they start to get flat spots on them, hence the clumping sound all the way home.

We turned in the keys and got the hell out of there before the attendant had time to figure out what we'd done.

After our day of sliding and spinning, Buck took me to Victoria Restaurant. A very nice venue located on top of the hill at Universal Studios. When we got there, we sidled up to the bar and Buck said to me, "Man, I could use an Irish coffee. Want one?"

"*Irish coffee?*" I'm thinking. "*This guy drinks Irish coffee. What happened to tequila and shots of Wild Turkey?*" But what I said was, "Sure, that sounds great!" I blurted it with boyish excitement, not wanting to let him know how un-macho I thought this drink was.

Well, I'm here to tell you that whatever was in those cups turned out to be plenty for this kid. We talked and drank for a little while . . . or a few hours. I still can't remember. I do remember pouring myself out of the chair and walking the mile and a half home. Driving wasn't *even* an option. I left him there, sitting in his spot at the bar, with the same big smile he had at the beginning of the day.

Today there are a number of great places in L.A. where young stunt people can go to train. But back then, there were only a couple of places to go. One of them was Paul Stader's gym in Santa Monica.

Paul was a talented stuntman who was renowned for his water work. I was also thrilled to learn that he doubled Lloyd Bridges in the '50s TV show, *Sea Hunt*, a program I had grown up with.

When I finally got the courage to go work out at Paul's (yes, although I was at the top of my game at Universal, I was nervous about fitting in with working professional stuntmen), I was surprised at its condition. It was an old beat-up gym that had been used and abused for years. The equipment was pieced together. I remember, in particular, the high-fall pad, also known as a port-a-pit, which was about eight feet wide by ten feet long and about four feet high.

The top of the pad, the part you landed on after jumping from the platform twenty feet above it, was a lattice of mesh rope that held down numerous chunks of foam that were stuffed into the pit. Every time you landed on the pad, you'd have to reconfigure the foam back to the middle of the pad. It was raw, but it taught you how to hit your mark.

I also learned to "picture fight" at Paul's.

Tom Morga, whom I met at Paul's and would later work with at the Tour as well as on dozens of TV and film projects, taught me the "dance" of the picture fight. Tom was Leonard Nimoy's stunt double through all the *Star Trek* movies and worked steadily for decades on such blockbusters as *Jurassic Park* and all the *Pirates of the Caribbean* films.

Tom taught me that it's all about your feet. "How you step. How you move your lower body," he would explain. "Then you incorporate your punches. Exaggerate your swing. Let 'em see it coming. Telegraph your moves for the camera to pick up. Action-reaction."

It sounds simple, but it takes a lot of practice and hard work to make a fake fight look real. I guess all the work proved helpful because in 1985 I was nominated for two fights in the first *Stuntman Awards*. I came away with a great-looking statue for a big-time brawl I was part of for an episode of *Knight Rider*, the 1980s action series starring David Hasselhoff and his high-performance, artificially-intelligent sports car, KITT.

There was a trampoline at Paul's place as well. This helps you with your movements and also helps you get your "air sense" which is knowing where your body is at all times while you're twisting and turning in the air. I had done trampoline work in high school and college and loved it, so I got on that thing whenever I could.

One day I was spotting on one of the sides of the trampoline while another stuntman was working on his flips. He was doing ok, but suddenly I noticed that he had shifted to the edge of the tramp bed. There was no time to say anything to him because he was in mid-air taking yet another flip. As his body headed down, I could see he was going to miss the edge of the bed and possibly hit the springs. Then I realized he wasn't even going to hit the springs. He was headed off the edge of the trampoline and right at me. So I caught him as he landed. No, not like a baby in a blanket, but more like a 180-pound man smashing into your chest and shoulders sending you both crashing to the ground.

He was shaken but not hurt, I was shaken but not hurt, and I learned. It was my first 'aha' about how dangerous a small mistake can be. It also came around. Years later, I would be 'saved' in much the same manner on *Extreme Prejudice* by a fellow stuntman and friend, Allan Graf. You'll find that story in the next few pages.

CHAPTER 7
HUSTLING STUNTS

You always pass failure on your way to success.

MICKEY ROONEY

T he dictionary describes hustling as follows.

hus·tle (hŭs′əl)

v. **hus·tled, hus·tling, hus·tles**

1. To move or act energetically and rapidly.

2. To push or force one's way.

3. To act aggressively, especially in business dealings.

4. *Slang*

   a. To obtain something by deceitful or illicit means.

   b. To solicit customers. Used of a pimp or prostitute.

   c. To misrepresent one's ability in order to deceive someone.

This pretty much sums up what "hustling" means as it relates to getting a stunt job in the movie business. That last item in the definition is the most frightening, but I'm sorry to say, it happens all the time.

There are many ways to hustle work in the entertainment business, and it's certainly changed in these modern high-security days, but no matter how you do it, it's something you never stop doing.

In those days, hustling stunts meant driving all over God's creation, tracking down working sets with a stunt coordinator in hopes you'd be able to steal five minutes of time to pitch yourself. Hustling was—and is—also spending time with other stunt people, sharing talent and knowledge.

Today hustling can be done via e-mail, Facebook, Twitter—or carrier pigeon for that matter—because the goal is always the same: reaching out to stunt coordinators and other stunt people, letting them know who you are and what you can do.

You do almost anything you can—in a professional way—to get yourself known so you can get to the next step.

If you choose to go out into the big cold world of show business, you'll most likely be asked the same set of questions again and again: Do you have your SAG card? Who have you trained with? Who are you related to? Why should I hire you when so many other qualified stunt people are out of work?

For most of us, this is when the little beads of sweat pop up on your upper lip, when your throat dries up, and your voice wants to crack. The trick is to prepare for the worst. That way you won't be disappointed by what happens.

Stunt coordinators come in all shapes, sizes and temperaments. Many of them remember how it felt to be put on the spot. Some are genuinely good people who will do what they can to talk to you and respect you as a human being.

But some are, let's say, "less kind."

I remember being on a set of a very popular TV show back in the early '80s. I had a worked a few jobs, but was still largely unknown—just another stunt guy trying to hustle some work. Then my guardian angel appeared in the form of a stuntman named Larry Holt.

Larry had been around for years, and had worked about every television show there was from the late '60s through the early 2000s. He doubled Paul Newman for years, and he helped create memorable action in films ranging from *The Towering Inferno* to *Pirates of the Caribbean: Curse of the Black Pearl*.

I had the good fortune of working with Larry earlier in that particular year, and he was one of those guys who was generous about sharing his stories and his secrets with you. He had taken a liking to me, and one day when I was hustling a set, he was there, too.

Larry noticed me standing off to the side waiting for the right time to talk to the *jefe* and walked right over to me. We shook hands and did some catching up, and then, without any prodding, he offered to introduce me to the coordinator.

"*Holy crap*," I thought. "*A personal introduction to The Man!*" There I was, ready with my headshot and my double-spaced resume. Standing tall with my chest proudly puffed up.

Larry says, "Joe, (no, not his real name) this is Carl Claifario (everybody always screwed up my name). He's a great new stuntman with talent and a good attitude." I was in!! I wiped off my sweaty palm and offered it up to Joe. And as he reached down to take my headshot from me, I said, "How do you do 'Mr. Quigley' (again, fake). I'm Carl Ciarfalio. I wanted to come by and introduce myse . . ."

I didn't even finish the sentence. Joe took a long drag from his smoke and turned and walked away. Leaving me standing there with my hand waving in the air.

I couldn't believe what had just happened.

By that time, I was used to being around really fine human beings—like Frank Orsatti who coordinated *The Incredible Hulk* series and Ron Stein, who coordinated *Airwolf* and gave me the opportunity to double Lou Ferrigno on *Trauma Center*—not somebody whose only acknowledgement of my existence was a cloud of carcinogens.

I glanced over at Larry and saw that even his mouth had dropped with amazement. But then he shrugged his shoulders, gave me a pat on the back and said, "Ya just never know."

Well, it's more than twenty-five years later, and I'm sure that "Joe" doesn't remember how he treated me that day. In fact, I'm sure he treated almost everybody he came across that way. But I never did work for Joe, nor did I ever hustle him again. I figured out early on that my time was valuable to me, and I quickly decided I wasn't going to waste it on people who wouldn't give me the time of day. I don't wish them any harm; I just want to spend my time with good folks.

So here is where I chalked up another important life and stunt lesson: Take Nothing Personally. Even if someone's a dick—and there will be dicks—you can't take it personally. Just accept the lesson and move forward, staying true to yourself and your goal.

BITTEN BY THE
PERFORMING BUG
AT AN EARLY AGE.
I EVEN PLAYED THE
ACCORDIAN UNTIL
SPORTS (THANKFULLY)
CAME INTO PLAY
FOR ME. *COURTESY:*
CARL CIARFALIO
PRIVATE COLLECTION.

CARL CIARFALIO

Height: 6' 1" / Weight: 230 lbs.
Hair: Black / Eyes: Blue
(714) 821-5275

SOME SIXTEEN YEARS
LATER, I CREATED MY
FIRST COMPOSITE.
BACK IN THE DAY,
WE'D HAND THESE
OUT AS CALLING
CARDS. *COURTESY:*
CARL CIARFALIO
PRIVATE COLLECTION

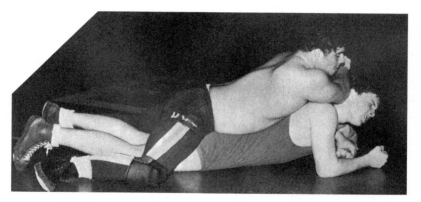

APPLYING A FOREARM ON MY WAY TO A WIN AND OUR TEAM'S LEAGUE CHAMPIONSHIP. *COURTESY: CARL CIARFALIO PRIVATE COLLECTION.*

MY SENIOR YEAR AS SIERRA LEAGUE CHAMP. THAT'S BLOODY COTTON STUFFED UP MY NOSE, THE RESULT OF AN ELBOW I CAUGHT IN THE FIRST ROUND. IT MEANT NO KISS FOR ME FROM THE 'MEDAL GIRL.' *COURTESY: CARL CIARFALIO PRIVATE COLLECTION*

PROUD PARENTS! NICK AND LU VISITING THEIR SON AT 'THE FARM.' *COURTESY: CARL CIARFALIO PRIVATE COLLECTION.*

GETTING SHOT OFF THE ROOF DURING A STREET PERFORMANCE AT KNOTT'S BERRY FARM. *COURTESY: CARL CIARFALIO PRIVATE COLLECTION.*

A STUNTMAN IN
TRAINING, I'M READY
TO TEAR UP THE TRACK
IN MY SHINY NEW DUDS.
*COURTESY: CARL CIARFALIO
PRIVATE COLLECTION.*

AT UNIVERSAL STUDIOS
TOUR'S "WILD WEST
STUNT SHOW." YEAH, I'M
A BIT OF AN INTROVERT.
*COURTESY: CARL CIARFALIO
PRIVATE COLLECTION.*

GIVING JOHN CASINO A LITTLE "LOVE TAP" AT UNIVERSAL STUDIOS TOUR. *COURTESY: CARL CIARFALIO PRIVATE COLLECTION.*

AFTER A LONG DAY OF GETTING BEAT UP, I'VE ALWAYS FOUND IT ENJOYABLE TO RELAX IN A HOT BATH WITH FINE LIQUEUR. *COURTESY: CARL CIARFALIO PRIVATE COLLECTION.*

ON SET WITH ALEX KARRAS AFTER A NIGHT OF DRINKING AND STORYTELLING WHERE MY YOUNG SELF MOSTLY LISTENED. WHAT A THRILL! *COURTESY: CARL CIARFALIO PRIVATE COLLECTION.*

HEADING OUT TO THE JUNGLE IN WARDROBE. I'M DOUBLING ALEX KARRAS, AND STUNT COORDINATOR GARY DAVIS DOUBLED JEFF BRIDGES. *COURTESY: CARL CIARFALIO PRIVATE COLLECTION.*

MY DAUGHTER CARLENE JOINED ME AT A PHOTO SHOOT AND THE
PHOTOGRAPHER WAS IMMEDIATELY CAPTURED BY HER. HOW COULD HE
NOT HAVE BEEN? *COURTESY: CARL CIARFALIO PRIVATE COLLECTION.*

ACT 2 :
CARL ON TELEVISION

CHAPTER 8
TELEVISION ACTION EXPLODES

I find television very educating. Every time somebody turns on the set, I go into the other room and read a book.

GROUCHO MARX

T
elevision in the 1980s and 1990s was a bonanza for stunt performers. Cop shows, detective shows, soaps and sitcoms—they all had bad guys who had to rough people up and then get vanquished by the good guys.

Back then, when my focus was all stunts, all the time, the big shows included *Knight Rider, Airwolf, The A Team, The Fall Guy, Sledge Hammer!, MacGyver, Charlie's Angels* and *Magnum P.I.* Each was pretty much the same in terms of action. It was good guy vs. bad guy with henchman. Stunt people would stand in for stars, handling the serious action; we would stand by the stars, ready to do their deadly bidding; some of us would even play roles, standing up against the stars only to fall victim to their heroism.

If bikers were the hot ticket, then I would find myself playing a biker on several different TV shows until the next wave of ideas made its way into the production offices.

Throughout those golden years of action on television, I played a cop, a killer, a shopper, an ice cream man, an elf, a sheik, a soldier, a rapist, a transvestite, a drunk, a drug dealer, a Pilgrim, a cowboy, a boxer, a biker, a thug, bully, mad dog, psycho, terrorist, hit man, baddie, cop and robber.

The thug uniform of the day was a pair of polyester slacks (usually slightly belled at the bottom), a patterned, polyester shirt (that may or may not have matched the pants) and a "Members Only" jacket complete with epaulets. Sometimes it was beige, sometimes black. Every stuntman who's played a goon on TV over the past thirty or forty years has worn the same uniform.

With that background, let's move on to talk about some shows!

CHAPTER 9
BJ AND THE BEAR

Never work with animals or children.

W.C. FIELDS

My first television job was on *BJ and the Bear*. Greg Evigan starred in this series about a truck driver and his pet/partner Bear, a chimpanzee.

My dear friend John Casino had worked for and befriended Gary Jensen, the stunt coordinator on the series. Gary has coordinated television and films for years, including the present-day *X-Men* franchise.

One night after work at Universal, John called to ask if I was available to play a part on the show, telling me it was about a week of work. This was huge! Finally! I was going to be on TV . . . on a hit show! As I picked myself off the floor, I yelled into the phone, "YES!"

The next day I met with Gary at Universal Studios. A man of few words and even fewer open emotions, he was very matter of fact with me. He told me I'd be doing a fight with the star, Greg Evigan—"*holy shi*t*"—asked me if I could do dia-log—"Sure I can!"—and then said he'd let me know when to report for a wardrobe fitting—"Yes, sir!"

I was so excited at the opportunity to work. Once on the set, I paid strict atten-tion to every detail and instruction, even if it wasn't directed at me. It was a new world that was soon to become my new home.

I remember being so impressed by all these people who knew their jobs and could do them well, yet still had enough time and personality to be human and kind. I remember thinking, "*You know, it doesn't take that much out of you to be good to the people around you. Look at some of these guys, even the actors are good people.*" (To be honest, the monkey was a bit of a pain in the ass.)

I concentrated on my "character," and I studied my lines endlessly—all three of them! I was working onstage in a boat that was rigged to sway with the waves that appeared in the beautiful ocean background. I was sprayed in the face with gallons of water to make sure it all looked real.

This was the start of a new life experience for me. This is where I got the first real taste of the biz in front of the camera. New people, new challenges and new opportunities.

I was on my way. I had successfully pulled off a real stunt job.

I thought I did great work! Stardom was surely ahead. But I sought out the video recently and realized that even though I had excellent hair, I was stiff and slow to react. Thinking back, others must have seen that too, because even though I never stopped hustling, I didn't work in front of the camera again for another six months.

Thank goodness I had my "summer job" at Universal. Although I subsequently worked more and more on camera, it was difficult to give up that steady paycheck. Ultimately, I hung onto the Universal gig for almost five years. I finally left when I could no longer juggle my live shows with my growing film and television schedule.

It was time to fall headfirst into the world of professional Hollywood stuntmen.

CHAPTER 10
SCARECROW AND MRS. KING

I think that to explore the uncomfortable and the politically incorrect is the job of the artist.

JARED LETO

Hanging around Chichen Itza waiting to do my dead man fall on *Against All Odds* led to my second job with Gary Davis.

About eight of us hung around together back in those jungle days— including Gary's wife, Madonna. We toured the marketplace, where horse heads were a dietary staple, and visited ruins. We had all kinds of fabulous experiences. But it was hotter than hell down there, so we'd always end up back at the hotel pool, drinking tequila margaritas. These were made by one of our very good friends on the show, Carrie, who had the good sense to schlep her blender from Hollywood to location. Good move, Carrie.

By then it was clear that I loved an audience, and for several days, I had a captive poolside crowd. I had perfected the against-type character I played at Universal's Wild West Show—a big sissy. I never played him over the top (okay, hardly ever). Instead, I tried to let the physical dichotomy of a muscled tough guy speak for itself. This challenged people's first impressions—they always expected the big guy to be a bad-ass and kick ass. It was a successful character, and it's been fun for me to pull him out from time to time.

So one hot and humid day as we were lounging around the hotel pool, Madonna began complaining that the weather was making her hair look bad. So I got up, stood behind her, and began to fluff, touch, stroke and manhandle her hair as only a hairdresser would. And the whole time I ad-libbed dialog in a voice that sounded like Nathan Lane wearing braces.

Just enough of a lisp, a slight cock of the head, my hands held just so with my little fingers crooked. There was a lightness in my voice, and I displayed a marked disdain for anyone else's suggestions for saving Madonna's hair. Okay, maybe I was a little bitchy. I just felt so trapped in my body. (Sorry, that's probably for another book.)

We all had a good laugh. And of course, for the duration of the trip, whenever the time was right, "Carlo" would come out and fix someone's hair. Good fun was had by all.

That experience came full circle when Gary called with the offer of work on the hit show *Scarecrow and Mrs. King*. The hour-long CBS series starred Bruce Boxleitner as a special government agent who enlists the help of a housewife, played by Kate Jackson of TV's *Charlie's Angels* fame. Gary explained that in an episode titled "Fearless Dotty," a bad guy—played by actor William Smith, then one of the best baddies in town—stalked series star Beverly Garland—who played Kate Jackson's mother—to a beauty salon, and intended to attack her as she sat napping under a hairdryer, oblivious to the action around her.

So I said, "And I'm one of Smith's guys, right?" Gary answered, "Oh no. You'll be playing the salon's owner, Mr. Emilio." Then he added, "He's a hairdresser, and I want you to play it just like you did in Mexico."

And play I did. Complete with tight red pants, a black sleeveless shirt, and a snappy red bandana tied around my neck.

I was to get in the way when star Boxleitner mixed it up with Smith. At one point in their fight, they would run into me, knocking me backward through a glass partition. Oh, the horror! I had a hoot of a time playing Mr. Emilio in all my—ah, his—glory.

Over twenty years later, I'm still amazed at how that job came about. All thanks to Gary, Madonna, and Carrie's blender.

Gary continued to be good to me over the years, hiring me for several episodes and placing me in some, might I say, 'tight' spots. "How tight?" you ask?

I was playing a henchman involved in a big fight on another *Scarecrow* episode called "Relative Situation" that we shot in an airport hangar in Van Nuys, California. At one point in the fight, Gary, doubling Boxleitner, sprints across the hangar floor and tackles me away from one of the good guys. Gary had me lined up with a free-standing eight-foot by sixteen-foot metal shelving unit filled with manuals, boxes, and spare, plane engine parts. When he hit me (like Ray Lewis blindsiding a quarterback) we toppled straight into—then over—the now-twisted monster. Then we got up and blew through it from the other side as we danced and grunted our way to another part of the hangar.

Ouch! Yes, ouch.

After that, the choreography had the actor, Boxleitner, and I pressed up against the wing of a plane with turning propellers. We were just a couple of feet away from the spinning blades, meaning that one slip, one heavy push, one moment of not paying attention could have meant a very ugly accident.

Some of the hardest hitting and vicious fights that I've done are from Gary's excellent action choreography. It's demanding, exhausting, brutal and really, really good!

CHAPTER 11
WILD, WICKED RATCHET RIDES

I hope I didn't brain my damage.

HOMER SIMPSON

I was working on a TV show in the early 1980s, and the truth is, I can't remember the name of the show. This isn't a failing memory. Rather, during that time in my career I was fortunate enough to be able to go from job to job almost daily . . . and they just kind of ran together.

On this particular show, several of us stunt guys were on board to do a shoot-out in a fast food restaurant. My gag was to take a hit from a handgun and launch myself back from the impact over a table to the floor. The stunt guy next to me was Allan Graf.

Graf was an All-American football player out of USC who became a go-to stunt coordinator and 2nd unit director—notably for a slew of football movies including

Any Given Sunday, The Replacements, Jerry Maguire, and *Friday Night Lights.* He's also run a range of shows from action to drama to comedy including *Magnolia, Boogie Nights, The Doors, Poltergeist* and *The Hangover Part 2.*

On this job, Allan was taking a shotgun blast to the chest. To ramp up his reaction, a ratchet was going to jerk him backward to the floor, then pull him several feet to the front of a counter.

What's a ratchet? Glad you asked.

Back then, you could walk up to a stunt guy and ask, "Have you done a jerk-off lately?" Or say to a stuntwoman, "I heard Fred took you for quite a ride the other night." (To be specific, you could ask this question on a film set—not so much at the grocery store.)

These terms—along with "nut buster" and "being snatched"—are how we stunters describe doing a gag called a ratchet. At times, the ratchet delivers the perfect "E-Ticket" ride—exhilarating, energizing, cool. At other times, it's the wreck of the week. "Film-at-eleven"-worthy footage of you getting your lunch handed to you.

Shaped like a car's shock absorber, only much larger, the ratchet is a mechanical device that can propel a full-grown man several feet backward. Landing him flat on his back if he's lucky—or flat on the back of his head if he's not.

A pressure regulator determines the speed at which the cable attached to you is "snatched" into the ratchet housing's tube, thus defining how fast you will void the space in which you were just standing. Today's computerized ratchets are so good they can pick you up and put you down in the same spot at the same speed every time.

Yesterday's ratchets—not so much.

Up through the mid-80s, the "hand pull" system was used. This is just what it sounds like.

Depending on how far you needed to fly or how high you needed to go, two, three, or six men would be on one end of a rope or cable, working to control you. That line was run through a pulley the stunt riggers would attach to something sturdy, such as a tall tree branch, an I-beam, a truss, a truck's trailer hitch or some other stable structure. The line would then be run to the ratchet housing. The other end of the cable was attached to what we call a "jerk harness" or "jerk vest." When the director called "Action!" the team of stuntmen would work in unison to pull on the line as hard as they could, thus "flying" you where you needed to go.

Let's talk a little bit about the jerk harness. It's a form-fitting vest made out of nylon and webbing that's worn as tight as an extra layer of skin. It's cinched by a set of straps that go through your legs at the crotch—which, I can tell you from personal experience, pulls your ya-yas up so high it looks like you have a couple of extra Adam's Apples. And then, just for the fun of it, you have to pull your chest strap so tight your mind's not sure you can still breathe. I think it's done this way because as long as you're gasping for air, you don't have time to think about never being able to feel your manhood again.

On this "vest of death" are strategically placed "pick points" where the cable is hooked to pull you in this direction or that. Sometimes they're positioned at your sides, but usually they're located in the spine area and at the base of the back of your neck, between your shoulder blades and dead center of your back. (Hmmm. Why do you think they call it "dead" center?)

Where you are picked will depend on how you are to be lifted out of the shot. It's like the story of Goldilocks and the bears' beds.

If the pick is placed higher than the ratchet, you'll be pulled directly to the ground, and will land on the back of your head with the force of a casaba melon being slammed to the floor. "Too hard."

If your pick is placed lower than the ratchet, you'll be pulled up and will flop forward like a rag doll and snap in half as you take a bite out of your knees. "Too soft."

But if the ratchet is lined up at the correct angle, and the wire is attached to the center pick on your vest . . . "Just right."

Even so, nothing is certain but death and taxes . . . and the fact that if you ride the rippin' rail enough times—aka the winged wire, aka the wicked ratchet—you're gonna' get slammed.

With that explained, back to my friend Allan.

The ratchet was positioned on the floor, and the pick was in the middle of Allan's back. Everything was properly set, but it was clearly going to be a thumper. He's traveling out of his chair at the set's table, straight to his back on the hard cement floor, and then he's going to get dragged about seven feet before coming to rest at the foot of a counter. Ouch!

The director called "Action," and when it was time, I hurled myself over the table as planned and came to rest on my chest on the floor, taking my squib hits with all the truthful force I could. (Squibs are battery-operated packets of fake blood that explode on your body as if you were being shot. Squibs are also used to explode items around the set such as plates, bottles, walls, and windows.)

From this position, I saw squibs and sparks flying all around me, and then I heard the shotgun of the ratchet go off. Bam! Allan—240 pounds of former-USC All-American, Rose-Bowl-winning pulling guard—got snapped back so hard that when he landed, I swear the floor rumbled.

From my vantage point—dead on the floor—I saw how hard he hit and heard the blurt of air that flew from his body when he struck the floor. But nothing prepared any of us for what happened at the end of Allan's magical ride.

The cable that was supposed to take him the final few feet to the counter was a couple of inches longer than it should have been. This meant that instead of ending up in a heap on the floor in front of the counter, Allan slammed into it with the force of a charging ram. The back of his head banged on the counter, and I heard the aforementioned sound of a ripe melon being thumped.

Allan survived to get jerked around another day; we'll talk more about him soon.

I've had the pleasure and the pain of riding the ratchet myself many times over the years. I remember one time, when I was a young pup, getting a job on a movie that had an extremely small budget.

The fight I was hired to do took place out in the middle of nowhere on the side of a road. The excellent stunt coordinator-turned-director, David Ellis, who set up the fight, explained that I would be hammered in the chest with a club, and that they wanted the blow to send me backward over the hood of a car. "Oh," he added, "and don't land on the car. It belongs to the producer . . . it's a 280 Mercedes convertible."

Now with a ratchet, the chances of me getting over the hood of the car are pretty good. But remember this movie had a small budget, so I was going to be pulled by a couple of stunt guys who were being backed up by a couple of hefty grips (grips are lighting and rigging technicians.)

Jimmy Haltey was the only stuntman on set with a jerk harness. Jimmy stands five-foot-seven and is 160 pounds; I was six feet and 225 pounds. He handed me the rig and off I went to put it on. I wanted to do the gag so badly that no way was I going to tell him that it fit me like the harness Lon Chaney wore to keep him from being able to stand up straight in *The Hunchback of Notre Dame*.

So there I was, standing as bent as the Elephant Man himself, ready to go flying up, up and over the producer's gold Mercedes two-seater.

The director called "Action!" and the club swung at my chest with the force of mighty *Casey at the Bat*. I took my reaction and began my backward momentum. I could feel the tug of the line pulling me up and I thought, *"Uh-oh. Not going up. Going back, but not going up."* And then I realized, *"Oh no. I am dragging across something smooth and shiny and gold."* And then I fell onto my back, and finally, I hit the ground.

"Hmmm. What to do."

"Son of a . . . !" I hear coming from off-camera. "Did he scratch it?"

It was the producer, hollering from behind the camera.

"No, it's just a little mark," hollered back one of the transportation guys. "We can get it rubbed out for you, sir."

Then the director spoke up.

"That didn't work. We have to do it again."

"Ok," the producer said. "But this time, put more people on the line to pull him."

So now there were six guys on the pull line. They had recruited a couple of bulky Teamsters to help out.

Here we go again.

"And *Action!!*"

As I lifted my weight off my feet this time, I felt the wind at the back of my ears and knew I was a fair distance up in the air. In fact, I was at least three feet higher than the hood of the Benz. But sure enough, tragedy struck. Team Big Boys had pulled me so hard that I had flown high in the air . . . in a prone position. The Boys had done one thing wrong. They didn't pull me far enough, and like a meteor dropping from the sky, I came down on the hood, fender, *and* the antenna.

"CUT! CUT! CUT!"

"Ah crap!" was what I heard from the AD.

Well, nothing we could do about it, so we moved on to the next shot. The show must go on.

Technology has grown tenfold in the last twenty years, and it's affected the business of stunts just as it's affected the rest of the world. We can jump from higher heights. We can light ourselves on fire for minutes at a time. We jump cars farther and get jerked off faster than ever before.

That's right, *jerked off*. See? You can't help but laugh when you say it!

CHAPTER 12
FAIR GAME

I got hammered plenty of times through the years. But you just get up and keep play-ing. I can tell you from experience, though. Sometimes it hurts like hell.

TERRY BRADSHAW

Many stunt folks have seen the ceiling of the inside of an ambulance at one time or another . . . and some of us have seen them more than others. My first ride came in the late 1980s when I was working on a Movie of the Week called *Fair Game*. It was a pilot that never made it to series that told the story of a retired police officer—Bruce Weitz of *Hill Street Blues* fame—who tracks down a bail-jumping ex-con.

I played a hit man posing as a parking lot toll taker. I was to step out of the booth at the bottom of the drive ramp, level my 45-caliber pistol and shoot the guy coming at me in a car.

Now if I was a hit man in the real world, I'd wait till my target stopped to pay the parking fee, reach in, and shoot him from six inches away. But instead, some good writer out there decided how it should be done, and thankfully so. Without that writer, there'd have been no car hit, no stunt adjustment and no hero story to tell you.

A stunt adjustment is a variable amount we are paid over and above our daily union rate for a particular stunt. Stunt coordinators budget these fees in the pre-production stage of a project. This practice is intended to acknowledge and reward a stunt performer's expertise and commitment to the action. It is also intended to compensate us for placing ourselves in situations that are too dangerous for an actor to undertake.

The stunt coordinator was once again Gary Davis. I was once again confident and scared spitless all at the same time.

Gary was going to drive the car, a Firebird with a low hood that would be easy for me to get on top of. So far, so good. Our location was a parking ramp at the West Side Pavilion shopping center in Century City, just outside of Beverly Hills. The ramp had a significant slope from the top down to the exit, where I was positioned.

I recall it was just before 9 a.m. when the 2nd Assistant Director asked me if I was ready to go.

I told him that I needed time to talk to Gary. I had to figure out what his speed would be when he hit me with the Firebird, and what first move I would make to get onto and over the car. The most important thing in a car hit is clear and concise communication between the driver, the director, the camera department, and the guy getting hit by the car. One beat off and it could mean needing to do it a second time . . . or disaster.

Gary said he wanted me to try to go the length of the car, then fall off the trunk to the asphalt. We covered every detail possible. I knew that this could be a thumper, so I wanted to make sure there'd be no surprises.

In our prep conversation, Gary said the car was a manual shift; that he would hit me while in second gear while moving about twelve to fourteen miles an hour; then he'd punch the gas to make sure that I got over the car cleanly—a little boost if you will. He said he'd drive through the gate arm, which would break on his wind-shield, and then drive away.

Okay? Okay. "Give me a few minutes to get myself ready," I told him, and he left me alone so I could visualize my movements.

The truth is that when you do a car hit this way—actually letting the car take you up and over as opposed to doing the action in four or five staged cuts—the first move you make is pretty much the only one you completely control. That first move is getting onto the hood of the car without being run through with the front bumper. After you're on the hood of the car, you're pretty much on a wild ride with a short stop at the end.

So I readied myself for the gag. But my preparation was interrupted when I noticed that there were five . . . FIVE . . . windshields quietly tucked away in the parking garage.

Now I knew that when doing a car hit like this, there's a great possibility that a windshield would break and a second or third take will be required. But *FIVE*?

"Hey Gary," I called to him, "why all the windshields?"

He flashed his sparkling smile and said, "I want you to get into the windshield and break it if you can. The rest are for backup in case we don't get it the first time."

No way I wanted to do this gag six times.

I smiled back and took a deep breath.

"Okay! We're ready for the stunt!" the call came over the megaphone. My stomach flipped, a chill went up my spine, and my butt puckered all at the same time. "Here we go!" I remember mumbling.

We had already shot the part where I step out and shoot at the car. Now all I had to do was hold a rubber gun and stand in front of a car that was coming down the ramp at me.

Easy.

Well, not really.

You see, it goes against everything that we as humans know is right. From the time we can remember, we are told to stay out of the middle of the street and out of the way of cars that are coming our way. So all the time you're doing a gag like this, your practical mind is saying, "*Get the hell out of the way!*" while your stunt brain says, "*Stay, stay, stay . . . NOW!*" Kind of like the "Devil" and the "Angel" on Tom Hulce's shoulders in *Animal House*.

Here we go. All four cameras are ready and running. Here comes Gary, out of the structure and down the ramp. I'm standing on my mark in the car's path, and I hear Gary shift into second gear. I'm ready now. I'm going to let the car take me by knocking out my right leg. I'll be on my toes and give myself a little boost to get up and over the hood. I'll go to the hood on my right shoulder, hit the windshield and let myself slide on top of the roof and off the trunk. Great plan!

Yeah, that's what I'm going to do . . . bring it to me, Gary . . . here we go . . . "*what the?!*"

With the car maybe fifty feet from me, I hear Gary grab another gear and come straight at me. Can't bail out now, he's coming and he's moving in on me. "*NOW!*" I tell myself. I get my feet off the ground and tuck my right shoulder to the hood of the car like I was doing a judo roll.

"*Bitchin! I got it . . . WOW! What the fu . . . !*"

I remember hitting the hood all right, and then I started spinning. I saw "sky, car, sky, car."

This confused me, because it's not what I had planned.

As it turned out, everything was on track when Gary hit me. I slid into the windshield, shattering it and punching it several inches inward. But when he gassed the car to get me over the roof, my left shoulder caught the car at the roofline, and it spat me up into the air like a marble being launched from a slingshot.

I got tossed about twelve feet or so in the air and made a couple of twists that would have gotten me a 9.7 from the Russian judge. I sort of remember seeing the car pass underneath me . . . and then it was gone. The asphalt was the only thing left to land on.

I hit the pavement like Superman. Arms extended and at a forty-five degree angle, like when the Man of Steel breaks through the cement and tunnels underground. Except for the fact that I'm not Superman and I didn't break through the cement, it was exactly the same.

I don't remember slamming my forehead into the street, but I do remember, as my friend and fellow stuntman Rick Sawaya puts it, seeing the "*FLASH.*" If you've ever been unfortunate enough to get smacked in the head by a bat or run head-on into a pole, you know what the *"FLASH"* is.

I didn't lose consciousness, and I had enough brains left to play dead until I heard them yell, "CUT!" Then I felt the warmth of my blood pooling around me, and I knew that I might be hurt. So I did what I always do. I took a quick inventory of my body.

"Fingers . . . check. Toes . . . check. Legs moving . . . check. Okay, not paralyzed. That's good."

With that established, I was ready to feel the pain without being so worried about it. I thought I might have fractured my skull—and so did the director, the medic and a few others. But after they came to my rescue, we decided that I had a really hard head and that I just needed some thread to put me back together.

Gary was the first one to get to me, followed by the medic and the director, and then by my good friend, stuntwoman Marian Green-Hofstein.

I had taken Marian to the hospital a few months earlier when she broke a toe doing a gnarly car hit for Gary. So she came out to support me, even though she was seven months pregnant at the time.

She walked over to see if I was okay, took one look and walked away. Head wounds bleed. *A lot.* That was okay because there was an ambulance standing by, and I had already—with superstitious reluctance—given them my blood type before the stunt. The boys wrapped up my noggin and laid me on a gurney for the ride to the UCLA Medical Center. By the time they got me ready to go, I was uncomfortable, but not in a lot of pain.

The 2nd AD—the position on a film that keeps track of stunt adjustments—came over to make sure I let them know what the outcome was at the hospital. He was a sweet young man, fairly new in the business. He looked to Gary to see how much to put down on the time sheet for my adjustment. Gary, who was several yards away at the time, held up two fingers. So the young AD turned to me and said, "Okay that's a two hundred dollar adjustment. Will you please sign right . . . *aackk!*"

From my prone position on the gurney, I had reached up and grabbed him by his shirt, up around the throat.

"Two hundred?" I questioned. The now terrified 2nd strained to turn his head to look at Gary and choked out the question, "Two hundred, right?" Gary flashed that megawatt smile and said, "No. Two thousand." With that, I released the youth and was on my way to the medical center.

I got lucky there because the doctor on duty just happened to be a plastic surgeon. He did a great job of sewing up the half-moon flap of skin hanging off my forehead just above my eyebrow. It took some time to get released that afternoon, but I felt pretty good considering.

As it turned out, this was one of those fortunate days I had double-booked myself, taking a second job that night as a "stunt doorman" on a TV show called *Nick Knight* that starred rock singer and actor Rick Springfield.

When I showed up on the set, I told the coordinator, Fred Lerner, what had happened to me that day. I said I'd understood if he needed to replace me because of the thread hanging out of my head. After looking me over, he decided I should stay, saying it added to the part.

So I once again dodged a bullet and was lucky enough to work two jobs in a day. I had a bit of a headache for the next couple of days, but the story I got . . . and the adjustment . . . helped balance the pain.

C H A P T E R 1 3
TRAUMA CENTER

Everyone has his own "little Hulk" inside him.

LOU FERRIGNO

I had a regular job doubling an actor only once in my career. It was the early 1980s and Lou Ferrigno was expanding his career after the end of the wildly successful *Incredible Hulk* TV series. Louie was penned to do a new action series featuring one of the first ensemble casts of its kind. The show was called *Trauma Center* and centered on stories about everyday traumas such as auto accidents, fire rescues, and work mishaps.

The show featured an ambulance rescue team made up of Lou and Alfie Wise. Alfie is the actor who played the smart-ass assistant director opposite Burt Reynolds in *Hooper*. If you haven't seen *Hooper*, do it now and then come back. Written and directed by stunt legend Hal Needham, it is the quintessential stunt movie.

Did you watch it? OK. So you saw Alfie. Which means you saw that he is the complete opposite of Ferrigno. Louie is about 6′5″, buff and dark. Alfie is 5′4″ on a good day, and although he was in great shape, he was the size of one of Louie's legs.

Doctors and nurses at the hospital's trauma unit also played a big part in the show, and their casting was terrific as well. Wendie Malick, Dorian Harewood, the great Eileen Heckart and award-winning James Naughton kept the tension going in the ER, while Louie and Alfie supplied them with the patients and their stories.

My opportunity to join this talented group began with a call from Ron Stein, a wonderful human being and a fine stunt coordinator.

Ron told me that he was doing a pilot out of 20th Century Fox and wanted to know if I was available to double Lou Ferrigno.

"Well, yeah, you bet, Ron! God, thanks for the call. What kind of stuff are we doing?" I asked him. "Oh, they've got Lou rescuing a construction worker from a high-rise building. And maybe a couple of other things," he said. "Great! That sounds great. That's great." I kept reassuring him, all the while trying not to let my voice crack.

See, to me, the words "high-rise" meant that I would need to be OFF THE GROUND. And I like it right down here where I am. Sometimes I even like a rail around me when I'm down here. On the ground. But I'd been up in high places before, and I figured this would just be one more dragon I'd have to slay to move forward in my career.

Ron and I talked a few times that week, and he let me know what the gag called for. A construction worker on the eleventh floor of a building gets his arm sliced off at the shoulder, and Louie has to go up, get him, and bring him down. My action was to walk a steel construction beam about twenty-five feet long to a platform, pick up the injured worker, put him on my shoulders in a "fireman's carry," then walk back across the beam with him on my back.

That's all. *Just* that. Oh. Great.

The minute we hung up, I called my dad, Nick, my hero. I told him I wanted to come over and get some professional advice about walking high steel.

My pop was an ironworker all of his life. He worked on most of the major high rises in Los Angeles from the early 1960s until he retired in the early 1980s. I had gone to visit him at work a couple of times, finding him up on a scaffold or walking across a beam a hundred feet in the air. Sometimes I'd find him hanging off the end of a building, welding a beam to a girder or a rivet to a steel plate, or whatever it is that those guys do. I'm not exactly certain, because my young self was too busy making sure I was standing on the biggest piece of whatever there was to stand on, and grabbing on to whatever would make sure I stayed there.

I remember watching my dad walk across the beams as if he was walking down the sidewalk. It was always impressive. And I needed to know how to do that *and balance a man on my back while doing it.*

His teaching was simple and direct. "Don't look down. Don't ever look down. Look at where you're going to, not down. You'll follow your eyes. If you look down, chances are you'll lose your balance. Look forward . . . and don't look down."

Okay. So you're saying "don't look down." Got it.

Turned out that was a very unnatural thing to "not do" when you're up in the air.

For the next few days, I walked on everything from a railroad track to a beam in a construction yard to the curb in front of my house. I walked anything that would help me get the feel of something that was about six inches wide. It's tough to not look down, but you better not. Every time I did, I'd lose my concentration and balance when I looked back up. My old man was right.

When I got to work that day, I was as ready as could be. I saw a couple of stunt friends there, and we started to talk about the day's work. This guy Dave says, "Ya, I'm playing the construction worker who gets his arm cut off." And I look at him for a long minute, the whole time my butt puckering like a year-old prune, and I say, "Cool. I better go get changed."

'Dave' was David Cadiente, a talented stuntman with movie-star looks who stood close to six-feet tall and weighed about 190 pounds.

We went up to the site of the scene—eleven floors up. Plywood sheets were laid out across the open beams, allowing us to move safely from the shaky scissor-lift ride to the opposite side of the building where the action was to take place.

Then I noticed one section waaaaay over there in the corner where there wasn't any plywood. Sure enough, that was going to be our spot. So I went over there and took me a look down. Okay, I admit it, wrong thing to do. It was a freakin' loooong way down!

The director, an energetic young man by the name of Thomas Carter, was setting up the shot while I was concentrating on just how to attack this animal with Dave on my back. Carter, who has since won a number of Emmy Awards for his directing, said, "I want you to go across this beam." And with that, he walked—practically skipped—across the freakin' steel beam like he was gliding across a dance floor!

"Well," I thought, "I'm hosed now! Not only do I have to butch up for this thing, but the stunt coordinator just saw the director do what most of us didn't want to do."

You have to understand that his little walk computed to a much lower adjustment at the end of the day.

I would guess the conversation would go something like this. Ron Stein to the Unit Production Manager (the one who manages production money): "I want to adjust Carl 'X' amount of dollars for his gag." UPM: "Come on Ron, it's not even worth half that. Hell, the *director* walked across the beam."

So we got ready to do this thing, this "walk of death" as it was for me.

Louie took the first step onto the beam and then the director yelled, "Cut! Bring in the stuntman." So I jumped right on the mark. One floor below me were two stuntmen who were to pull a port-a-pit along the left side of the beam. In case I fell, I had better fall to my left, because to the right of me was a long way down.

I took my first step and immediately focused on the point that I was walking to. It was hard to not look down, but Nick's gravel-soft voice never left my head. I made it to the other side fairly easily, made the move as if to pick up Dave, and then we cut.

It was half-time for me. The sweat was just now starting to show on my forehead.

The cameras were reset for the trip back with Dave on my shoulders. We preset him up on me, so all I would have to do is find the beam and start my way back. He was perfectly still. One arm was hidden under his jacket because the story was that his arm had been severed from his body. He was laying across my shoulders like a buck I had bagged on a hunt. I was looking straight ahead while he was only able to look straight down below us. The port-a-pit was now on our right side, and I've already told you what was now on our left. That's right . . . *nuttin'!*

The first step was the hardest to take. It took everything I had to concentrate on making my foot move out onto the beam solid and sure. *"There it is . . . trust yourself, Carl. You can do this."* That was my mantra for the moment. In fact, it's been my mantra several times throughout my career.

Right step (I always lead with my right side, be it air rams, high falls or high steel beams) . . . balance . . . left step . . . balance. I got it now. Dave's weight is nicely centered on my shoulders, and he was as still as a dead man.

Right . . . left . . . rig . . . *"OH SHIT! DON'T LOSE IT NOW! YOU GOT IT. GRIP. BE STURDY. GET CENTERED!"*

I had just officially learned what it was like to be scared to death. I had taken a step with my right foot and started to lose my balance. The footage onscreen shows me making a little stumble on the beam. It wasn't two seconds between stumble and recovery, but it felt like forever. I gathered every inch of my strength and straightened without jerking my body around.

I caught my breath, moved forward to the end of the beam and stepped onto a thick piece of plywood.

Now, I don't know if anyone can relate to what goes through your mind at a moment like that. True, you have all the thoughts that I've given you above. But it's that second voice that really kicks in. You know, the one that talks you down to common sense when you're in a "fight or flight" mode. Mine said, *"Carl, you have a man on your shoulders and his life is in your hands. Make sure that IF you fall, he ends up on the pad."* I was very lucky.

In truth, it was Dave who saved us. He committed himself to the job he was doing and the trust that he had for me. Dave didn't even flinch when I stumbled. If he would have jerked or stiffened, we would have had a much harder time recovering. He was truly a pro. And am I thankful for that.

At that time, I was the best double in town for Lou—as long as I didn't stand next to him. He's an easy four inches taller than me, and even back in the day, my waist was never as small as his and my arms were never as big as his twenty-plus inch guns. My legs are also shorter than his so my strides aren't as long or smooth as his are.

But through the magic of Hollywood, with all the smoke and mirrors we used, and mindful that people want to believe what they see . . . I was a great double for the Big Guy.

I have to say the whole "Stunt Double" experience for me was a little strange at first.

You want to be respectful. You never know if you should stand next to the actor that you're doubling. You don't want to make it look like you think that you're equal to him in the eyes of the cast and crew. I'm not saying that all actors are like this, but I think that's it's best to find out a little at a time. Plus, back then, stunt performers were very much in the background. The publicity machine avoided any indication that stars were not doing everything onscreen.

Eventually, Louie and I became very close working friends. I helped him learn to trust me to have his back by always knowing when he might need to be spotted from a ledge or a tight spot. I also knew whenever he might need a kneepad—for his elbow. The man's arms are huge! Fortunately for me, so are his talent and his kindness.

We did more than a few uncommon gags on *Trauma Center*.

There was the time that I had to wrangle a cobra that had gotten loose in a game arcade. And, the time I had to wrestle a steer that had escaped its corral.

"Just clamp on right here. Yep, like your bulldoggin' her," is what the steer wrangler told me in his best cowboy twang. "Don't you worry 'bout a thing. She weighs near to six hundred pounds, but we're gonna give her a shota' this here drug to slow her down some," he reassured me. "Oh yeah," he added, "be sure to bury your head deep into her neck thar, so as not to get smacked in the mouth ifin' she snaps her head back."

That got my attention.

I grew up in West Covina, California. The biggest wild thing we had seen was a kid on the block named Randy. I definitely didn't know from wild animals. So they shoot this big cow up with a big ol' syringe, and I finally see him start to slow down a little. He hung his head just a bit lower, and his horns, each about two-and-a-half feet long, didn't look quite as deadly.

Okay, we're ready, and I'm locked on him. Head tucked in, a death grip on the horns and the camera starts to roll. I'm doing my best acting, trying to make it look like I'm really wrestling this guy into the pen, when he gets a boost of bull adrenaline and comes to. He snapped his head up and shook it side to side, flopping me around like a flag in a hurricane. Just as suddenly went back to being more subdued, and I guided him into his pen. He must have had a good laugh with his friends that night, telling them how he flipped this stuntman around with a mere flick of his head.

Then there was the Bengal tiger.

Appropriately named "Tigger," this cat was a beautiful specimen of God's creation. He was still growing when I worked with him, so he only weighed around 350 pounds.

The script called for Lou and Alfie to rescue a model at a photo shoot who was being mauled by the cat. Trainers Monty Cox and Glory Fiormonte—both also outstanding stunt performers and very good friends of mine—told production that I needed a play session with Tigger to make sure he would work with me once we got on the set.

So I set a date to rehearse with the tiger in an open field near Valencia, CA. It was a late morning, and I took a friend and her teenage son to watch and get some pictures. I prepped them about the dangers of the cat, emphasizing that they should do exactly what the trainers said.

When we arrived at the rehearsal spot, the cat was in his cage and Monty, Glory, and their assistant were there and ready to start. They explained that Tigger needed to know he could play with me and be the victor of each of our wrestling matches, or he wouldn't want to play or work with me once we got to the set.

I absorbed everything they told me, including their instructions to go down the first time he knocked into me—and that whatever else I did, "*DO NOT . . . DO NOT EVER . . . LET HIM GET HIS MOUTH CLOSE TO YOUR NECK!*"

Why? Turns out it's a natural instinct for the cat to bite down on an animal's neck to render it helpless before the kill.

Well okay and crap!!

"Oh yeah," Glory added in her sweetest little voice, "when he's on top of you, make this sound (she then demonstrates a guttural purring sound made in the back of her throat) so he knows you're talking to him."

I stood at the ready in the middle of the desert, like the last wildebeest at the watering hole—the one the tigers sit and wait for. Everyone else was at least twenty-five yards away. My friend, her son and Glory were in one spot; Monty was a few yards from them; and the assistant was on the other side of me, manning Tigger's cage.

Tigger was beautiful. He was a big puddy cat, with huge eyes and thick fur you wanted to bury your face into. He appeared to be a pretty good size (standing twenty yards away) and had gorgeous colors and markings.

When his cage door was opened, Tigger came out slowly. At first he sniffed the air, catching all the new scents that were blowing around. He then walked a few steps and looked around. He didn't make eye contact with any of us, but you could tell he was completely aware of his handler's presence.

Next, Tigger began a playful lope around the field as if he were chasing butterflies from the bushes. How magnificent he seemed to me—powerful and graceful all at the same time.

Then, as if he were tracing a question mark in the dirt, he turned a wide half circle, and at a bounding lope, shot out like a dart heading straight for the group of three. Tigger toppled my friend in a nanosecond, then immediately turned and put his sights on me.

Come to find out that Tigger's animal instinct was working. He had taken a look around, found what he considered the smallest and weakest target—someone unlike his handlers, who had no power over him. He didn't hurt her when he ran over her; he just wanted to let his prowess be known.

It only took a moment for the dust to settle. Monty urged me to not lose my focus on the cat. He told me to call the cat by name, then skip and run and let him chase me and catch me.

Okay, here I go.

"Tigger!" I called to him in my best Tarzan-like voice. "Here Tigger!" And with that I started to jog away from him. I figured I'd get several steps before I would need to brace myself for his tackle. WRONG! I took two steps, turned to look and call him again, and then I witnessed the strangest thing. Tigger's eyes zeroed in on me like those of a cartoon character, and then he moved more quickly than anything

I had ever seen. Before I could get "Here Tig . . ." out of my mouth, he was on me. He knocked me down with powerful grace then just kept moving forward.

We did this a couple of times to teach him that he could easily take me down to play. Then the fun started. I'd call to him, and he'd pounce on me and lay on top of me like I was his slave doll. "Protect your neck!" Monty would call to me. "Talk to him, Carl," Glory would chime in.

So face down with my hands locked around the back of my neck, I started to talk to the powerful beast.

Only thing was, I had cottonmouth so badly that I couldn't get enough spit in my mouth to drown a gnat. So the sound I was making was more like a snake hissing than a tiger purring.

We did this drill a few times. I got to the point that he would let me turn over onto my back and play with him face to face. And if you thought my mouth was dry before, it was now the Gobi desert. I literally had no saliva. Glory had to keep making the purring sound for me from several yards away, just to help keep Tigger happy.

As I laid there, with my arms crossed at the wrists and placed between me and Tigger, my senses were working. I took it all in.

That cat's head was massive, and his teeth were huge and white. His breath wasn't bad, and although his fur looked soft and inviting, it was coarser than I had expected. Funny the things that go through your head at times like these.

Tigger, meanwhile, could have gotten past my crossed arms with one swoop of his catcher's-mitt-sized paw, but he was playing with me. He was having fun.

However when he tired of me, he was simply done. He just walked away.

When we got to the set a couple of days later, Tigger and I said hello. (I had been drinking lots of water and practicing my 'Tigger talk.') When it was time to shoot Tigger jumping on me, it all went fine until he realized I wasn't going to fall down this time. He gave a couple of half-hearted attempts at making it look like an attack, but became uninterested pretty fast. We managed to get the shot, and then we were done.

Kids and animals, you have to watch out who you're working with.

Toward the end of the season, the script called for me to do a rappel and rescue of a world-famous building climber who was attempting to scale one of the twin towers in downtown Long Beach.

As the story went, a famous thrill-seeking mountain climber—played by George Willig, an actual mountain-climber who ascended the South Tower of the World Trade Center in 1977—was about halfway up the building when he suffers an equipment failure. He falls several floors, only to be suspended like a spider at the end of his silk thread. Louie and Alfie are the first ones on the scene and devise a plan to rescue him.

George's fall happened around the fifteenth floor, sending him down about twenty-five or thirty feet, where he was to hang until rescued. Fortunately, a window washer was working on top of the building. So Louie takes the washer's bosun's chair and makes it his own to perform the rescue of Willig. A bosun's chair consists of a waist strap and rope attached to each end of a flat seat board. The rope is locked off on a pulley system tied to a stationary object on the roof. You lower the chair down the building by feeding the rope through the pulley.

I strapped on the seat, and we ran the rope to a safe anchor on top of the roof. I also had a secondary safety line manned by another stuntman in case anything went wrong. I perched myself on the edge of the building and took a very deep breath.

There I was, some 220 feet up in the air, about to step off of a perfectly sound surface. Not my most favorite thing to do. Ron did set up an airbag for me at the bottom, in case George or I went down. But I gotta' tell you, hitting that airbag from that height would have been like dropping a dart onto a balloon from your roof. Even if I had managed to land on it, "POP!" would have been the last thing that I heard.

I knew as soon as I stepped over the side that I would be okay, because I was belted into the chair. I also had a safety stuntman whose job it was to slow my descent if all went awry. I was also anchored to a very sturdy object on the roof.

Even so, I admit being so scared that my butt was stuck to the seat. Come to think of it, that was good too, as it helped to secure me even more.

I lowered myself down to George, who had done a tremendous job of acting out the slip and plunge. He had already bounced off the building and was hanging there like a wet washrag. Once I reached him, I maneuvered myself in position just below him, hooked him to my harness by means of a carabiner, and then unhooked him from his harness.

This all went just fine.

Next I had to move George's 175 pounds or so through the air. This was a challenge because he was just hanging there like a big dead fish. But I had successfully secured him, so down we went.

I lowered us the first few floors at a brisk pace, but then my right arm began to seize up from the rapid movement, so I stopped for about thirty seconds or so to regain my strength. I could hear the hush of panic from ten floors below.

I learned later that the crew thought I had frozen a hundred feet up with George Willig tied to my lap. Once I continued my descent, everyone sighed in relief and welcomed us down to ground zero.

The following week, just when I thought we were on our way to a seven-year series, the word came down to the set. "This will be the last show. We're cancelled."

What the . . . ?

As quickly as it came, it was gone. The network bought thirteen episodes, shot ten and showed nine. No reruns. No residuals. Just R.I.P.

CHAPTER 14
IN THE HEAT
OF THE NIGHT

I've run into some S.O.B. directors, but I gave them back as good as I got.

CARROLL O'CONNOR

n late 1980s, I was fortunate to work several times in New Orleans on the show *In the Heat of the Night* starring the great Carroll O'Connor as the sheriff of a small Mississippi town. You will remember O'Connor from his Emmy-winning performances as Archie Bunker in the 1970s TV series *All in the Family*.

I was truly looking forward to working with O'Connor. Not only was he an icon in the industry, he also looked and acted a lot like my dad. Nick was of similar build and hairline, and like O'Connor himself, he spoke pretty much only when he had something to say. It was always gruff and to the point, it was usually the right thing to say. I will admit that Nick was often a little more Archie Bunker than Sheriff Gillespie.

O'Connor was a pro who knew what was needed to make a scene work. He was also quite personable and approachable on set. I found myself standing next to him one day and started a little small talk. Of course, I told him how much I enjoyed and appreciated his work. I also told him how he reminded me of my dad, which seemed to touch him a little.

Then I said I had a bit of an odd question. I told him that throughout many years of watching him on the big and small screen, I'd noticed that he always wore a silver ring on his middle finger of his right hand. I asked him, if he didn't mind sharing, why he never seemed to be without it?

He looked at me a little sideways, as if to say, "You noticed that?" and then explained the ring was once his grandmother's and that he "never takes it off." Nothing earth-shattering, but to me, interesting nonetheless.

Each episode of *Heat* I worked on had its challenges. For instance, in one episode I played a hit man who used a pillow to smother a patient in his hospital bed. This particular week of shooting had been very tense and a strain on everyone due to the director who was hyper and wound as tight as a two-dollar watch. He was scattered and sweating and grinding his teeth like he was a gristmill. Not surprisingly, he was barking orders at actors and crew alike.

It took me a while, but then I recognized what I was seeing. It was the same way I'd seen other people act on set during the drug-fueled industry of the early 80s.

The day I was to perform the smothering, this director gave me specific directions on how he wanted the pillow placed onto the victim's face. He spit and sputtered his instructions regarding the sequence that he wanted to shoot. I acknowledged that I understood his direction, and we were ready for camera.

"And, action!" was the call from the first AD. I made my move to the bed with the pillow. But as I placed it over the actor's face, just as I was directed to do, a gravelly British voice bellowed out, "No. No. No. Cut, cut, cut!"

It was the director. "What the fuck do you think you're doing?" he barked at me in front of the cast and crew. "I specifically told you to do it this way! Can't you take fucking direction? If you can't do the bloody scene right, then we'll find someone who can! Can you do this fucking right this time?"

"Yes sir, I understand" was all I said to him, and we were off for take two.

Action was called again, and I performed the scene just as I had the first time—according to his direction. This time, the only voice that rang out was that of the first AD. "And, CUT," he called to the cast and crew. "Let's go to lunch."

That was my chance to walk over to the director and ask him if he would please come out behind the set with me for a minute. He obliged me, and we found a shaded spot behind the building.

I remember him looking at me as if he were granting me an audience, the little prick. I said to him, in my best character-driven bad guy voice, "Who in the fuck do you think you are? If you ever speak to me like that again, in front of the crew or in private, I will rip your head off and shit in your neck."

His eyes got very wide as he looked up at me, there was a visible lump on his throat, and I swear I smelled a little dookie in his pants.

He was silent, so I looked him square and said, "Do you understand me?" He nodded. I said "Good," and off to lunch I went, fully expecting to be stopped by security and asked to leave the set.

That didn't happen.

Later that night I got a call in my room from production, and again I just knew they were going to tell me I was fired and would be leaving in the morning. But that didn't happen either. Instead, they told me the director had been admitted to the hospital for "the flu," and we'd be on hold, or standby as it's called, until further notice.

"Flu" my ass. I've been around plenty of people with the flu. I've had the flu. You've had the flu. You don't act like he did when you have the flu. You act like that when you have powdered white shit packed up your nose. And "hospital?" I don't buy it. No one said where he went to get better, but we had several days off in New Orleans while our director was most likely getting dried-out.

It just so happened that this went down during Mardi Gras, so I took advantage of the time off. I headed downtown, drank a few Hurricanes and caught some beads. Had myself a nice little paid vacation right in the middle of work.

We were all called back to work several days later and finished the episode without any yelling, cursing or surreptitious snorting of powder.

I had already done a couple of *Heat* episodes and had hoped to do more, but figured my little confrontation with the director meant an end to things. But a few weeks later I got a call from the coordinator asking me to come down again and play another part on a new episode.

Hell yeah!

This time I played the part of a politician's bodyguard, who is also his hitman. Another stretch.

Part way through the week, we switched to night shoots in the swamp. Night work is not my favorite thing, and a swamp just might be my least favorite thing closely behind heights . . . but it's all part of the job.

The scene called for a shootout with Sheriff Gillespie and Detective Virgil Tibbs, played by Harold E. Rollins, Jr.

Rollins was a terrific actor with huge credits to his name, including *A Soldier's Story* and *Ragtime*. I remember he was a big man about my height and had a strong presence both in person and onscreen.

The scene called for me and another bad guy to split up in the swamp as we tried to escape capture. O'Connor's character chased the other baddie while Rollins followed me. Our foot chase turned into a fistfight and then ended with a shootout.

The fight with Rollins went great. Stunt coordinator Chuck Hicks took us through a rehearsal first. Then it was time to shoot. Rollins got the best of me, as planned. Then I broke loose from him, as planned. We engaged in a shootout, as planned. And then I got killed. Which meant I had to fall down and die. Which meant I did a face plant into the muddy swamp; the stinky, wet, muddy, alligator-infested swamp.

I don't recall that being planned.

When all was said and done, Rollins and I were both wet and cold and covered in swamp water and ooze. It was the last shot of the night and when the AD finally called "wrap!" the wardrobe people brought Rollins a sound blanket—also known as furniture pads—and wrapped it around him. They were kind enough to bring me the same thing. I thanked them, said goodnight and walked over to the passenger van that was loading up with cast and crew to return to the hotel where we all were staying.

Meanwhile, three town cars drove up to take O'Connor, the director, and Rollins home for the night. Rollins happened to be staying at the hotel complex with the rest of us. As I made my way to the van with the rest of the group, we passed Harold and amidst the good-nights, I extended my hand to him saying, "You did a great job out there, thank you."

"And you as well. Really a nice job," he replied. Then he asked, "Are you going back to the hotel?" It wasn't like I could go anywhere else, swamp monster that I was, but I smiled and said, "Yes, I am."

"Well then," he said. "Why don't you ride back with me? There's plenty of room."

Let's see . . . I could squeeze into a van full of tired people while being wet to the bone and cold and stinky. Or, I could jump into the Town Car and be warm and cozy for the twenty-minute ride.

Town Car wins!

So I said "thanks," and went around to the back seat on the passenger's side while Rollins got in behind the driver. And we were off to the comforts of the Swamp Valley Inn and Suites. (No, that's not the real name.)

Harold and I did a little chatting about the show and the day. I asked him about his career and what he thought were his best moments onscreen. He told me he was most proud of his work and association with *A Soldier's Story* and *Ragtime*.

We finally pulled into the dark parking lot of the hotel, and the driver stopped to let me out first as Harold's place was on the other side of the complex.

I reached out my right hand and shook with Rollins, thanking him again for the day and the ride. In response, he nonchalantly reached up with his left hand, put it on the back of my neck, and masterfully pulled me in for a goodnight kiss.

"Wait! What the fuck? Oh, no, no, no. Halt! Thank you but no thank you! Nope, not gonna' do it!"

My head was spinning during those couple of seconds it took me to realize what he thought was about to happen. Then my mind cleared, and I pulled away. I didn't jerk away—it's not like I felt threatened—but I did make it crystal clear that I wasn't going to move in any closer.

He looked at me with such kind eyes all I could say was, "No thank you. Thanks for the ride."

Wet, chilled to the bone, and surprised by the night's events, I shuffled to my room. I thought about the previous week and how I'd seen Rollins walking around the hotel grounds in long flowing kaftans. I understood now that he had been expressing more of himself than I had originally realized.

Rollins passed away in 1996, a talented actor, and a good man who succumbed to struggles with alcohol and drugs.

CHAPTER 15
RESCUE 911

I guess I thought I was Elvis Presley, but I'll tell ya something. All Elvis did was stand on a stage and play a guitar. He never fell off on that pavement at no 80 mph.

EVEL KNIEVEL

n the late 1980s through the mid-1990s, I worked on a few episodes of *Rescue: 911*, a reality-based television series hosted by William Shatner. Yes, Captain Kirk.

The show would hire actors and stunt people to reenact harrowing real-life emergency situations. I played a father who rescues his son while scuba diving, a man whose single-wide catches fire, and a motorcycle officer who had a horrific accident.

For that last one, an episode titled "Motor Cop Down," the call came from Conrad Palmisano, a stunt coordinator and second unit director known for his creativity and ingenuity in designing action. I worked with "Connie," a number of times over the years, including on the films *Out For Justice, Robocop 2* and *Robocop 3*. But after *Out for Justice* wrapped, I worried for a time that Connie would never hire me again due to the way I handled a situation with the film's star, Steven Seagal.

In the film, I played Paulie, a bad guy who was paid to ambush Seagal's character, Brooklyn detective Gino Felino. William Forsythe hires me for the hit, asking me first if I had the balls to do it.

Connie worked out a scene between me and Seagal, a martial artist, that had him best me by hitting me with a double chop to the neck before cracking me in the groin then nailing my hand to the wall with a meat cleaver.

I remember Seagal was especially insistent that the director get a close-up shot of him giving me that double karate chop. The director pretty much had no choice but to agree, so we got down to it. I stood up against the wall where my hand was to be embedded and the crew set camera as the director and Conrad looked on.

We rehearsed the scene, finessing the action to make the assault look right for camera. We worked it out that Seagal's hands were to come down squarely onto my upper chest and collar bones just below my neck. Thanks to the angles involved, it would look like the brutal blows Connie and the director intended.

Take one. And action!

Seagal came down with the double-chop and cracked me right where he was supposed to.

Perfect! We reset for take two and Action! was called.

Conrad, seeing that things were under control, went to check on the other stunters that were readying themselves for their gags.

That's when things changed. On takes two through twelve or so, Seagal became increasingly heavy-handed, landing his blows with way more force than was needed. Additionally, every second or third take, he'd actually catch me in the throat, instead of the planned collar bone hit.

Now that kind of "accident" would be expected and understandable from an actor untrained in martial arts. But Seagal was a 7th degree black belt and Aikido master. Not only did he know what he was doing, he was getting some sick kind of pleasure doing this. How could I tell? Because with each inappropriate blow, he smiled. Smirked, really. Every single time he caught me in the throat.

When we reached take twenty, after he had caught me in the neck yet another time, I'd had enough. As they were setting up for take twenty-one, I looked over at the director and said—in a voice that was strained and gravelly from being hit so many times—"If you don't have it by now, you'll never get it." And with that, I walked off the set.

Stunt people don't do that. Nobody who isn't a star does that. So as I wrapped for the day, I was fully prepared to get fired and be put on a plane home the next morning.

But I wasn't fired. So that night I went to dinner with a few other stunt people, as we'd done nearly every night. As we walked into our regular restaurant, we saw that Seagal and then-wife, actress and model Kelly LeBrock were there, too, seated near the back. Our group had barely made it through the door when Seagal stood up and yelled out over all the noise and music in the place, William Forsythe's line to my character: "Hey Paulie! You got da balls?"

The place went quiet. Far from angry, I just shook my head at this pathetic display, as did much of the rest of the crowd. I have a vivid memory of seeing Kelly drop her head in embarrassment as we and all of the restaurant patrons got an uncomfortable glimpse of the real Steven Seagal.

The next day on set, not a word was spoken about the previous day, and on we went to finish the film.

When he called about this *Rescue 911* project, Connie asked if I wanted to fly to Reno, Nevada to reenact the story of an officer who laid down his motorcycle and ran into a truck during a high-speed chase.

Of course I wanted to do that!

My first order of business was to head straight for AMSPEC, a San Fernando Valley company that designs and produces products for the stunt community. I had them make me a pair of sliding shorts to wear under my wardrobe that would protect my hide while helping me slide smoothly on the pavement.

Next I went out and rode a couple of Kawasaki 900 motorcycles to get used to the weight and power of a police motor unit. Then I was off to Reno to do my thing.

It was January and Reno spared us no winter mercy. It was cold and snowy and wouldn't you know, we were shooting at night, which is when the accident occurred.

Conrad told me the story. He said the officer I was playing and his partner would occasionally play a game of "let's see who can get more speeders" while on patrol. The two of them would park where they couldn't easily be seen, and when a speeder shot by, they would race to see who would reach the offender first.

On the night of the crash, a white Ford Mustang raced down the street, flying past the officers. The cop I was playing was first to chase after the speed freak. His partner followed closely, but backed off when he saw what was about to happen.

You see, as the first officer shot down the street, in excess of 60 mph, a truck pulled out in front of him. The officer got on the brakes and laid the bike down to avoid a disaster, but it was too late. He was too close to scrub off any speed. He plowed into the side of the truck, and a rear tire rolled up on him.

His partner was the first one there to help. The downed officer survived, but spent several months recouping from some very serious injuries. He was lucky to be alive.

When I reached set the night of the shoot, I met both of the officers. Although they were actual lawmen, these gentlemen looked like they were straight out of Central Casting. Prototypical police officers, they each had big chests, thick necks, crew cuts above their shaved whitewalls and each had an unmistakable "cop stache" planted above his upper lip.

I introduced myself, and we started to talk about the accident. How it happened, what led up to it, how it ended. I wanted to get a feel for being this guy.

They told me of their antics chasing speeders and confirmed they had made a game out of it. As they spoke, I could tell that the partner who didn't crash had more experience and was a little older and wiser. He clearly wasn't proud of how they had acted back then, and told me that since that night, he had sworn off the games and put his full concentration on the work.

Now the other cop, the one I was playing, was in his twenties and still full of piss and vinegar. When he told his part of the story, his eyes sparkled with excitement. Plus he was chomping at the bit to get back on his bike and catch speeders with his partner. He told me he had recently been cleared to return to work and in fact was scheduled to start up again in just a few days.

After getting all the information I needed, it was time to get geared-up for the gag. I slipped on my sliding-shorts, then my Reno Police Department uniform, then took the bike for a little ride to get the feel of it. I was riding a fully-equipped Police-Issue Kawasaki 900.

Here's how it was going to play out.

A Mustang speeds down a dark street.

Two Reno PD motorcycles pull out to chase.

One pulls ahead as the other slows.

The truck pulls out, and we cut.

Next setup is me, laying down the bike and hitting the truck.

This was not an easy task.

We decided I would lay down the bike into the truck in one shot, and then on the next setup, my body would be dragged into the rear wheels of the truck as if I had slid into them.

All right. Ready to go! The first scene went well. Then it was time for the lay-down. They wanted it to happen at about 40 mph, which is good because the bike is heavy, and we wanted it to slide as far as possible. If all went well, I'd be separated from the motorcycle after the first ten to fifteen yards, having kicked it away when I laid it down.

The last thing the senior motor officer told me before I grabbed a handful of throttle was to pull the bike all the way to the pavement and make certain to get away from it ASAP. The reason being these big bikes tend to stand themselves back up and then flip to the other side. This slams the rider to the asphalt, then traps and drags him several yards and many layers of flesh down the highway.

That was NOT going to happen to me. I planned to pull the bike down as hard and fast as I could and kick it away as far as possible.

"And action!"

I got to third gear pretty fast and saw the truck, driven by stuntman Bruce Barbour, pull out in front of me down the road. I stayed steady at 40 mph and spotted my mark on the street where I would start the lay-down.

I pounced on the rear brake pedal and leaned to my left a little, allowing the rear end to slide around. Then I pulled back and down on those handlebars like I was pulling on the reins of a runaway stallion. I pulled with all my might, trying to get that motorcycle down to the street that was passing underneath me. Once I got it down, the rear tire whipped around like it was seeking vengeance. I used my legs to push hard on the bike, working with all of my strength to get away from the metal beast.

It worked. The stunt went just as planned and we did it in one take. I stood up when I heard "cut" and joined the small crowd that had gathered around the fallen black-and-white steed. It looked bereft, just lying there on its side with jagged evidence of the action strewn all around the street.

One of the officers said, "You sure weren't gonna' let that thing jump up on you, were ya'?" He pointed to the handlebars on the downed bike, and I saw I had yanked on them so hard I had pulled them level with the gas tank.

Told ya' I wasn't going to let that thing get away from me!

Next it was time to get my head slammed into the truck wheel.

We didn't know exactly how to pull this off. We had to get my momentum going in order to be dragged or pulled along the pavement and into the tire. All the stuntmen on the scene started sharing ideas, and we finally decided to get all MacGyver on the situation and jerry-rig a little something.

Our solution was a great example of the genius of teamwork.

Stuntmen Richard Hancock, Eddie Matthews, and Rick Sawaya tied one end of a fifty-foot rope to my ankles then tied the other end to the rear bumper of a pickup truck. On "ACTION" Richard would hit the gas and pull me to a pre-designated spot and by doing so, drag me into the waiting truck tire.

We got the shot in two takes, and the finished product looks just like I'm getting my head slammed into the rear wheel of the truck. Everyone was happy—the director, the stunt coordinator, the crew, the cops and me.

In fact, the cop I was playing was so happy and so very excited about what we had done, that he talked his commanding officer, who was there that night as well, into letting him get on the bike and take it up the street "just to get the feel of it again."

After a little discussion—and after his partner raised a red flag saying, "I dunno if it's such a good idea"—that young officer grabbed a helmet and jumped on the bike. He cranked open the throttle and went through the gears like a pro.

Then it happened.

About two hundred yards down the street from us, we could see the taillights of the motorcycle snap back and forth in the dark. Then they turned sideways and were lost in the explosion of sparks that were shooting off of the sliding motorcycle.

Yep, the same cop who had slammed into a truck while playing a game of speed-chaser had managed to crash his motorcycle once again, right where he wrecked a year earlier. Once again, his partner was the first one to get to him. That great officer jumped on his bike and tore down the street to help his buddy, who was already up, hobbling around and cursing like a sailor.

The ambulance came and took the guy back to the hospital with everyone hoping he hadn't torn apart all the work the doctors had done on him. As it pulled away, the commander and the second motor officer shook their heads and the officer confided in me, "He'll be ok, but he'll never get on another motor unit. He'll be in a squad car or at a desk until he retires."

CHAPTER 16
WALKER, TEXAS RANGER

If Chuck Norris roundhouse kicks you, even Google won't be able to find you.

INTERNET MEME

L et me tell what it was like to get beaten up by the one and only, world-renowned, 8th Degree Black Belt Grand Master Chuck Norris.

In 1993, it was announced that a hot, new, action TV pilot starring Chuck Norris had been picked up and would be shooting in Texas just outside of Dallas. I was anxious to get a chance to work on *Walker: Texas Ranger.* My call finally came in the show's second season when Chuck's son, Eric Norris, took over the stunt coordinating responsibilities.

Eric is a fun-loving and talented stuntman, stunt coordinator and director whose skills are punctuated by a remarkable ability to drive anything as fast as it can go. Like NASCAR. Yes, he's that good. So when Eric called asking me if I could come to Dallas and work with his dad, Chuck, my "Yes!" was immediate and enthusiastic. This kicked off the first of many wonderful adventures on *Walker.*

Over the seasons I was handed—yes handed, no auditoning!—several stunt acting roles and numerous other roles as a 'nondescript' stunt player. A nondescript, or ND player, is a performer who has an integral part in the scene but doesn't have a specific character name. Typically, Eric would bring me in to play a part and then keep me for the next episode to work as an ND stuntman.

I say I was lucky to have been brought from Los Angeles because there were already several qualified and experienced stuntmen in Dallas. One is Russell Towery, the brilliant stuntman inside *Robocop*'s suit who recently coordinated TV's *The Walking Dead*. Another is the talented Randy Fife, a forty-year stunt veteran who unselfishly shared his wisdom and experience with the production whenever he was asked. Not only has Randy done it all, he knows how it works and how to engineer it. We became fast and close friends, working with each other whenever we could, and I see him as one of several key mentors in my career.

Eric and the show were also fortunate to have the legendary Greg Elam as the stunt double for Clarence Gilyard Jr., who played Walker's sidekick, James Trivette. Greg, who brought a couple of decades of experience to his work on *Walker*, is the quintessential stuntman. He worked with great directors like Speilberg, Gore Verbinski, and Norman Jewison; he doubled some of our greatest stars including Gregory Hines, Michael Jackson, and Richard Pryor; and he is a founding member of the Black Stuntmen's Association. Not only has Greg given us unforgettable entertainment—like that heart-stopping 370-foot slalom off a high-rise building in *Superman III*—he has passed on his tradition of excellence to his three immensely talented sons: stuntmen Kiante K. Elam, Ousaun Elam and Kofi Elam.

Actor Clarence Gilyard was also a dream to work with—a real professional who knew his work and did it well. He was extremely coordinated and in great shape. Between Greg teaching him all he could about action and Chuck just being there, Clarence became a tremendously proficient action actor.

So as you can imagine, getting the chance to get to work with Chuck—as well as guys like Eric, Randy, Greg, and Clarence—was superior on-the-job-training for me. I watched and learned as they handled a set, developed and managed stunts, and worked with actors, writers, and producers.

During these years, I also got to meet another of Chuck's sons, Mike Norris, who is the spitting image of his father. Mike is an accomplished actor, writer and director who has launched several of his own projects. I had the pleasure of sharing the screen with him on a thrilling action movie he wrote and starred in titled *Death Ring*.

The best thing about working on *Walker*? I got to work with Chuck *effing* Norris, a great guy on top of being a pure professional and a lethal martial artist. Chuck must have liked my acting as well as my fights, because it never seemed to bother him or the producers when I was cast in yet another episode. In fact, I secretly think Chuck especially liked to do fights with me because my chest made a really good target for his drop kicks.

Let me tell you about the episode I remember the most. It was titled *The Prodigal Son*, and the guest star was Tobey Maguire. Yes, Tobey Maguire of *Spider-Man* fame, back when he was just a young Tobey.

I played a mafia-type thug who tries to kidnap Tobey. My boss in the show was Frank Vincent, the same actor who cut my throat when my head was in the vise in *Casino*. Vincent's first in charge was actor Rick Aiello, son of actor Danny Aiello and brother of the late Danny Aiello III, one of the finest stuntmen and gentlemen I've ever met.

At the end of the episode, Walker comes in and cleans up by beating the crap outta the bad guys, one of whom was me.

My particular fight with Chuck took place outside a makeshift squatter's home, which was located on dirt that slanted slightly downhill to a lake. Chuck was to use one of his famous drop kicks to send me flying over an old lawn chair and onto my back.

When the fight reached the point where Chuck was to kick me, I found myself standing on a slight downhill slope. I was facing him with my back to the lawn chair, which was a good ten feet from the water's edge.

Chuck came at me and landed his kick square into my chest. I immediately realized that the impact of the kick was a little harder and deeper to my chest than normal. (Yes, after being the subject of numerous flying kicks throughout my career, I can tell the difference.) Consequently, as I "took" my reaction to the chest kick, I found I was flying a little farther back with slightly more force than I had expected. Instead of correcting by pulling in my legs or throwing myself to one side, I decided to accept the movement of my body and just go with it. I flew over the lawn chair to my back. The momentum of flying downhill then caused my body to roll into a backward head stand, sending me ass-over-teakettle and ultimately landing me flat on my face in the mud with my legs flopping into the lake.

They loved it. Eric laughed really hard as the first AD called, "Next setup!"

I'll be the first to tell you that Chuck was always on his mark in his fights, and I know, because I did dozens with him. But this time, I think that because he had a little extra inertia coming downhill, and the fact that I was leaning back already, the kick just took on a life of its own. The kick didn't hurt . . . it just showed me yet again the power of "A Man Called Chuck."

After the end of its ninth season, *Walker* went off the air. It was the end of an era. A really great era.

Chuck was busy doing his Total Gym® equipment commercials with Christy Brinkley when *Walker* was coming to an end. At the same time, I had become the first co-Governor of the newly-formed Stunt Peer Group at the Academy of Television Arts & Sciences.

I had worked long and hard with stunters Spice Williams and Lane Leavitt as well as actor Conrad Bachmann to lobby the Academy members, to convince the television Academy that stunt coordinators deserved recognition for their excellence. After more than a year of lobbying, we finally prevailed, meaning from that day forward, an Emmy would be presented to the outstanding stunt coordinator of a prime-time television show. It was a huge achievement for the stunt community.

After gaining this approval, I suggested to the Television Academy Governors that this new award should be introduced by someone of great significance to the stunt community, as well as the television audience. They thought that was a good idea and asked me who I had in mind.

Without a minute's hesitation, I blurted out, "Chuck Norris. Who else?"

There was a momentary hush and then, like a well-scripted movie, the ahhhs and ooohs started to filter around the room. The president of the Academy spoke up. "You go ahead and make that happen, Carl."

I could tell the majority of these folks didn't believe I would even get close to Mr. Norris.

"Holy crap! What the hell did I just do?"

Not unlike a stunt, my next task was to figure out how to make it happen.

I chose to start by contacting Eric. He loved the fact that stunts would now be recognized by the Academy, and he put me straight through to Chuck. It was only a matter of minutes after I proposed my question, that Norris accepted my request to tape him introducing the Emmy for Stunt Coordination for the very first time. He even told me we were welcome to film him at his spread in Encino, California.

Chuck's sprawl of a property included a main house as well as a smaller home that had been partially converted into a gym. This is where Chuck and his wife Gena first met me and my crew. They had just finished their workout and were headed to the main house.

After we all introduced ourselves, Chuck politely asked me if he could have a few minutes to clean up. Right. Like I'm gonna say 'no' to Chuck Norris about anything.

When he came back out, Chuck put his hand on my shoulder and asked me if I'd like to see the gym. So in we went as the crew waited outside.

Yep, just me 'n Chuck. I'm not too jaded to admit that was a huge thrill.

The gym was fantastic—in fact, you can see it in some of his commercials. But what struck me dumb was his trophy case.

It was like being at the Smithsonian. There were rows upon rows of medals, belts, ribbons, patches, certificates and statues. It looked more like the display of an entire University athletic team than that of just one man. What stood out the most was a huge trophy right in the middle of the case that made the Heisman look like a third place ribbon. It was Chuck's World Karate Championship trophy, and it was nothing short of spectacular.

Most of all, I remember Chuck Norris as being humble, gracious and the very definition of a gentleman.

We finished our taping and Chuck was once again a pleasure to work with. Hey, come to think of it, this was the first time I'd worked with him that he didn't beat the hell out of me!

CHAPTER 17
TREKKIES & FIVERS

Stuntman's Log, Stardate 46001.3. My career enters the Star Trek universe.

CARL CIARFALIO

'm a huge fan of the *Star Trek* phenomenon, but sadly, the original was before my time. I finally had the opportunity to be at least a small part of the tradition in two of the spin-off series.

My first foray into Roddenberry's world was in 1992 on an episode of *Star Trek: The Next Generation* titled "Time's Arrow, Part II." I was so looking forward to being made up as a great alien character. Maybe a Klingon like Lieutenant Worf, or my favorite, the Ferengi! Not exactly tough-guy aliens, but the makeup was excellent. Alas, when I got to work I discovered that my job was to double an actor who gets punched out during one of the crew's visits to planet Earth.

The second time I got the call, it was for "Fistful of Datas." Perfect! Clearly, I thought, since Data was the main character in this episode, I'd at least be made up as an Android. I was really looking forward to experiencing that enhanced skull. Once again, it was not to be. This time hair and makeup slapped a bushy mustache above my lip and darkened me down a couple of shades. Then wardrobe stuck me in a serape and sombrero. Turned out the crew had traveled back in time to the American Old West and I would be doubling an actor who gets killed in a western-style shootout.

The third and final time I got my *Trek* on was in 2001 on "Shadows of P'Jem," an episode of *Star Trek: Enterprise*. The Andorians mounted an attack on the planet of P'Jem, and I was one of a group of rebels that took Archer and T'Pol hostage. Finally—makeup!

I also worked on several episodes of the science fiction series *Babylon 5* where I got into some good makeup. I particularly remember playing a Drazi Merchant and having a good "negotiating" scene with the talented Stephen Furst, a series regular who played the Centauri diplomatic attaché, Vir Cotto.

I had a ball, was proud of my work, and although I should have known better, I put the word out, letting all of my friends know that I had this great scene coming up.

We watched together the night it aired, and my friends were appropriately congratulatory when I appeared onscreen, then got quiet to listen to the scene I was so proud of.

When it was over, all was quiet until one finally said, "You didn't tell us you used an English accent." Then another friend piped up, "Yeah—hey, uh—was that your voice?" Indeed, it was not. The producers had decided it was appropriate to have my lines looped by someone with a voice like John Cleese.

And so it goes.

CHAPTER 18
DAYS OF OUR LIVES

Know your lines and don't bump into the furniture.

SPENCER TRACY

A t the beginning of my career, I played bad guys on *The Young and the Restless*, *The Bold and the Beautiful* and *General Hospital*. Soaps didn't typically include a lot of action, and it showed. I remember getting beat up by some of the most uncoordinated actors I've ever worked with. There were actors who couldn't throw a punch and actresses who had to be taught how to react to a slap. Then there was the woman who got so involved in our fight scene, that instead of throwing her purse at me as written, she picked up a vase and cracked it across my temple! Good times.

The most fun I had working on a soap opera were my years on *Days of Our Lives*. My dear friend Mike Adams brought me in to double Joe Mascolo, who played the evil Stefano DiMera.

Mike was one of the best men I ever knew, and I'm so fortunate to have been his friend. He was a rodeo cowboy who was tougher than any horse or bull he rode and as kind as any man could be. He was also an excellent race car driver, an unstoppable bullfighter and a boxer who could crack you open with his right hook.

Mike coordinated *Days of Our Lives* for some twenty years. He was tough and talented and extremely safety-minded—and expected his people to be the same. Thanks to him, I learned soap opera style from the best. He also helped transform me into a stunt coordinator by sharing his insights and expertise and by trusting me to run the show when he was busy on another project.

I doubled Joe for over twenty years, making friends along the way with everyone at Corday Productions including the actors, directors and producers. In turn, they got to trust my work and would ask Mike to call me in for roles that had dialog as well as some action—typically a fight or a fall. I was chosen because I had proven to the show's executives that I was able to handle myself on a "daytime TV" schedule. That was important because soaps work against grueling deadlines. Every day they deal with a huge number of scenes, including walk-through rehearsals and blocking, dress rehearsals and blocking, script changes and blocking, and then performing in front of the camera.

One role I was given was playing Stefano's minion. It came with a short speech, then a little scene with an actress. I worked so very hard on that dialog to make sure I would get it on the first take. Our rehearsals went well and then cameras were ready. I had reached my chance to shine. I got on my mark, knowing exactly what I was going to do and how I was going to do it. All I needed was to hear the stage manager say "action."

Now one would think that after several years on soap sets, I would remember that the stage manager doesn't say action. Instead, he or she counts down from '5' and you start your action after you hear 'one.'

But no.

I heard, "In 5,4,3,2,1 . . ." but no "Action," so I waited. Time stood still for a moment; then the director's voice came booming over the onstage loudspeaker. "Carl? Carl? Is there a problem?"

"*Shit, shit, shit, a thousand shits!*" is all I could think. I was concentrating so hard that I missed my cue. I got it on the second take, but I'll never forget that voice booming from the heavens.

In recent years, Mike and I formed a production partnership, and we were deeply involved in bringing new movie projects to the screen. Then we suddenly and unexpectedly lost him.

Mike Adams was a truly good man and mentor I was lucky enough to call friend. I miss him every day.

CHAPTER 19
24

If you are lying to me, I'm going to make this the worst day of your life.

JACK BAUER, *24*

had already worked on a couple of episodes of Kiefer Sutherland's award-winning action series *24* as a stuntman, when I got a call from stunt coordinator Eddy Donno offering me an acting role. I was to play a very bad guy who is interrogated by Sutherland's Jack Bauer.

My character was a slime ball who preyed on innocent children, but because they needed his testimony in another case, he was going to walk free. The scene called for me to be handcuffed to a chair in a tiny room. Sutherland, who was not only the series star, but one of the producers, would be my interrogator.

I needed to be on my game.

When Kiefer came onto the set for rehearsal, we said our hellos, then took our marks as director Jon Cassar walked us through the scene. Kiefer and Cassar had worked together for years, so no time or words were wasted. We were entirely focused on building to the moment when Bauer finally becomes fed up with this low-life scum.

When you watch the episode—Season 2, "8am to 9am"—you can see the camera catch the instant Jack Bauer transforms from Government Agent to outraged citizen.

Feeling his murderous intensity, my arrogant confidence wavered. It showed in the subtlest manner as I bit my lower lip, then Bang! Kiefer pulls his weapon and shoots me point-blank in the chest. The gun fired, the squib on my chest exploded, and I threw myself back to the ground, making sure that the chair and I moved as one.

Afterwards, dead and chained to the office chair, I held my breath and stared at the ceiling. I could only hope they thought it went well.

"And, cut! That was great, moving on."

Those words were music to my ears. I was helped up and unchained from my metal anchor. The first person to come up to me was Eddy, telling me it was a good take. The second was Kiefer, hand extended and a smile on his face. "Are you ok? Cuz that was really great," he said. "Yes. I'm good." I replied. "Glad it worked for you." With that, he was off to conquer the next scene, something he did repeatedly for nearly two hundred episodes. As of this writing, Sutherland is doing it all over again in a series renewal, *24: Live Another Day*.

CHAPTER 20
HEROES

At best, life is completely unpredictable.

CHRISTOPHER WALKEN

Recurring guest star status refers to characters who regularly appear on a series. With the obvious exceptions of star and co-star status, this is the Holy Grail of acting roles. It's something I've come close to but am still chasing to this day.

In 2006, I got a call from Ian Quinn, then the stunt coordinator for the series *Heroes*, asking me to audition for the role of "Jumpsuit." Finally, a show where I don't get killed! In fact, he told me my character might never get killed off.

"*Hooray!*" I leaped at the chance. I mean, I was going to read for a major casting director for a hit show for a part that was going to be recurring . . . great!

I won the part and showed up on set the following week. Jumpsuit was a bad guy who, in this episode, was posing as an exterminator in order to break into the home of Sendhil Ramamurthy, who played Dr. Mohinder Suresh. Sendhil catches me and demands to know why I'm there. I mumble something about a dog with a cough, he knows it's bull, and a fight ensues.

Sendhil starts things off by clubbing me in the leg with an elephant statue. I kick him in the chest and send him flying backward. This was a stunt performed by stuntman Anthony Molinari, who completely committed, slamming himself to his back from eight feet away after flying three feet in the air. We got that part of the fight in a couple of takes. Sendhil was so easy to work with, and Molinari made the action look wonderful.

Our struggle then moves into the building's hallway where we get interrupted by another character, causing my character to back off and make his escape.

The show's director/writer/producer loved what he got on film. Afterwards, he told me to make sure that production had all my information because we had a long hard season ahead of us. I was all over it like a cheap suit. I made sure that I went to the office and gave them what they needed; I went to casting and made sure that they were completely updated; and whenever I'd get another job, I'd let *Heroes* know in case they might need me.

Well, one week turned into two weeks, then became two months with no word. Right around the third month, I found out the show got a new producer and a new stunt coordinator and it was decided to not bring back the Jumpsuit story line.

I was so close!

CHAPTER 21
STUNTS AND THE EMMYS

It's really an honor to be nominated. But it is much better to win.

SUSAN LUCCI

J ust as the dust was starting to settle around the success of the Taurus World Stunt Awards©, which I'll tell you about a few chapters from now, I got a call from my friend Spice Williams-Crosby. I've known Spice for most of my career, and you know her work, too. Spice is a fine stuntwoman and actress whose credits date back to 1985. She is also a Doctor of Nutrition and a hard-working activist for her friends and peers.

Spice said she was a registered member of the Actor's Peer Group at the Academy of Television Arts and Sciences, or ATAS, which is the organization that brings us the Emmy Awards. She explained that the Television Academy recognized just about every department in the industry except stunts. In addition to acting, peer groups had been established for television disciplines including producing, directing, wardrobe, make-up, props, special effects, camera, and lighting departments. But there wasn't any representation for stunt people.

Spice said that once she became a member of the Actor's Peer Group, she began lobbying ATAS to establish a Stunts Peer Group. She said she came up against all the same ignorance and prejudice that I had experienced while trying to get the Taurus Awards underway. But now, with that recognition in place, she felt it was the right time to make a major push forward, and she asked me to participate. Spice also contacted a mutual friend and fellow stuntman, Lane Leavitt. She asked both of us to speak to the heads of the peer groups—known as Governors—about the inclusion of a peer group for stunts.

And so began the education of a room full of people representing each production department in television. These were people I worked with one way or another every time I was on set. Some I knew personally. But it was by no means an easy task.

The Television Academy created the Emmy awards in the first place to honor the art and the science of television production. Spice, Lane and I had to prove and defend that our specialty fit that criteria. We literally had to take these Governors through the steps of how we work.

How a stunt is defined.

What it takes to set up a stunt.

The technology we use to create action.

How we hire people to perform the stunt.

The art it takes a stunt performer not only to do the physical action, but to play his or her part as well.

How we price the stunt adjustment.

How we are a 'stand-alone' department that works with every other department on the set.

It took us well over a year to convince these folks that stunt people deserved the same recognition as all the other departments that ATAS represented.

The Governors finally came to their senses once a couple of heavy hitters from the floor weighed in on the topic. Veteran actor Conrad Bachmann—who is known for *Tremors* and *Portrait of a Killer* with Jack Palance and Rod Steiger and who also stunt doubled Bing Crosby in *Stagecoach* in his early career—eloquently addressed the floor with reasons why stunts should be included in the Emmys. Also speaking up was writer/producer Bryce Zable, who was then president of ATAS.

A vote was taken, and the first part of our goal was finally accomplished. ATAS created a Stunt Peer Group, and Lane and I became the first co-Governors of the first Stunt Peer Group at the Television Academy. This was a huge step in the progression of stunt people in the television industry.

It took us another year to convince the Academy that stunt professionals were worthy of an Emmy as well. Everyone finally agreed and an award for Outstanding Stunt Coordination was established. Today the Academy of Television Arts and Sciences honors our stunt community with two Outstanding Stunt Coordination awards. One in the Comedy Series or Variety Program category and the other for a Drama Series, Miniseries or Movie.

The inclusion of stunts in the Emmy organization is an accomplishment I am truly proud of. I remain grateful to Spice and Conrad for involving me and will always appreciate walking alongside the two of them and Lane down the long, hard road to Emmy recognition.

Postscript: In 2007, the Screen Actors Guild stepped up to commend the work of the stunt community by adding awards for us. They now recognize Outstanding Performance by a Stunt Ensemble in a Motion Picture and Outstanding Performance by a Stunt Ensemble in a Television Series. The Guild also includes stunt performers in its awards for outstanding performance by a cast.

What about the Oscars™? Well, despite a heroic, ongoing, 20-year effort led by prominent stunt coordinator Jack Gill; despite calls for just such an award by a number of leading celebrities including but not limited to Steven Spielberg, James Cameron, Arnold Schwarzenegger, Martin Scorsese, Jessica Lange and Jason Statham; despite the fact that stunt professionals are central to many of the most successful movies of all time . . . the Academy of Motion Picture Arts and Sciences refuses to honor stunt people with an Academy Award.

Stunt professionals *have* been awarded Honorary Academy Awards and Technical Academy Awards. In 1966, Hollywood stunt legend Yakima Canutt was awarded an honorary Oscar "For achievements as a stunt man and for developing safety devices to protect stunt men everywhere." In 2012, Hal Needham, another legend discussed elsewhere in this book, was honored as "A pioneer in improving stunt technology and safety procedures." Stunt professionals Vic Armstrong, Kenny Bates and Scott Leva have also been honored with the Academy's Scientific & Technical Awards. Each of these was a highly deserved award for each individual and also reflected well on our stunt community.

But as for the annual Oscars—which the academy says is intended to reward "the previous year's greatest cinema achievements as determined by some of the world's most accomplished motion picture artists and professionals"—nada. Zip. Nothing.

MY BUSHY WIGGED SELF WAS PERFECT FOR THIS JOB ON *GREATEST AMERICAN HERO* WITH STUNT LEGENDS GENE LEBELL AND TONY BRUBAKER. *COURTESY: CARL CIARFALIO PRIVATE COLLECTION.*

TAKING A TRAY OF CRAB LEGS TO THE FACE ON *TENSPEED & BROWN SHOE*. ACTOR BEN VEREEN HIT ME SO HARD I FLEW BACK AND CRACKED MY HEAD OPEN. ONE HOUR LATER, I WAS ALL STITCHED UP AND BACK AT WORK. *COURTESY: CARL CIARFALIO PRIVATE COLLECTION.*

HIGH FALL IN THE MALIBU
CANYONS FOR AN EPISODE
OF *AIRWOLF. COURTESY: CARL
CIARFALIO PRIVATE COLLECTION.*

GETTING "MACGYVERED" BY SERIES STAR RICHARD DEAN
ANDERSON. *COURTESY OF CARL CIARFALIO PRIVATE COLLECTION.*

DOUBLING TELLY SAVALAS—BALD
IS BEAUTIFUL! *COURTESY: CARL
CIARFALIO PRIVATE COLLECTION.*

ABOUT TO FLY ONTO THE
SET OF *THE GOLDEN
GIRLS*. OH, HOW I
LOVED THOSE LADIES!
*COURTESY: CARL CIARFALIO
PRIVATE COLLECTION.*

YOU'RE LOOKING AT THE MOMENT I REALIZED THIS CAR HIT GAG MIGHT NOT
TURN OUT AS I HAD PLANNED. *COURTESY: CARL CIARFALIO PRIVATE COLLECTION.*

CHICKS DIG SCARS.
COURTESY: CARL CIARFALIO
PRIVATE COLLECTION.

WITH LOU FERRIGNO ON *TRAUMA CENTER*. COURTESY: CARL CIARFALIO PRIVATE COLLECTION.

RAPPELLING DOWN A LONG BEACH
HIGH RISE WITH A WOUNDED MAN
IN MY CONTROL. *COURTESY: CARL
CIARFALIO PRIVATE COLLECTION.*

THIS STEER HAD ME JUST
WHERE HE WANTED ME.
*COURTESY: CARL CIARFALIO
PRIVATE COLLECTION.*

"PLAYING" WITH TIGGER IN THE DESERT. *COURTESY:
CARL CIARFALIO PRIVATE COLLECTION.*

SPARKS WERE FLYING WHEN I LAID DOWN THIS POLICE MOTOR UNIT ON *RESCUE 911. COURTESY: CARL CIARFALIO PRIVATE COLLECTION.*

ABOUT TO GET THE CRAP BEAT OUT OF ME ON HUNTER BY STAR AND FORMER ALL-PRO NFL DEFENSIVE END FRED DRYER. *COURTESY: CARL CIARFALIO PRIVATE COLLECTION.*

WITH THE GREAT CHUCK NORRIS ON *WALKER, TEXAS RANGER*. YA'LL KNOW
WHAT'S COMING . . . *COURTESY: CARL CIARFALIO PRIVATE COLLECTION.*

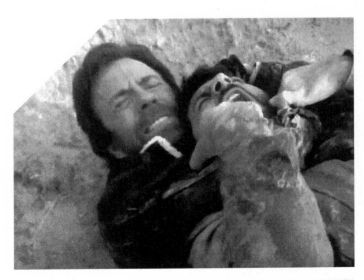

I GOT HIM JUST WHERE I WANT HIM. *COURTESY:*
CARL CIARFALIO PRIVATE COLLECTION.

YEARS AFTER I PLAYED A DRAZI MERCHANT ON *BABYLON 5*, I FOUND
MYSELF ON THIS COLLECTIBLE CARD. DEFINITELY A COOL BIT OF
MEMORABILIA. *COURTESY: CARL CIARFALIO PRIVATE COLLECTION. ©2000
WARNER BROS. GAME DESIGN ©2000 PRECEDENCE PUBLISHING. WHEEL OF FIRE.*

AS THE WOODSMAN ON AN EPISODE OF CHARMED. AN EVIL
WITCH BROUGHT ME TO LIFE OUT OF THIS ILLUSTRATION.
COURTESY: CARL CIARFALIO PRIVATE COLLECTION.

PLAYING A NASTY DRUNK
COWBOY ON *DR. QUINN,
MEDICINE WOMAN. COURTESY: CARL
CIARFALIO PRIVATE COLLECTION.*

DOUBLING THE EVIL STEFANO
DIMERA (JOE MASCOLO) ON *DAYS
OF OUR LIVES. COURTESY: CARL
CIARFALIO PRIVATE COLLECTION.*

WITH ALEX DANIELS AND
BROOKE DILLMAN ON *THE
WAYNE BRADY SHOW.*
*COURTESY: CARL CIARFALIO
PRIVATE COLLECTION.*

WITH FRIEND AND
CO-GOVERNOR LANE
LEAVITT AT OUR FIRST
EMMY AWARDS HONORING
STUNT COORDINATORS.
*COURTESY: CARL CIARFALIO
PRIVATE COLLECTION.*

ACT 3 :
CARL IN THE MOVIES

CHAPTER 22
GETTING MY SAG CARD

Movies are a fad. Audiences really want to see live actors on a stage.

CHARLIE CHAPLIN

received my SAG card on an independent movie in 1978—and let me tell you, getting your SAG card is a big deal for a performer.

SAG, or Screen Actors Guild, is the labor organization for performers. Now formally known as SAG-AFTRA, it is a guild that negotiates and enforces rules and contracts that govern fair pay and safe working conditions.

The double-edged sword with SAG-AFTRA is this: performers can't get hired by union productions without a union card, but they can't get their card until they have a role in a union production. So when a performer is lucky enough to get hired for his or her first union project, he or she can accept the job and use it to become a SAG-AFTRA member.

That said, you can imagine how excited I was to finally get a job that would get me my SAG card!

The project was *Do It In The Dirt*, a motorcycle movie starring Frank Sinatra Jr. Co-starring was Darby Hinton, a Disney child actor who starred as Fess Parker's son, Israel, on TV's *Daniel Boone*, which ran from 1964 to 1970.

I found this opportunity in a production listing in Dramalogue magazine that read "Looking for biker/stunt types. Must be able to ride. SAG." So I sent in my headshot and a resume—triple-spaced, in my rookie attempt to camouflage a lack of credits—and got a call to come in and meet the producer.

We hit it off, and he liked my look, which was then burly and bearded with a thick head of Italian curls. The only problem was my lack of a SAG card. But the producer explained to my eager young self "how things worked."

He told me that while it wouldn't be easy, he figured he could *probably* get me my card *if* I would agree to give him my two-day paycheck. He said he needed it to cover the fines imposed by the union for not hiring a union person.

I didn't know what the hell he was talking about, but of course I said yes!

Go figure: I got the job.

During the shoot, I rode some motorcycles, did some fights and over-acted my ass off in three whole scenes. Afterwards, I happily handed my check over to this producer, then called the guild to see about getting my SAG card.

The representative at SAG told me to bring in my pay stub along with $525 in cash to cover initiation and the first six month's worth of dues. That's all it would take: I'd be a card-carrying member of the Screen Actor's Guild. I stuffed my pockets with *all that cash* and made my way to SAG's office in Hollywood.

Boom! Done deal. Carlo is in the Screen Actor's Guild.

You may already have guessed that the producer ripped me off. The situation was naïve on my part, and highly unethical on his part. But the reality is there will always be someone out there who is willing to take advantage of hungry young performers.

The experience taught me that you've got to learn how your industry works. From that point on, I made it my business to understand how sets work and to understand the details within our contracts. I also focused on helping my stunt community and perhaps the entire industry. In short, I got involved. At SAMP, SAG, Taurus, and the Television Academy. To this day I contribute where I can, I pass on my knowledge and experience, and I focus on paying it forward.

If you're coming into this business, I hope you'll take the opportunity to do the same. It's a pretty special feeling.

But it all took time. As you'll see in the upcoming chapters, I still had a lot to learn.

CHAPTER 23
BLACK
MOON RISING

I'm a hedonist.

TOMMY LEE JONES

I n 1986, I got to work with the great character actor Keenan Wynn in his final screen role. Also starring was a young Tommy Lee Jones and the even younger Linda Hamilton, fresh off her success on *The Terminator*. The film was *Black Moon Rising*, a story about a retired professional thief, Jones, who is forced back into action by the FBI to steal incriminating evidence against a company they are investigating.

I played a hired thug for the company and after killing Keenan, who played an innocent businessman, I was supposed to kill Tommy Lee. Of course my nameless thug character wouldn't succeed in killing the movie's star!

The fight, which was choreographed by stunt coordinator Bud Davis, stands today as one of the most brutal onscreen fights ever.

My fellow thug in the fight was second-generation stuntman Don Pulford, whose mother, Lee Pulford, was a famous stuntwoman. We performed the whole fight with intensity and grit as we executed orders from our boss to put the hurt on Jones's character any way we could.

We started out punching him a few times in the trailer we'd tracked him to. Then we took him outside and threw him over a stair railing and onto the hood of a car below. That stunt was performed by stuntman Clifford Happy, who doubled Jones.

After Jones staggered to his feet, Pulford battered him down with another powerful blow, then it was my turn again. I hauled him partially up, only to send him sprawling with a vicious knee to the head. Then I picked him up from the ground—'him' once again being Clifford. I reached through his legs and grabbed onto his belt buckle with one hand while grabbing his jacket with my other hand. Then I rammed his head into the car door.

Tommy Lee took over at that point, and began dragging himself under his car in what seemed to be a pathetic attempt at escape. But when I reached down to pull him out by his legs, it turned out he had retrieved a hidden, large-caliber handgun. He promptly used it to shoot me at close range, exploding my body back some fifteen feet.

How'd that happen? You guessed it. I was jerked back on a ratchet line to a stack of waiting port-a-pits intended to stop my movement at the end of the cable. If you haven't done it yet, be sure to read the earlier chapter titled "Wild, Wicked Ratchet Rides" where you'll learn that the "jerk off" is not an exact science.

The ratchet needs to be anchored to something very sturdy. At this location, our only option was to attach it to a girder on the second floor of a building that was about two hundred feet away. That's a long way to run a cable. If the line developed any bit of slack, it would cause quite a snap.

Ever game, I put on my jerk vest (by now I had one that fit me) and waited to get hooked up. Job one was to rehearse so we could get dialed in on the amount of pressure we needed to use.

And so another wild ratchet ride began.

We used a light pressure for the first rehearsal, and it pulled me about eight feet. The pressure was increased for each subsequent rehearsal until we reached our goal of fifteen feet. Finally, we were ready to put this puppy on film.

"And, Action!" was the call from the AD.

Tommy Lee sat up from the ground we'd beaten him down to and fired his gun right at my midsection. This cued the ratchet and *Zing!* Off I went, flying backward into the pits.

"Okay! Let's do it again, folks. Let's get set for one more."

"*So they want another one, eh? Okay, let's go.*" I could do another one . . . as soon as I caught my wind. And so it went for the rest of the afternoon. Again and again I was zipped out of there like I was on a rocket. "*Uhhh . . .*" was the sound that came out of me every time I hit the port-a-pit.

In addition to all the rehearsals, we shot over a dozen takes of that scene. Each time I was cranked into the waiting pad, fifteen feet away. And each time I made the same noise. I went home that night a little sore, but very pleased with my performance and glad I was given the opportunity to do a fun gag.

The next morning my alarm went off at the usual time. I reached over to shut it off and noticed that the top of my shoulder had a bit of a twinge. Thinking over the previous day's work, I realized the twinge was most likely from getting jerked off so many times. (There's that phrase again.)

Then it was time to get up.

"*And here we go. Ah . . . here we go. And a-one, and a-two . . . What the hell?*" I couldn't get out of the bed!

I did my quick inventory. Wiggled my toes. Clenched and opened my hands. Took a deep breath. I was sore, but everything seemed to be working.

I finally realized what was going on. I couldn't raise my head off the pillow. As hard as I tried to, I literally could not pick up my head and neck from the bed. I ended up using my hands to lift my head up off the pillow. When I finally got myself to a sitting position, I realized just how tight my neck and back muscles were.

Out to the spa I went, pretty much living there for the next week. Whenever I wasn't bubbling in the jetted tub, I was packing ice on my neck and taking copious amounts of over-the-counter pharmaceuticals.

I spent some of my recuperation thinking back on the production. I had been warned that when rubbing elbows with Hollywood, there's always the possibility you'll find out that an actor whose work you appreciate, whose characters you relate to, is a real dick. This film marked the first time it happened to me.

Tommy Lee Jones and I met for the first time when we rehearsed the scene. Bud introduced us and talked us through the fight, then stepped away so we could work on it. The minute Bud left, Mr. Jones began telling me how to do my job—how to throw a punch, how to react, and even how to aim my gun. Mind you, he chose to do this all out of earshot of the coordinator.

Now I don't have a problem with someone pointing things out if what I'm doing isn't working—and it doesn't matter whether that someone is a stunter or an actor. And for an actor, Tommy Lee was a pretty good physical actor.

But don't tell me how to do my work sight unseen. That just doesn't float for me.

It wasn't just fight instruction he pontificated on. Jones went on to relate some "old time" wisdom he received from his pappy. Now that sounds like it could have been a nice, human conversation, but it wasn't. Instead, it was shared in the context of how unfortunate I was for not having a wonderful upbringing like him.

Wow. Before I could say a word, this guy demonstrated what a jerk he was. I decided to keep my admiration to myself and just get on with the work.

Cut to years later on *Natural Born Killers* where this same actor was on set, talking with Woody Harrelson and Juliette Lewis. I thought maybe the first time we met he was just young and brash and full of himself, so I left the past where it belongs and walked over to say hello. When he was done talking with the others, I stepped up and said, "Good afternoon, sir, been a long time, good to see you again." He looked up at me through his saggy-ass hound dog eyes, glanced down at my out-stretched hand, looked me in the eye again . . . and turned away.

During 2012's *Men in Black 3*, we were on set together once again. By now, I'd heard enough stories to not take anything he did or didn't do personally, so I didn't put myself out to even say hello. I still enjoy and appreciate his work, but finally learned to distance myself from him personally.

Will Smith, on the other hand, couldn't have been more pleasant. He openly and professionally greeted me and everyone else who came his way. Great guy, that Will.

C H A P T E R   2 4
EXTREME PREJUDICE

You can't help but learn something from this experience.

NICK NOLTE

. . . and learn I did.

In 1987, as a young-ish and excitable stunt man, I was offered a job by stunt coordinator Bennie Dobbins on a Walter Hill movie called *Extreme Prejudice*.

Bennie was a tough old salt whose credits dated back to 1955's *Cheyenne* television series, in which he performed a weekly parade of street fights, bar brawls, and horse gags. For a good while in his career, Bennie was Elvis Presley's stunt double. He had also hired me two years earlier for *Commando*, one of Arnold Schwarzenegger's early films.

Walter Hill is an icon in the industry. He's a writer, producer, and director and in those various capacities is the powerhouse behind some of your favorite blockbusters. This includes the *Alien* movies, Eddie Murphy's *48 Hours* franchise, Schwarzenegger's *Red Heat* and several television projects including the *Tales from the Crypt* series throughout the 1990s. As of this writing, Hill is producing Ridley Scott's *Prometheus* franchise.

Clearly Walter is known for his work in action films, which translates to stunts, which translates to fun and opportunity for stuntmen and stuntwomen. He's a well-prepared professional who knows what he wants when he gets to the set and keeps people around him who are like-minded. Walter is also one of those "regular guy" directors who will say good morning to you and actually make eye contact when he has a couple of minutes to shoot the breeze.

Extreme Prejudice is a story of love, lust and deceit starring Nick Nolte, Powers Boothe, Michael Ironside, Clancy Brown and Maria Conchita Alonzo. It was a modern-day film set in a southwest desert town that was overrun by bad guys—vigilantes and murderers led by Boothe, a truly outstanding actor who played a drug lord this time out. Good guy Nolte played a Texas Ranger, who comes into this hell-hole guns-a-blazing. He saves the town and, of course, gets the girl, who was harassed and groped throughout Boothe's short reign as *jefe* of the town's bad guys—which included me.

All this meant there was going be a ton of shootouts, falls, squibs and all-around mayhem for the stunt people to create. I worked for a couple of weeks on *Extreme Prejudice* and was happy to be there. I put in some very long hours on this shoot with my buddies including Rick Sawaya, Marian Green, Allan Graf, Jimmy Ortega, Tommy Rosales and Dave Cadiente. You'll remember Dave as my partner for *Trauma Center's* high-rise rescue.

The movie had a lot of gun battles, and when you're filming these, preparation is everything.

There are "bullet hits" that need to be placed on the ground and tables and walls—all hidden from camera.

There are the squibs—miniature explosive devices that special effects people place under a performer's wardrobe to create the illusion of being hit by a bullet.

Wardrobe people need to "scuff and score" the performer's clothing over the squib packs to ensure they explode properly.

The special effects department has to run hundreds of feet of wires to connect the explosives to the battery box that makes them blow.

Makeup artists have to apply blood to faces and secure wigs and beards all in support of the action scene.

There's also the importance of getting the camera in the right position and protecting the camera operators from being harmed by the squibs and explosions.

All this and more is what's involved in filming each and every take of each and every scene. When you work on a production like this, you have to be part of the team that helps make it all happen.

I was killed at least five times, as five separate characters, on this shoot.

We would go into the makeup trailer first thing in the morning where I might start out with a wig and a mustache. Then I'd go out and do the scene, get killed and break for lunch. After lunch, we would change our wardrobe, go back to makeup and get a different wig and beard, and after shooting that scene, we'd repeat the dance, this time with sideburns and a scar. This went on for several days.

As the good stunt team members we were, there was no complaining about how raw our faces were getting from the spirit gum glue they use to attach the facial hair. No complaints about ill-fitting wigs pinned on so tightly, they'd stretch back our faces and distort our eyes.

One day on set, I was slated to do a "flat back" to the cement, which is just as the name suggests. I was sitting with the stunt guys, getting ready by putting on my elbow pads, when Bennie walked by. He stopped, pulled the stogie out of his mouth, pointed to the pads I was sliding up my sleeves and said, "What the hell are those?"

"My, uh, elbow pads," I muttered to the boss.

Bennie looked at me, gave his head a little shake and said, "Elbow pads. Shit." And he walked away.

We all kind of laughed; he was from a different era, a different mind-set, a great pro.

Like every stunt person on this movie, I did a lot of gags. And some kinda' bit me in the butt. Let me tell you about two of them—involving bib overalls, a hot bullet shell, and a button.

One of the gags Bennie asked me to do was a high fall. Now I don't like heights, but hey, I'd trained to do them and had done several by then. I was confident I could do what he was asking for.

Bennie explained I'd be falling through a second-floor balcony railing—a stunt that would set off the film's big shoot-out.

"Yes, sir, I'm good for that," I said to him.

"And," he continued, "I want you to go through it backward. You're getting shot in the chest and going backward."

"You got it, Bennie."

Well, I just about pooed myself. *"Let's see, high fall, through a railing . . . backward?! I mean, backward?! Ok. We're talking—what—fifteen, twenty feet? Ok. I got this."* I'm better when I can see where I'm falling, but I was certain I could handle this gag just fine.

The day we shot this, I was in position as a guard on the second-floor balcony of the bad guy's fortress. The action was set off by an argument that got out of hand between Michael Ironside and actor Clancy Brown.

As the scene escalates, Clancy points his machine gun at Michael but gets distracted, and his shot finds me. The force blew me backward through a doorway, across a balcony and against a wooden railing that was scored (meaning that the wood was pre-cut) and ready to break at my body's insistence. On the cement deck below was a six-foot by eight-foot foam fall pad that was about eighteen inches high, just waiting for me to float down onto its spongy goodness.

It all went well up to the point it didn't.

I got shot, the blood spurted, and I flew across the deck into the breakaway rail . . . which didn't break.

And "Cut! Cut! Cut!" was what we heard.

The special effects crew didn't score the breakaway rail deeply enough for it to break when I hit it. So in they came to re-score the rail for the next take.

Now, here's where the "human factor" comes into stunts.

See, I had my movements, my speed, and my force all set to hit that rail and go to my pad. But it didn't break on take one. So, on take two, I *should* have done everything exactly the same, knowing that this time the rail was properly scored and ready to go and would break as planned.

But I didn't do that.

Instead, I got the "ACTION" call for take two, made my initial moves the same way, but when I got to the rail, I made a fairly common "take two" mistake. I pushed a little harder, just to make sure that the rail would break this time. Pushing just "that much more" was all it took to carry me off target. I overshot my mark. I ended up flying a foot farther than I had planned, which meant that while my body was still headed toward the pad, my head was streaming straight for the cement.

Thankfully, "safety" stunt people are always assigned to big gags. They are there to hold a fire extinguisher or stand ready next to a fall pad just in case something goes wrong. Bennie had a few stunt guys spotting the pad for me on this shot, one of them being Allan Graf.

In the short time it took for me to fall less than twenty feet, Allan saw what was about to happen—I was going to hit my head on the cement deck below—and took action. Graf was already on his knees so he could stay lower than the camera frame. From this position, he swooped under my head with his hands cupped and caught my head before I hit the deck. Saving my head, my career and possibly my life.

On impact, my knees bounced to my chest at the same time my chin tapped my sternum. Allan and the crew got me to a seated position and helped me to catch my breath.

Needless to say, I'm thankful for Bennie's foresight and Allan's quick reaction.

Afterwards, as I sat there tasting my blood and trying to define just what the hell went wrong—and feeling grateful that I had survived the ordeal—Bennie came up to me. Through his cigar he asked, "How much do you want for that?"

Here's where I learned how important it is to know your worth.

While spitting blood, I said to him, "Oh, Bennie, whatever you have." What I didn't know was that Dobbins was known as "Bennie the Penny" for his tight-fisted adjustments.

As he turned away, he said, "Okay. Two hundred." It took a couple of seconds for me to realize that the going rate for the gag on this feature should have been about $500. But there was nothing to be done. Bennie was doing what was best for production and his budget, and I was learning a lesson.

"Next setup!"

Another scene had a bunch of 'bad guys' surrounding an innocent townsperson who was already on the ground. We gathered around this poor devil and sadistically emptied our automatic weapons into him, laughing all the way. In this particular scene, I was wearing a pair of bib overalls.

Now if you know a little about automatic weapons, you understand that they eject their empty shells to the side. All of us were aware of that fact and placed ourselves accordingly.

"And ACTION!"

The call came from Walter, and as directed, each of us emptied our full clip. But about one-third of the way into the scene I felt a scorching pain in the middle of my back, and then another. This was nasty, burning, repeated doses of pain. "*Gotta keep on going,*" I thought to myself, "*gotta get through this, it won't be long,*" hoping the painful expression on my face helped my character look even more like a mad man.

"CUT! CUT! CUT!" Came the yell from the assistant director. "*Oh thank God!*" I remember thinking, "*I'm on fire here!!*" Before the dust cleared, I was doing "the dance" trying to get out of my bib overalls.

You probably guessed what happened. A few shells found their way inside my overalls and stuck to my back. Maybe one of the guys turned his gun sideways, or maybe the shells bounced off someone else.

I think it was Brian Williams—not the news anchor, but a fine stuntman with blockbuster credits exceeding thirty years—who helped me out of my bibs to check on the damage. He found two new tattoos burned into the small of my back. The shells hit the ground just as I looked up to see the entire crew staring as I stood there with my shirt off, overalls around my ankles, and a fellow stuntman behind me checking out my butt.

All I heard from Walter was, "Next setup!"

A few days later I was set to take a shotgun blast to the chest. This was cool because . . . well, it's just cool. Again with the bib overalls, but this time they had sewn into them one of the biggest squib packs I had ever seen. The scene was me, firing my rifle from behind a short wall, then rising slightly only to get blasted in the chest.

I even had the "button" in my hand.

The button is what sets off a squib charge. Sometimes the special effects team will do that for you, but when the shot calls for it, you get to do it yourself. This task brings with it a little performance pressure. You have to be on your mark, face the camera, fire your weapon, hit the button and then take your reaction to the squib.

You have to "press" the button, which is a small red object about the size of a pencil eraser, to set off the charge to the squib. It won't go off if you just brush against it or touch it lightly.

Usually.

Do you see where I'm headed here?

By this point in my career, I had been squibbed hundreds of times. I always did—and still do—listen as the special effects people go through their how-to and safety spiel, to make sure all bases are covered. The last things they say to you is, "Okay, you're hot," meaning that your squib is ready to go when the button is pushed. Then they give one final warning: "Don't hit the button . . . careful of the button . . . don't touch that button till you're ready to go!"

Okay, gotcha. Got it. Ready to go!

The button was in my left hand, which was cradling the barrel of my weapon. As I walked so very carefully to my final position for the shot, I saw Walter and his staff positioned around the nearby camera that would capture my "close-up."

I stood on my mark, gave a quick look over at camera, began to kneel into position behind the short wall, and then it happened.

My thumb "brushed" against the button and my chest exploded—with such force that the blood sprayed across the wall and onto Walter, the assistant director, and the script supervisor.

There was utter silence. I had nowhere to hide, no hole to crawl into.

I looked up—as astonished as anyone—directly into Walter's blood-splattered face. He stood and said in a very calm and directorial voice, "Next setup."

I was left there to get cleaned up, muttering all the while some inane thing about the button being touchy.

Walter never came back to get the shot, and as for me, I went about my remaining days on the show being as professional as I could. I was a little concerned that every day would be my last, but felt generally philosophical about the whole incident. After all, nobody got hurt, and everybody knows that shit really does happen.

C H A P T E R 2 5
HALLOWEEN 4: THE RETURN OF MICHAEL MYERS

Execution is everything.

JEFF BRIDGES

n 1988, I was in Utah working on *Halloween 4: The Return of Michael Myers* with the great Donald Pleasence, Ellie Cornell and stuntman George P. Wilbur, who starred as the murderous Michael Myers.

The movie's stunt coordinator was Fred Lerner, a highly successful stuntman and stunt coordinator. Fred took a shine to my stunt pup self four years earlier when I worked with him on an episode of *Cover Up*, a television series that ran for only one season.

Cover Up starred then-supermodel Jennifer O'Neill as a fashion photographer turned government agent. Her co-star was Jon-Erik Hexum, who played her former Green Beret bodyguard posing as one of her models. Jon-Erik was a handsome young man on a fast rise to stardom when he died by his own hand in a tragic on-set gun accident.

The first time Fred and I worked together, he asked me to consider joining the Stuntmen's Association of Motion Pictures, more commonly known as SAMP, saying he would like to be my main sponsor.

It was an incredible honor to receive an invitation to become a member of the oldest and largest stunt group in the business.

Fred recruited fellow SAMP members Hubie Kerns Jr., Dick Warlock, Dick Durock and Bennie Dobbins as my sponsors for the group. He then escorted me through the anxiety-filled process of being accepted by dozens of stunt professionals who didn't know me from Adam. Long story short, all went well, and I was inducted into the Stuntmen's Association.

I was a proud member of that group for twenty years, making lifelong friends and brothers and serving as its president for two terms from 1990 to 1994. But I chose to leave the organization in 2005. I was part of a mass exodus of some twenty working members who left the group around that time. Although each of us had our unique reasons, a common thread was the lack of "brotherly support" which was once the glue that held this group together.

Back to *Halloween 4*.

I was to perform a couple of gags, and both were real fartknockers. In one, I'd be doubling an actor whose character was thrown by Michael Myers from the bed of a truck traveling about 20 mph. The other gag had me doubling a different actor whose character was yanked from the driver's side of a moving truck and flung down an embankment.

On the very cold night we shot our scenes, I found myself in the back of the truck with George, as Myers, and a stunt guy I didn't know. He introduced himself and said he would be doubling another actor in the scene. When Myers threw me out of the truck, his job was to drop the tailgate so I could fall out, then he was to follow me to the pavement.

Stuntwoman Debbie Evans was driving. Debbie is a superior stunt player who is unstoppable in any vehicle. I had full trust in her to pilot the truck in a straight line down the highway. As she got up to speed, George gripped onto my jacket and belt and got ready to give me the heave-ho out of the truck. The other stuntman was in position, hanging tightly to the tailgate, ready to drop it as I took my last step before exiting to the pavement.

The cameras were ready, the truck was up to speed, and my heart was thumping a mile a minute as I watched the dark, cold street pass beneath me. I heard George count it off. "Three, two, one . . ."

Confident the tailgate would drop, I took my three steps and hit the back of the truck. But instead of dropping the tailgate like he did in rehearsals, this fool just leaned on it. Of course, it didn't budge one inch. It was like hitting a steel wall.

Instead of the fall we had planned, I crashed into and over that tailgate and landed like a lawn dart into the pavement. My right arm was above my head (an unconscious move I made that probably saved me from cracking open my skull) and my body did a "scorpion."

A scorpion is what we call it when your face is stuffed flat into something hard, like pavement, and your feet whip over and smack the back of your head, curving your body backward like one of those invincible little predators.

I immediately knew I'd torn my shoulder pretty badly and that the real pain would settle in as soon as my adrenaline wore off. But I had another gag to do, so I told Fred that if they wanted to get that shot, they needed to set it up ASAP so I could give them what they wanted. "But please," I emphasized, "hurry."

The crew got the shot together as fast as they could. Meanwhile, I sat with an ice pack on my shoulder, a blanket around me to stay warm, and a mug of coffee to wash down the handful of ibuprofen given to me by the set medic.

In the upcoming shot, I would be driving the truck with Debbie beside me, and George would be positioned on top of the cab. He would break through the driver's side window, grab me by the head and throw me out and down a thirty- to forty-foot embankment as Debbie simultaneously slid over to take the wheel.

Whew!

It had been about forty-five minutes since I hit the street, and the stiffness was starting to set in. My hot flashes and sweats were turning into chills and shakes. It was time to get it done.

Fred loaded me into the truck, and he put George on the top of the cab. I drove the truck to the number one position and the director called "action."

I accelerated, brought the truck up to our planned speed of 15 mph then veered to the side of the road to the spot where I was to be flung out. Without a second thought (because common sense was all but gone at this point) I opened the door, stepped onto the running board, and launched myself out into the rocks and brush that were waiting to cushion my fall.

"Cut! Print! Let's get him to the hospital." This is what I heard as my friends Fred and George helped me up the hill and into a waiting van.

Here we go: emergency room, doctors, nurses, confusion, hectic-ness. The drill was familiar. I came out with some x-rays, a sling and a torn and separated right shoulder.

Production let me stay a few more days in case they needed my services, but in all honesty, I think Fred pulled a few strings and had them keep me on the clock. He was a class act that Freddy. I miss him.

CHAPTER 26
GLORY

Making movies is much more dangerous than people appreciate.

BILL MURRAY

I n 1989, I traveled to Jonesboro, Georgia, to work on *Glory*. This movie told the true story of the heroics of black Union soldiers in the American Civil War. The film won three Academy Awards® including a much-deserved Supporting Actor Oscar for Denzel Washington. Director Ed Zwick did a fantastic job telling this heart-wrenching story of our nation's history, including executing grand battle scenes that were filmed on actual Civil War battlefields.

The coordinator on the show was Bob Minor. Fans of 1980s television will appreciate that Bob, once a champion bodybuilder, coordinated the Tom Selleck TV classic *Magnum, P.I.* He also doubled Roger E. Mosely, who played TC, Magnum's sidekick.

We filmed our *Glory* battles in July and August. Now summer anywhere is hot, but summer in the south is HOT and HUMID like nobody's business.

Like most historic battle scenes, reenactors were hired to support the action called for in the script. This film pre-dates today's practice of using computers to morph fifty actors into five hundred, so we had several hundred reenactors on hand. Each brought his own authentic uniform and weaponry, representing a particular branch of the military from the Civil War. These guys also wore the long hair, mutton chop sideburns, beards and handlebar mustaches that were popular at that time.

And it wasn't just soldiers. Their wives and children came along, too, wearing authentic, homemade costumes as well. And almost all of them . . . ready for this? . . . brought tents and stoves, pots and pans, and camped right there on the fields where we were shooting. These dedicated men, women, boys, and girls came to the battle site ready to work.

I remember it was a bit surreal for me to arrive in the production van, to a real battlefield, and see soldiers in Civil War uniforms having coffee with their families outside of their tents. It was reminiscent of the photos taken by celebrated nineteenth-century photographer Mathew Brady of the soldiers he visited in the 1860s.

Each of these guys knew the history of the war and most of the individual battles. Their stories were amazing. At the same time, it was like having five hundred technical advisors on set, each with a multitude of opinions about such topics as weapons, battle plans and wardrobe. "Oh, you'd *never* wear your pants on the inside of your boots if you were with the 151st. But you would if you were with the artillery of the 134th."

There were Union and Confederate reenactors, and each one brought an invaluable feeling of authenticity to the picture. Interesting side note—years later, when I married the one true love of my life, I discovered that one of her nephews, my buddy Michael Berger, is a passionate Civil War historian and reenactor.

Several of my close stunt friends were there with me. I remember we were all so excited to go play Civil War! Somewhere inside, when we get a chance like this, we're all just big kids having the time of our lives.

Wardrobe and makeup came to us each morning, bringing our facial hair and costumes for the day. Although it differed each day, pretty much an even number of us was assigned to be either Union or Confederate soldiers.

We had elaborate battle scenes to choreograph and perform. There were horses charging down slopes and running into soldiers, cannons were blasting, and explosions went off all around. The field was littered with ankle-breaker holes, and at the center of each shot were actors with dialog. We all knew that for all the fun it was going to be, there would be plenty of hard work ahead.

The first day of shooting, we felt an unusually heavy air around us. 98% humidity was not the kind of air we westerners were used to. Running through the fields, explosions going off everywhere you stepped, trying to keep your focus—all the while struggling to get enough of that thick Georgia air in our lungs so we could reach our final mark—was definitely a challenge.

As the day turned into early evening, we were faced with another challenge: how to not be eaten alive by mosquitoes that were the size of Huey helicopters. I mean these monsters had ID numbers stamped on their sides.

That first day finally ended, and the director got the shots he needed. But we were all hot, sticky, tired and bitten. Movie war definitely is hell!

Day two started a little differently.

You see, we had all discovered a critical wardrobe secret. The Union uniforms were made out of cotton. Cool, breathable cotton. But the Confederate uniforms were made out of wool, just like the real soldiers wore. Thick, heavy wool. And we stuntmen were to trade off roles every day—one day we would be Union, the next day Rebel.

But come the second day of filming, when wardrobe asked the stuntmen what we played the day before, you'd better believe we all yelled "Rebels!!" Some of us lucked out and got to play Union soldiers for two or three days in a row before the wardrobe department got wise to us. Oh well, it was nice while it lasted.

Somewhere in the second week of filming the battles, I was involved in a huge charge across the field with about 150 other Union soldiers. Of that group, only about five of us were stuntmen, the rest were reenactors, all of whom carried their own weapons or were issued rifles from the prop department . . . with bayonets attached! "The bayonets must stay on," the A.D. told us. "Just get them to point away from you when you get blown up."

It was my job to gather some forty reenactors in my vicinity and clue them in on what was about to happen. So my stunt buddy H.B.—Harold Burns—and I lined these guys up and in the nicest, but most professionally stern voices, we told them that by no means were they to ever, *ever* point their rifle skyward during the shot, because H.B. and I were going to be hitting air ramps.

Air ramps are nitrogen-powered contraptions that launch stunt performers high into the air. The device uses hydraulics and compressed air to send us soaring. The air ramp is triggered by us stepping on a foot-plate; the height and distance we travel depends on the amount of air pressure that's set at the controller.

We carefully explained to these reenactors that if they didn't follow these important instructions, we could be impaled on those long sharp suckers on our way back down.

But as I looked into their faces, I saw men who wanted to be unleashed. I saw soldiers who were ready for battle. I saw forty men who didn't hear a word we were saying.

So we repeated ourselves, again and again, until we got the nod from them. Unfortunately, it was the same kind of nod you get when you tell your texting teenager to take out the trash or do the dishes or do just about anything.

Nonetheless, we soldiered on.

The stage was set for the double air ramp gag. I was running on the left side of the cannon and H.B. was on the right. The mortar bombs were loaded with chunks of cork and pounds of fuller's earth that was packed on top of cubes of black-powder set to explode at the same time we hit our air ramps. Fuller's earth is a clay silicate that special effects uses to make explosions and blasts look even larger.

The reenactors had their instructions and were ready to go. Special effects gave the "all clear" sign to the A.D. The camera operators confirmed that they were ready to go. My heart was beating a little more rapidly than normal as I got ready to make my charge. I counted my steps to the ramp. I visualized my action in my head. I was ready. H.B. was ready.

Zwick called out his directions to the troops just like a field general, using a bullhorn from his vantage point on top of the highest mound on the battlefield. "AAAAND ACTION! ACTION! ACTION!!"

I was off, and out of the corner of my eye I saw that H.B. was moving into his mark as well. The extras were all around us, screaming those ungodly war cries that pierce your ears. I was three steps away, two steps away, and then everything became zeroed-in and slow-motioned. I could see the air ramp one step in front of me. It was the mark that I needed to hit to get off and fly into the air. I could see H.B. getting to his mark. I could see and feel the extras around us. The battle was raging on, and then the final step.

KA-BLAM!! I hit the ramp. Just as planned, the explosion blew dirt, grass, and chunks of cork into the air all around us. I was several feet up in the air . . . coming down fast.

THUMP! ERG! OOF! "*Good God the ground's hard,*" I thought. But I got to it and didn't get jabbed with a pig sticker. Life was good.

Then I heard somebody say, "Oh thit! Thon-of-a-bith!"

"CUT, cut, cut!" came the call from camera.

I jumped up just knowing that someone got stuck, but I couldn't see past my hand because the smoke was still so thick in the air. I followed the voice; it was coming from near H.B. As I raced over, my mind raced, too, wondering what might have just happened. When I got to him, H.B. was laying face down in the grass. I put my hand on him and turned him over, oh-so-gently. "H.B., what's wrong? What happened?"

As he rolled over and half sat up, there was blood coming out of his mouth. "*Oh my God,*" I'm thinking. "*Internal injuries! He's spitting up blood!*" I took a closer look and saw that his lips were starting to swell under the blood. Yes, he was spitting blood all right, but it came from a mouth injury. Throughout, he continued to cuss. "Thit! Thon of a bith!"

"H.B." I asked with great concern, "Did one of these guys get you with their bayonet?" I asked.

"No." he confessed to me. "I fogot to dwop my wifle when I hit da wamp. I frew it up in da air inthead, and da latht thing I rememer theeing wath da butt of my wifle coming down from da thy. Then BANG! Rite in da mouff."

It was off to the hospital for a few stitches for him, and then a couple of weeks later, new caps for his front teeth.

We all learned lessons that day. The reenactors finally understood how dangerous filming stunts could be. And we all got an unforgettable reminder that stunts are complicated.

In this stunt, for example, H.B. and I had to hold our rifles in our left hand, then drop them as we stepped on our ramp plates with our right foot while looking up and forward so we could hurl ourselves into the air knowing that a black-powder bomb was exploding up our asses.

Most important of all, H.B. learned to ALWAYS drop your gun when you hit an air ramp! *Or elf you migh loof your teef!*

CHAPTER 27
DIRECT HIT

My job is to defy the normal.

ERROL FLYNN

've only been around a couple of mishaps on sets where someone other than me was taken away in an ambulance. One of them occurred in 1994 when I was working on a film called *Direct Hit*. The movie starred William Forsythe, an actor I've worked with several times in my career. I very much respect how he brings "tough guys" to life.

I was working in a restaurant scene with about thirty other stunt people of all ages and sizes. The scene called for a car to come crashing through the front picture window of the restaurant, and for all the patrons to scatter out of the way. We used a closed-down car dealership for the restaurant, so you can imagine the size of that front window!

I played the concierge, the guy at the podium at the very front of the window. I had a direct eye line on the car as it approached the ramp that led into the window and then into the restaurant.

A bar was set up about three or four steps behind me, and the rest of the place was filled with tables. Stunt people were positioned throughout the space as bar patrons. About thirty feet into the room from the window was a small set of stairs, three or four at the most, which led to another level that was about ten feet deep ending at a wall.

We were all placed for the camera, and we all knew where our "bail out" point was and where we were going to end up. The bail out is the point in a gag when you need to make your move to get out of the freaking way of what's coming at you. For example, *"When the car gets to this particular spot on the ramp leading to the window, it will be going about 25 mph. That means I'll have approximately 1.2 seconds to get the hell out of the way, or pay dearly for it."* I planned to bail out up and over the bar and crawl to a far corner just in case the car veered off to the side and took out the bar.

Everyone else had his or her spot as well, knowing where to go and how not to get in anyone else's path.

It was dark and time to get it done. The car was set, the cameras were set, and stunts were set. Everyone was literally on their toes, even those who sat at tables.

When the director called action, everything started out at regular speed and then, for me, turned into a slow-motion dance. I happened to be the first guy. I see the car hit the mark, which lets me know that it's time to bail, which in turn lets everyone else know that the car is here. Because when the first guy goes, everybody goes. Well, I jumped over that bar like I'd been shot out of a cannon. I don't even remember touching it as I cleared it.

I do remember the front of the car hitting the huge picture window. I heard tables and chairs being flung and dragged around and the sound of the car hitting and screeching to a stop. Then there was dead silence.

"CUT! CUT! CUT!" was called over a bullhorn, and I popped up from behind the bar to see the aftermath. Everyone was just coming out of their end marks, doing self-checks and also counting heads to make sure that no one was down.

Suddenly the stunt driver yelled, "Where is he? I didn't see him get out of the way!!" A horrific realization settled on the room: someone was down. One of the stuntmen was pinned under the car.

You know, I'm sitting here recalling that evening, and I've got the chills just thinking about it. Sure enough, a stuntman who had been sitting at one of the tables in the back of the room at the base of the steps had been hit. He and several others who were manning those tables had their own bail out time and place to go when "action" was called—but this gentleman encountered a problem.

We all ran to the car, which had traveled all the way up the stairs and was now resting on the upper level, and found one of our own. Some of us lifted the car up and off of him while others pulled him ever so gently out from under the Jag. He was like a rag doll. He was broken and bloody and awake enough to be in pain and shock at the same time. We kept him warm and still until the paramedics came and jetted him to the hospital.

That gentleman did what we all know we can't do. He blinked. He hung in for that extra nano of a second, that fine line between decision and indecision. I don't know if he got hung up on something, or he thought that he was a little faster than he really was.

What I believe happened is this. He got distracted for an nth of a moment. He thought too hard about how he was going to do this gag. He thought too long about how he was going to land. Thought too much about how close he was going to let that Jag get to him before he bailed. A stunt person has to learn how to let the thinking go when it's time to perform. From my experience, once your thinking is done, you have to let your instincts take over. Or else you could think yourself into the hospital . . . or worse.

That stuntman is up and around these days, a miracle by anyone's standards. He doesn't walk as well as he used to, doesn't stand quite as straight and has a mouthful of new teeth. But he's up and amongst us, and for that we're all thankful.

CHAPTER 28
THE FANTASTIC FOUR

It's Clobberin' Time!

THING, *THE FANTASTIC FOUR*

remember getting a call from our secretary at the Stuntmen's Association saying only that I had an audition and that casting was looking for a stuntman who was six feet tall and had blue eyes.

The interview went something like this.

"How tall are you?"

"A bit over six feet tall."

"How much do you weigh?"

"About 235."

"How long have you been doing stunts?"

"Oh, better than fifteen years."

"If you get this, you'll be doing the stunts for the Ben Grimm character after he turns into The Thing."

"That sounds great."

"Have you ever worked in a full body suit?"

"Ah, no I haven't."

"Are you claustrophobic?"

"Um," (deep gulp) "no . . . I'm not."

"Do you know anything about *The Fantastic Four* comic books or characters?"

"No. I don't know much beyond *Superman* and *Batman*."

"Hmph . . . mumble-mumble. Thank you, we'll let you know."

A short time later I received the call that I was selected to play Thing in a Roger Corman film titled *The Fantastic Four*.

Word gets around fast. Within the day, I was getting calls left and right from friends telling me how cool it was that I was going to play Thing. I thanked them and then got busy doing homework about *The Fantastic Four* and the Thing character. At that point in my career I had already worked on *The Incredible Hulk* and *The Flash*, so I knew how passionate comic book fans were. I knew they'd be outraged by characters who weren't correctly portrayed onscreen.

Once I started reading the *Fantastic Four* comic books, the exciting stories and multi-dimensional characters hooked me. Physically, I discovered that Thing was right up my alley. He was described as six feet tall, blue eyes, built like a stack of boulders and weighed five hundred pounds.

Height . . . check! Blue eyes . . . check! A five-hundred-pound stack of boulders? Well, I've been compared to a refrigerator, a moose, and a bear, so why not a stack of boulders?

First order of business for me was to be fitted for the Thing costume. I reported for duty at Optic Nerve, a special effects house in the San Fernando Valley that was building costumes for Thing as well as Dr. Doom.

On that first day, I walked into their "circle of scrutiny."

Those guys took measurements of everything that I have. They measured me from my ankles to my crotch . . . from my wrists to my neck . . . and then my face and my head. They looked at their drawings, at images from the comic book and looked at me. Then they huddled several feet away from me and had a little pow-wow. Every once in a while, heads would pop up and look over at me, then they'd drop back down into the huddle.

When they finally broke, the group once again gathered in front of me and stared at my face some more. I began to realize they were staring at my nose. Their expressions showed they didn't know what to think about it or what to do with it. The previously upbeat creative vibe in the room was gone.

The head honcho, Jon Vulage, took my chin in his hand, turned my head to profile, and shook his head. He said, "I don't think that this is gonna work for Thing's head." He then turned my head to reveal the other side of my face. Then everyone in the group shook their heads. "It's your nose," Jon explained. "It won't fit into the mask we need to make in order to have the Thing look authentic."

I felt like I had been punched in the gut. I realized that the run of work I was about to embark on was going to get yanked out from under me. And for what? Because my freaking dago nose was too big!

But I knew something they didn't.

"Wait a minute," I said. "You mean if my nose was smaller, maybe a little flatter to my face, as if I'd been in too many boxing matches, that would be better for you?"

"Yes," he said in a kind but regretful tone. "I'm afraid so."

With that, I raised my right hand, stuck out my "pointer finger" and proceeded to press sideways on my nose until I flattened it to my cheek.

"Oh my gawd!" someone said. Another exclaimed, "What the hell is that?" They all laughed and gawked at my squished nostrils.

Then John spoke up. "You can breathe like that? Are you ok to work like that?"

"Yep," I told him. "I'm good to go!"

Whew! Thanks to my oddly flexible dago nose, I got to keep my job and make a little Hollywood history—or at least Hollywood lore—while I was at it.

The whole making of Thing took several visits to Optic Nerve. Everything progressed quickly and efficiently. I didn't know at the time that speed was necessary due to behind-the-scenes moviemaking machinations.

First, the artists brought me in for a full-body cast session. Every inch of me was covered in plaster as I stood in the middle of the room, propped up by 1x2 and 2x4 boards so I wouldn't and couldn't move until the plaster dried. Once it was finally set, the cast was cut off the same way they remove a cast from a broken leg or arm. With that little circular saw. The one you're secretly terrified will slice off your most vital parts.

Then it was time to cast my head—my whole head, neck to crown. They sat me in a director's chair, stuck a couple of straws up my nose and proceeded to slop me up with cold plaster. It was like falling into a big mud puddle on a cold October night.

Next they focused on fitting me for my suit. It took several sessions to make sure the suit fit correctly and would allow me enough movement to handle the action I needed to perform. This all went down during the holidays, so I had to make sure I didn't put on any Christmas pounds.

The making of the headpiece was especially interesting. A remote-control device enabled movement of the mask's brows, cheeks, and mouth. The device's electronics were housed in a contraption that was placed across the bridge of my nose, which kept it pretty much flattened down. They made it work, and in my opinion, it looked better than any Thing mask since.

The process was as pleasant as could be. Everyone in the shop had a "fantastic" attitude. Recognizing that I was, in fact, more than a little claustrophobic, they did everything they could to make me comfortable.

I had a friend record the entire process with my handy Super-8 video recorder. (C'mon, it was 1992!) I compiled that footage into a DVD I creatively titled *The Making of The Thing*, which is available on my website. Additionally, some of the footage is highlighted in the documentary, *Doomed: The Untold Story of Roger Corman's The Fantastic Four*. The film was made by film studies professor and director Marty Langford and casting director Mark Sikes, who was Roger Corman's casting assistant.

There was one fly in the super-suit ointment—an extremely hot and sweaty fly.

I had seen a "super-suit" in action when I worked on *The Flash* television show in the early 1990s. Stuntman Dane Farwell wore it when doubling John Wesley Shipp, who played Barry Allen/The Flash. On that show, the suit was made with a built-in cool suit layer that got its energy from a little hand-held unit. He'd plug it in, and it helped keep his body temperature normal, thus preventing overheating.

This was important, because it gets really friggin' hot in a suit that's made out of a couple of inches of dense rubber, sealed in the back like a wetsuit, with a rubber headpiece that's sealed with snaps to the shoulders of the costume.

Let me repeat: it's really friggin' hot.

But Corman's production didn't have enough money for a cool suit. So I bucked up and made it work.

It wasn't easy.

Most of my scenes were shot on a stage where the temperature—thanks to closed doors and high-power movie lighting that was on for hours at a time— reached a stifling eighty degrees or better. With the full suit on—which covered my hands, feet, head and body—the only way I could get any fresh air to breathe, was to have someone direct a small fan at me between takes, and blow it into the open mouth of the mask.

Additionally, once I was in the suit. I couldn't sit down. I could lean, but because of the way the suit was designed, I couldn't get off of my feet. In fact, it took three people at least five minutes to get me out of the suit. As you can imagine, taking a pee in that thing was a full-blown ordeal!

Filming finally got underway. We shot in December and January at Corman Studios in Venice, California. As impressive as that might sound, the B-movie legend's studio was actually an old, run-down building both inside and out.

I remember the days being long, director Oley Sassone keeping everyone strong, and playing Uno on the dressing room floor with Rebecca Staab, the wonderful actress who played Susan Storm.

I worked in tandem with Michael Bailey Smith, who played the Ben Grimm character. Michael, who is known worldwide for his memorable work in the horror and science fiction genres, was extremely giving and generous as an actor, helping me play his counterpart in the Thing suit.

Michael and I have since worked together several times—notably in 2010's horror film *Chain Letter* starring a host of young actors including *Twilight*'s Nikki

Reed and the great character actor Keith David. Michael played the Chain Man. As his name suggests, his preferred mode of murder was industrial steel chain. As stunt coordinator on the film, I worked with writer/director Deon Taylor to create uniquely gruesome death scenes. Go rent or buy the movie, then come to my website and we can talk about the stunts.

Shortly after *The Fantastic Four* wrapped, we learned that the movie we had all put so much sweat and blood into was not going to be released. No theater debut, no television replays, no residuals.

What? How could this be?

It turned out that the guy who owned the rights to the story was going to lose them if he didn't act on his option to make the film. As the story goes, he decided to make the low-budget movie with Roger for the sole purpose of preserving those rights. He never intended to release the film. Instead, this production gave him the ability to sell the rights to 20th Century Fox for about twenty times what it cost us to make our version.

And that, my friends, is how business is done in Hollywood.

I have a little P.S. to this story.

The Fantastic Four wasn't my only association with a comic book hero. I was tickled pink to get to work on a reunion movie of the week called *Return to the Batcave: The Misadventures of Adam and Burt.* I grew up watching Adam West, Burt Ward, Julie Newmar and all of the iconic guest villains on the show. Adam was as charming as hell, always with a smile or a wink. He truly enjoyed mixing it up onscreen and was a joy to work with. Burt? Not so much.

Performing with people I raced home to watch on television every day of my youth was a remarkable experience—one that I'll never forget.

CHAPTER 29
CASINO

Death comes in a flash, and that's the truth of it. A person's gone in less than 24 frames of film.

MARTIN SCORSESE

I n 1993, I got a call from stunt coordinator Doug Coleman, who asked if I could make an audition for a movie starring Robert De Niro, Joe Pesci, and Sharon Stone. And, oh yeah, it was directed by Martin Scorsese.

Doug, highly sought-after as both a stunt coordinator and second unit director, said that the role called for some dialog and added that if cast, my head would get crushed in a vise. Then he wanted to know if I was interested.

"Hmm. Let me think about that. Do I really want a chance to work with these people? Hell yes!"

"You bet, sure," I said to him. "Thanks for the opportunity."

A couple of days later, off to the *Casino* audition I went. I showed up with a few other guys and was the last one to go in. There were two women in the room. One operated the video camera; the other gave me direction, which went something like this.

"We're going to videotape you and send this to Martin Scorsese for his pick for the part of Tony Dogs. We want you to swear, cuss and mostly say "fuck." We want you to be telling somebody off. Telling them to "fuck off." Call them a "fucker" and defy their authority by getting in their face. Can you do that?"

"Fuck yeah!" was the answer I gave.

Once the tape was running, I said the "F" word as many different ways as I knew how. I remember my audition included numerous references to mothers and families.

A couple of days after that, I got the call that Marty (that's right, Mr. Scorsese) picked me for the part of Tony Dogs. Needless to say, I was pretty effing excited.

The role called for me to be in two scenes. In one, Tony would shoot up a bar, killing people in the process. Unfortunately for my character, the bar was under the protection of mob boss Remo Gaggi, who sent his muscle after me. His avenging gang was led by brutal mob enforcer Nicky Santoro, brilliantly played by Joe Pesci. In my other scene, my character would endure a brutal death.

I traveled to Las Vegas where the film was being shot, and on my first day was shuttled directly to the production's wardrobe warehouse for a fitting. With me were two other stuntmen—Rick Sawaya, incredibly talented and the best friend a guy could have, and the gifted stuntman Jim Wilkey. Both were there to play my "gang" of bad guys. They had both read for the part of Tony Dogs as well, and Doug, being a class act, gave them each a week of work on the film.

The next day we shot the initial scene, where I come into the bar guns-a-blazing, flagged by Rick and Jim, who were also firing weapons. We shot the place up, killing stuntmen Jack Verboise, Rick Blackwell and Richard Hancock as well as Eliza Coleman, an experienced stuntwoman who also happens to be Doug's wife.

Before we shot the scene, coordinator Doug took us through the barroom set and showed us what the shootout was going to look like. Who got shot where; where the body squibs were going to be placed; where the squibs were placed on the bar, the bottles, and the furniture; how large the explosions were going to be; and the order in which they would be set off.

After that, we got to meet Mr. Scorsese! A small entourage surrounded him as Doug introduced us. He was polite and business-like as he talked to us about the scene. He made certain we understood how this scene fit in the overall story. He also talked to me about what a badass Tony Dogs is and the intensity he wanted for the scene.

Beyond that, this kind of scene called for me and my gang to hit our marks for camera and for our victims to know when and where to fall. It would be in my next scene that I'd get to experience a little "one-on-one" direction from Marty . . . uh, Mr. Scorsese . . . as you'll soon see.

My death scene began with me being dragged into a warehouse by two goons, one played by Frank Vincent. The same Frank Vincent you've seen in every Italian movie in the last thirty years.

As the story goes, these guys had been beating on me for two days and nights—during which time they also stuck an ice pick in my balls—all to find out who else was with me in that bar. I refused to talk, so they upped the ante.

They were to lay me on a table fitted with a cast iron engineer's bench-vise at one end and clamp it onto my head. Then Pesci would grind its sharpened jaws into my skull to finally get me to talk. The brutality of this scene came from real life. It's said that mobster Anthony Spilotro, on whom Pesci's character is modeled, stuck Billy McCarthy's head in a vise (Tony Dogs in the movie) and cranked it until his eyeball popped out of his head! Yeah, for real!

We took a close look at the vise. It was practical (real), but it had been fixed up to protect the actor (me!). The inside of its "jaws" was lined with foam that had been shaped to my head. It also had a safe stop on it so even if Joe got carried away as he tightened the vise, it wouldn't close beyond the point of my safety.

Then it was off to hair and makeup where I would be transformed into the seriously messed-up Tony Dogs.

I got a bit of a surprise when I first walked into makeup. There on the counter was my "already tweaked" head. Before leaving for Las Vegas, I had sat for the special effects team so they could take a cast of my head. At the time, I didn't realize exactly what they were going to do with it. There it was, bloodied and battered—ready to stand in for me! I have to say that it looked amazing—my fake head was seriously crushed. But it didn't make me happy.

In an unusual turnabout for a stuntman, I experienced the actor side of the equation. I didn't want them to use a double for me! Even if that double was a cast of my own head. I wanted to do it all myself. I knew that a part like this wouldn't come around too often, and I wanted to do everything I could as an actor to pull it off. As hair and makeup worked on me, I made up my mind to get in there and do such a great job that they wouldn't need the head.

In order to accomplish the script's call for Pesci to crank the vise so hard that it popped my eye out, I was fitted with a piece of skin-colored latex that fit over my left eye from my eyebrow to my cheek. They attached a prosthetic eyeball, colored like my own, under the latex and connected it to tubes that ran down over my ear and under the vise. One tube would fill with air from a pump with enough pressure to push the eyeball out of the latex, creating the illusion that my eye was erupting out of its socket. The other was the blood tube, which dispensed copious amounts of movie blood out of the latex eye every time the vise was cranked.

Three-and-a-half hours later, I was ready.

First we shot several different angles and takes of the boys dragging me into the warehouse and putting me on the table. And here, dear reader, is where I experienced my most humiliating professional moment.

I was so eager to get my head into the damn vise that I forgot about this pivotal opening scene. I forgot how important the entrance was in establishing just how tough and dangerous Pesci was as he takes over the town. So when Scorsese called "Action!" and Pesci's two goons dragged my battered and testicularly-damaged body into that warehouse, I practically skipped into the room, like a kid walking into a toy store.

Yes, I did that. In front of Martin Scorsese and everyone else in the room.

"CUT! CUT! CUT!"

Nobody ever just says "cut" once. They all say it at least three times.

Like Oz himself, Scorsese emerged from behind the curtain of video-village where he was watching the monitors, fast-stepped right up to me and said in his rapid-tongued speech, "Whatdayathink you're doing? Dis guy's been beat up! He's broken! He's barely alive! They stuck icepicks in his balls for crissakes! You can't come in here with that much energy! I wanna see you're barely hangin on! Let 'em drag you in. You can hardly stand on your own. Two days they've been beating you."

"Yessir," I said to him.

"Oh my gawd," I thought. *"How could I have a brain-fart like that?"* I realized I had only been thinking about getting to that table, and the only thing on my mind was, "Can these guys really carry or drag me that far without me helping them?"

Acting 101: don't think, act.

We moved on to take two. This time I concentrated on everything Scorsese had said to me. I adjusted my brain-tapes and let my instincts take over, and the scene worked.

Then it was torture time. I spent the next several hours on the table with my head in that contraption. My sole job at that point, as Marty explained it, was to resist giving Pesci's character what he wanted. I can't tell you how many times I told Pesci to eff himself in one way or another over the next nine or so hours I was in that vise. (It had been made clear to me that once I was locked into position, I would stay there until we had accomplished all the shots that Martin needed.)

Pesci threw his best 'effin New Yorker dialog at me time and time again, building his anger and frustration with each take of the scene. To me, Pesci doesn't get the kudos he deserves. He is an incredible actor. Audiences see him as "that guy from *Goodfellas* with that snappy comeback attitude." But he was spectacular in the *Lethal Weapon* series as well as in *My Cousin Vinnie*, both great comedies.

Scorsese and Pesci go a long way back, so their on-set banter was reminiscent of a couple of cousins who grew up around each other and know what the other wants or needs with no words spoken. On the other hand, they also lobbed a heavy raft of obscenities at each other—but it was in a loving manner. For example, Martin told Pesci he needed to stand on a "fuckin' apple box" so he could be in the shot. Pesci retorted something like, "Yeah, get me a fuckin' box, but I'm still taller than you."

I can tell you that Martin likes blood. He likes lots and lots of blood. Every time we would do a new angle, the voice from the camera monitor would say, "Blood.

He needs more blood!" So on the blood flowed . . . and flowed . . . and flowed some more.

I can also tell you that every actor gave 100% in each and every take. We shot many takes each of the master, two-shots, close-ups, and over the shoulder shots. On some projects, actors will only give full performances for their own single, then lower their intensity when the camera isn't on them. Sometimes they leave altogether, and lines are fed to the remaining actors by someone off-screen. That didn't happen here. Everyone in the room was fully involved in each and every take.

At the end of the scene, after finally giving up the name he was after, I strained up from my bloody imprisoned posture and spit out a whisper to Pesci, "Kill me you fuck." He obliges, telling Frank Vincent, to do me "a fuckin' favor" after which Vincent pulls out a knife and cuts my throat.

"More blood! Bring me some more fuckin' blood!"

In the original director's cut, the camera caught all the gruesomeness of the eye popping out of its socket and dangling on my cheek, something that happened in almost every take. Each time, the effects guys would stuff it back into the latex, and we would start again. Well, as the story goes, when Scorsese showed the film to the MPAA, the board that gives out movies ratings, that particular scene caused the movie to get an NC17. At that time, an NC17 was the kiss of death at the box office, so Scorsese was forced to re-edit the footage and cut the scene just as my eye started to pop out.

It was a long and trying day and night of work for everybody, but Mr. Scorsese was pleased with the result . . . and that's what matters.

I got wrapped off the set at about 7:30 a.m. and was told that production had rented a room in a hotel across the street from our warehouse location so I could shower. How nice was that of them to do?

So I said good night/good morning to the cast and crew and thanked them for making the whole day and night possible under some extreme emotional and technical circumstances. Then off I went, led by a production assistant into the brightness of the morning sun. As we left the parking lot to cross the street to the hotel, cars screeched to a stop and swerved to avoid us. *"What the heck, what's the problem here?"* I thought.

Then it hit me. I was covered in blood, bruises, and stab wounds, and part of my face was hanging down! So what else could I do? I waved.

Working on *Casino* was one of the better experiences I've had as a performer for several reasons. Chief among them was the ability to work with such a great production team. The cast was gracious and energetic. Mr. Scorsese was pleased with the footage, and stunt coordinator Coleman, was pleased with my performance. The producers were happy that Doug brought in a stuntman/actor who nailed the action and the dialog—always great for a coordinator. Doug rewarded me handsomely with a generous adjustment for everything that I was able to bring to the table . . . so to speak.

Oh, as for the prosthetic head? They decided not to use it, and offered it to me as a gift. How very cool. I accepted, of course, and still have it today. I've set it out for Halloween a couple of times, and I show it to friends when the topic comes up. But my daughter says it "creeps her out," so I keep it in a plastic box in the garage.

But if you want to see it . . . all ya' gotta' do is ask.

CHAPTER 30
FAR AND AWAY

I disagree with people who think you learn more from getting beat up than you do from winning.

TOM CRUISE

t was 1991, and work was plentiful for me. I was hired on some great TV shows and got a couple of long runs on some hot features. One of those was *Far and Away* starring Tom Cruise and Nicole Kidman. It was their first film together after getting married.

Word had gotten out that the production was looking for bigger stunt guys who could box, preferably "Italian looking." That sounded just like me, and sure enough, I got the happy call from the secretary of the Stuntmen's Association saying they wanted me to audition for the part. I still belonged at the time, as did Walter Scott, who was coordinating the film. I was instructed to wear trunks and a tank top and to be prepared to show the producer that I could picture fight.

I was always comfortable doing fights. It's the first thing that I learned and perfected doing live shows at Knott's Berry Farm and Universal Studios Tour. I won an award for Best Fight Sequence at the 1985 Stuntman Awards for my work on the television series, *Knight Rider*. I played a bare-knuckles boxer on the western TV show *Guns of Paradise*, and also portrayed a real-life boxer in *Dempsey*, the life story of Jack Dempsey, "the Manassa Mauler" who held the World Heavyweight Championship from 1919 to 1926.

Auditions for *Far and Away* were held in a production office in Hollywood. When I walked in, I noticed on the sign-in sheet that they had already seen at least twenty-five people. Another five or so were still waiting their turn, like me. As I looked around, I saw that everyone was bigger than average; everyone there could do a decent fight, but no one else was Italian.

Nice. I'll take any advantage I can get.

Those big boys went into the small interview room one at a time. And from the waiting room, each audition sounded the same. We could tell they were blocking out a fight and then going through it for the producer and coordinator Scott.

As each stuntman came and went, I could see Corey Eubanks inside, playing Tom's role in the fight. Corey, son of TV legend Bob Eubanks, is famous for his stunt driving, but he is also a fine horseman, writer, producer, director and an excellent boxer. He was hired to be Tom's stunt double in the film's fight scenes.

I was licking my chops to get into that room.

The last man to audition before me was John Clay Scott. John is Walter Scott's younger brother and a very good stuntman. And he's a big man! John is as strong as any two-and-a-half men I know. He is a rodeo bulldogger and has a grip like a shop vise. I stopped shaking hands with him in 1992 because I didn't want to lose the feeling in my fingers.

I was the last guy waiting when I heard an enormous boom and felt the whole room shake. It was like someone dropped a desk from the ceiling. Shortly afterwards, John Clay walked out of the audition with a big smile on his face.

"Carl, you're up," came a call from inside. So in I walked. There, at a long table, sat Walter Scott and Todd Hallowell, the executive producer.

I said my hellos and Walter looked at me with a question in his eye. Then he says to me, "I know who you are. Where do I know you from?"

"Well," I told him, "you and I are both members of the Stuntmen's Association, and we've talked several times over the last seven or eight years."

"Oh, right," he said. "They told me you were a big eye-talian."

Corey took over then and explained that we were going to set up a little five- or six-punch fight so the coordinator and the producer could see my movement. I turned around to see how much room we had, and there, in the back wall, was the hole the size of a VW bug!

I gave Corey a "What the hell happened?" look. He explained that John Clay had taken a reaction from a punch that sent him into the wall a little too hard.

That explained the earthquake.

I did the audition, and later that same evening I got the call asking my availability to play the Italian boxer in *Far and Away*. I made them wait for my answer— maybe two or even three seconds—before accepting the job.

Rehearsals started the following week in a downtown LA warehouse. Several stuntmen were there to do bare-knuckle fights with Tom. Walter was there to oversee and help choreograph the fights. The producer was there to explain the progression of the fights leading to the final match between Tom and my character, who at that point was known only as the Italian boxer.

Tom showed up a little later with just one assistant and introduced himself all around the room. I have to say I was impressed. He is one personable guy. Hellos and handshakes all around, looking everyone in the eye, and he was ready to work. He made it clear in actions and words that he'd do whatever it took to be convincing onscreen as a bare-knuckle boxer. Tom did surprise us with one requirement—he wanted to box left-handed to differentiate his character from the rest of us. An excellent move by a smart actor, but it did add a whole new dimension in terms of teaching and blocking.

Corey was there as Tom's double as well as being the one who would help Tom with his boxing skills and moves. Tom worked the room and talked to the other stunters about their individual fights. Then he came up to Corey and me as we were working out the fight that Tom and I would be doing.

As Tom, his assistant, the producer and the stunt coordinator watched, Corey explained the basics of throwing a picture punch. He told Tom that it was important to know your distance from your partner before throwing a punch.

Cory said, "you never need to come closer than six to eight inches from your opponent's face." He moved on to discuss types of punches. "You can throw a cross." He demonstrated a cross, and I reacted. "Or you can throw an uppercut." Again he demonstrated the punch with precision and ease, and as his fist passed my face I reacted to the punch.

Corey then stood directly in front of me and said to Tom, "Now this is a straight punch, and whether you throw a right or a left, it should stop about six inches in front of Carl's face." And with that, Corey threw the most perfect straight right punch I've ever seen. As it came close to my left eye, I was about to react when there was a huge flash in the room! And with the flash came the sound of raw hanging meat being beaten, like in *Rocky*.

It took me a nanosecond to realize what had happened. Corey let his punch fly but didn't pull it soon enough. My left eye immediately swelled shut, and there was a half-inch gash under it.

The whole place got very quiet, and everyone—everyone—looked at Tom and waited for his reaction.

I wish I had a picture of the look on his face, his beautiful, unmarked face. He stood there, a little in shock, staring at the swelling building up under my eye and the blood trickling down my cheek.

Tom didn't say a word.

He looked at us; he looked over at his assistant, who was also in complete shock; and he walked away. We all thought—and I know this for a fact—that we were all going to be fired.

After Tom left, another stunt combatant, Cole McKay—a one-time professional boxer—stepped up with some ice, sat me down and asked for someone to find a spoon. It tickles me to this day that I didn't know why. I remember thinking, *"I'm sitting here with my head swelling up, I'm gonna' be out of work in about ten minutes, and this guy wants a spoon! What, is it time for yogurt?"* Come to find out that an old boxer's trick to reduce swelling is to freeze a spoon and then repeatedly press the backside of it against the swelling, pressing and wiping it away.

As for Corey? Once he realized that I was going to be all right, he started laughing. You have to know him—great guy with a good sense of humor, though a little sadistic.

The frozen spooning worked. The bleeding stopped. And we didn't get fired. We started rehearsing the fights again and after a while, Tom came back in with a smile on his face.

We rehearsed at that warehouse every day for about a week-and-a-half before we left for Billings, Montana.

Once we got to location, we checked into the hotel, got a bite to eat, then headed off to set to block the fights. We would be shooting at an abandoned train station that served as the saloon in the film.

We met Ron Howard that day . . . what a great guy, just as regular as Opie, but all growed up. (If you younger readers don't understand that reference, go find *The Andy Griffith Show* and enjoy Ron as a young man in this idyllic portrait of America's past.) Ron was welcoming to all of us and let it be known that he was open to our thoughts and suggestions in the fight scenes—which meant, of course, if the stunt coordinator cleared it.

Tom jumped into learning all the fights, of which there were several, and insisted on doing them himself. This guy loves to work. In fact, I have to say that he is one of the hardest working actors I've ever had the pleasure of performing with.

The next day we started rehearsing what we had blocked. The fights would be shot over a week's time, but we weren't scheduled to be on camera for over two weeks. So every day we would go to set just before lunch break and rehearse with Tom. It was an intense and physical couple of hours. All of the fight rehearsals were recorded for Tom, who watched them during his down time to make sure he would remember all the different moves he had to make.

Here's one thing that impressed us about our star. Outside the station was the most beautiful motorhome I'd seen to that point in my career. It was Tom's trailer, of course, and in a very un-diva-like fashion, he would invite us into that luxury home-away-from-home pretty much every day after fight rehearsal. He served us cold drinks and played back the takes so we could all watch and critique our rehearsal fights. With Tom as the leader, we all kept a laser focus on making things as real and engaging as possible.

Billings is a perfect little western/cowboy/historic town that holds many wonderful surprises. One of them was its people.

Production decided to hire locals as background extras, playing saloon workers, bar patrons, and fight enthusiasts. The script calls for the Irish boxer, Tom, to be supported by the white Irish types, while the Italian boxer, me, would have a following that resembled people from the Mediterranean part of the world. Well, I'm here to tell you that extras casting did a bang-up job of hiring. They found enough of both types of people to make up the full, enthusiastic crowd we needed.

Those background players were fantastic! They came to work every day and did an extraordinary job for Ron. They stayed in character, they took direction, and they kept their energy up hour after hour after hour.

It was a joy to be surrounded by nice people who wanted to be there and were intent both on doing a great job and making the day as pleasant as possible for the cast, crew, and friends.

Throughout this period, my days consisted of breakfast, a good workout at the local gym, fight rehearsal with Tom and the boys, lunch, more gym time, hanging out with some friends, bed. That was pretty much it for two-and-a-half weeks.

I have you tell you about my wardrobe fitting. This is where the costume department gives you your wardrobe, you try it on and then they make any necessary adjustments or changes.

I introduced myself to the wardrobe department, as did the other stuntmen, and they handed out our costumes, which were on hangers and covered with clear plastic. I took mine, which consisted of a pair of old time boxing shoes and two hangers that held my boxing wardrobe. Both were covered by a terrycloth robe.

I got to my honey wagon (a small trailer assigned to performers that includes a bathroom and a small space to get dressed and wait between scenes), hung up the hangers and stripped down to my underwear. I took the robe off of the hangers to access my wardrobe. What I found was a pair of spandex bottoms that reached down to about my mid-calf and a . . . oh wait, they forgot my top. So I put on the bottoms, the boxing shoes, threw on my t-shirt and headed back to wardrobe.

When I got to the wardrobe trailer, the costumer asked me how everything fit. I told him everything fit well, but he had forgotten to give me my top.

"Top?" he said, "You're not wearing a top, you're the main event."

Panic had just set in. "*Shirtless onscreen? Oh . . . my . . . God!*"

Tom was twenty-nine when we did *Far and Away*. I was thirty-eight and wasn't going to embarrass myself if I could help it. But *shirtless*? This was not something I was happy about. But again, like always, you do what's called for, so I had to suck it up.

It's not like it was first time going topless. I had done it when I played a bare-knuckle boxer on a TV show called *Guns of Paradise*. I played a Native American chief on *Remington Steele* complete with headdress, a loin cloth and a pair of queen-sized panty hose so I wouldn't scrape up my knees on the canvas wrestling mat. I also played a shirtless boxer on an episode of *The Fall Guy*, and one of Jack Dempsey's many victims in *Dempsey* starring Treat Williams.

Even so, it always panicked me to even think about taking my shirt off onscreen. Every time a shirts-off part came up, I'd hit the gym as hard as I could. I was also always worried that someone would say something about the six-inch scars on each of my shoulders—the product of bicep repair surgeries when I was younger. When *Far and Away* came along, I was on a mission as it was, working every machine I could to exaggerate my size over Tom. After seeing my wardrobe, I doubled my workouts.

When we finally got to shoot the fight scenes, we were chomping at the bit. Tom had rehearsed and memorized seven fights with seven different stuntmen. And he had worked hard to sell that he was a left-handed scrapper.

When you watch the film, some of the fights consist of only one or two punches. But I'm here to tell you that we shot those fights for hours to make sure Ron got what he and the editors wanted and needed to tell the story.

Speaking of the film's editors, one of them, Mike Hill, wanted very badly to be one of the boxers in the film. Ron brought him to us and asked if we'd teach him a few things that would make it to the screen. We gladly took Mike in hand and struck up a deal with him.

We would teach him everything he needed to know to let Tom punch him out, and in return, he would give us the editor's cut of the fights. Now it's a really, really big deal to get footage before it's been edited for the screen. What a prize. And Mike came through. He did a bang up job fighting with Tom, and he kept his part of the bargain. I still enjoy watching that film.

We spent a few days shooting the preliminary fights that were called for in the script. Then it was time for Tom and the "Eye-Tai," as they called my character in rehearsals, to put on a show.

I'll start by saying that Tom and I filmed that fight for three days. Not three hours a day, but three extremely long, hot and physical days. We shot the fight in its sequence to help keep the continuity of the scene, which meant we started with my entrance.

Ron decided that he needed an entrance for the Italian boxer that would capture the tenseness of the scene. So he set it up for me to be carried into the saloon on the shoulders of my supporters. And since the scene called for the crowd to be divided into two factions—one was the fans for "Joseph" and the other was fans for the "Eye-Tai"—Ron further decided that each group needed to chant the names of their fighter as they entered. But since "Eye-Tai" wasn't a very film-friendly chant, Ron decided to rename the character and had the Italians fans chant "Carlo! Carlo! Carlo!" to drown out the crowd that was chanting for Tom's "Joseph!"

I thought it was pretty cool to have my named used for my character. It happened once before in an episode of *Falcon Crest*. I was playing a chauffeur/bodyguard for an actor who has a confrontation with the character played by Lorenzo Lamas, one of the series' stars. In that show, my boss introduced me as "Carl." Then Lorenzo kicked my ass! The first of many times Lorenzo kicked my ass. He's another class act.

Back to my entrance on *Far and Away*. I was around 240 pounds by the time we shot in Montana, so I expected to get some flack from the local extras, who were going to have to lift me up and carry me. But those great sports jumped right up without hesitation, and without asking for a "bump" in cash for having to carry the big dago.

That entrance is one of my favorite parts of my screen time. It turned out to be a lot of fun to play that character's arrogance as I shrugged off my silk robe and stretched out my chest to intimidate Tom's character, Joseph. Tom's reaction, when he sees me, is exactly the way I envisioned it. He acted startled and a little scared.

I knew this was going to be a good opportunity for me to show my wares. And the bonus? I was going to come out the winner of the fight! Just like it said in the script!

I don't know if anyone outside the stunt business can understand that in our profession, winning a fight onscreen doesn't happen very often. And if it does, there's almost always a payback before the end of the film.

In fact, for me to even survive a film or TV show is pretty miraculous. I've been beaten up by men half my size and by women three-quarters of my size. I've been killed with a pistol, a shotgun, a machine gun, and a missile. I've been run over by cars, stuck with arrows and had my head crushed in a vise. I've had my neck broken, been hanged, blown out of an apartment building . . . and then had the building fall on me. I've been pummeled to death by a twelve-year-old, pitched across the room by a female demon, eaten by a giant alligator, pushed off a cliff, blown to bits with a cannon ball and kicked in the nuts!

I even got beat up by Steve Urkel, for crissakes!!!

So as I said, winning a fight—with a major star no less—is a BIG DEAL!

The first day of filming the scene went well. There was so much to do. The fight needed to be shot from as many different angles as possible to show the impact of the physicality. The crowd needed to be captured as they cheered and booed. Little skirmishes in the crowd needed to be covered.

And then there was the fact that this wasn't real. The fact that you can't get so caught up in the yelling and cheering so that you don't hear the director. Or get so involved in the fight that you forget the routine you've rehearsed. Or—and this is the one that gets stunters at least a couple times in our careers—you have to watch out in case the actor you're fighting with gets caught up in all the hoopla and forgets where he or she is in the fight. So when you're set for that big right cross and all of a sudden you get a left hook, you have to adapt . . . or everything will shut down, and you'll have to start again.

The other thing that happens in a big fight where your footwork is as important as your punches, is that you might come too close to your opponent. Someone who does fights all the time knows how to adjust to make the moves work. But actors, who don't do all or even most of their own stunt work, don't know to watch out for these little things. Other problematic occurrences include getting punched in the nose or getting the air knocked out of you because someone didn't remember to pull his or her last gut punch.

Guiding actors through a fight scene is a technical and creative process and is an important part of a stunt performer and stunt coordinator's job. But Tom? He didn't make any of those mistakes. He was spot on with his footwork, punches, and reactions. If we got to a place that wasn't comfortable or something wasn't going to work for camera, he would stop and we would reset to start again. He knows camera, he knows action, and he knows himself.

Another element of this particular fight is that he and I were going to have to make some good body contact to show the power of our punches. This meant that when Tom hits me in the mid-section or side of my body, he was going to need to show force because there weren't any gloves to absorb the punch or accentuate the hit. Additionally, Ron's plan called for filming some of the fight in slow motion, so it was even more important to create impact with body punches that would make the flesh ripple.

Said another way, the punches were going to have to connect to flesh.

Of course we're talking about my flesh, not Tom's.

Let me be clear; I did make contact with his body, but I had to be careful not to throw too many connecting body punches. Not because he couldn't have taken it. Trust me, he could have. Tom was dedicated and committed to doing whatever it took to make things as dramatic and realistic as possible. But punches like that leave marks and cause deep pain that would have prevented him from being prepared for all of his other scenes. Which would mean delays, and delays cost money. A lot of money. Which is a huge negative for production companies and their insurance carriers.

I was the perfect example of bruising. I spent nearly two weeks of rehearsal in L.A., three more weeks rehearsing on location, and three full days of filming the *Far and Away* fight. That's more than a month of getting popped in the stomach and sides on a daily basis. My body was a mottled mess of purple and yellow from one side of my rib cage to the other. The bruises lasted for sixteen days after I had finished the show, a fading badge of courage that I wore proudly.

I have a little P.S. to share about *Far and Away*.

Months after production ended, I went out to enjoy an afternoon movie. When the film was over, I headed out to the lobby where I saw it for the first time. It stopped me in my tracks. I'd never imagined it. I didn't know anybody on my level that had one of their own. I was proud and bashful and excited all at the same time.

Right there in the middle of the lobby was the poster for *Far and Away* featuring Tom Cruise, Nicole Kidman, and Meeeee!

I couldn't believe it. This does not happen.

I looked and looked again just to make sure.

"Yep, it's me alright!"

The poster was on a sandwich board positioned on the floor in the middle of the lobby, and hundreds of people were walking past. I walked right up to it to take a closer look. Then I looked around to see if anyone else saw what I saw. Well, they weren't looking so I thought I'd help them out a little.

If you look at the poster, I have my back to the camera but my face is at about a three-quarter turn to camera—enough to recognize that it's me. So I stood as tall and strong as I could and tried to catch the eye of passersby. Nothing. Then I struck the same pose that was in the poster. But people just walked around me. Nobody said excuse me, no one looked me in the eyes, and certainly nobody made the connection. They just went on about their business and chalked me up as just another "loony" in Hollywood.

Oh well. Didn't matter. I was thrilled.

CHAPTER 31
NATURAL
BORN KILLERS

Natural Born Killers is a misunderstood romantic comedy.

WOODY HARRELSON

n 1993, I was offered a job on *Natural Born Killers*, which called for two or three weeks of work in Chicago. As is typical for such stunt jobs, I didn't get the sides (the portions of the script in which I'd be performing) until I arrived on set. As it turned out, having them might have helped me better prepare myself.

The coordinator was Phil Neilson, someone I had admired as a coordinator in the past. Phil is a tough block of a man, a former Marine, who would just as soon intimidate you with his piercing eyes and wad of chew in his cheek, than talk to you directly. Still, I somehow got past that part of him and found him a friendly family man who knew his stuff when it came to stunts.

I was to play the part of 'Mallory's Guard' and work alongside New York stuntman Douglas Crosby. The script called for us to guard a cell as Detective Jack Scagnetti—played by Tom Sizemore—violated Mallory, the brutal killer played by

Juliette Lewis. Mallory waited for the right moment to retaliate, then she went to town. She smashed Scagnetti's head against the prison block wall and kicked and punched him while Doug and I desperately fumbled for the keys outside the cell. We finally got inside and separated them. Sizemore then flooded her face with pepper spray, hitting me with the bitter liquid in the process.

As the scene progressed, a riot breaks out, giving Mickey and Mallory their chance to escape. In this scene, Doug and I were the first guards to be killed. Woody took us out with shotgun blasts.

So here I was, working on an Oliver Stone film with huge stars and lots of action. In addition to Woody Harrelson and Juliette Lewis, I got an up close and personal look at the intense method acting style of none other than *Ironman* himself—Robert Downey Jr. What else could I ask for?

Well, in truth, darkness hung over me on this job.

This had never happened before and has never happened since. But it happened then. We shot inside a small, cramped prison cell set, and Stone chose to blast this gawdawful music at decibels that permeated our entire warehouse location. It was a looped tape of techno heavy metal—but to me it sounded like screaming baboons being castrated.

I presume Stone orchestrated this level of mayhem to get the actors to live in the skins of their messed-up characters. But this continuous sound coming from the enormous on-set speakers, with Stone yelling out direction through a bullhorn from outside the cell, combined with the actors continually one-upping each other between takes with comments that were as ugly and intense as they were graphic . . . got to me. I would get back to my hotel room after wrap and feel moody and frustrated out of my skin at what the day had been like. I'd call my friends at home just to hear their voices.

We finally finished the cell scene and moved to a prison hallway for the riot scenes. Unfortunately for me, the music continued to throb in our ears, day after day after day. I steeled myself to get through another week of shooting.

Then I got a call from Doug Coleman—remember him from *Casino*—asking me if I could come to Washington, DC to work for him on *Pelican Brief* with Julia Roberts and Denzel Washington. He needed me in a couple of days.

I told him I was in Chicago on *NBK* and that my scenes were completed, but that Phil had asked me to stick around for another week to play a stunt prisoner during the riots. I told Doug that if it was any other show at any other time, I would never consider leaving before I was wrapped from the picture. But this time, I felt in my heart that I needed to make an exception for my own good. I promised I'd get him an answer in twenty-four hours.

When I got to the set the next day, I put on my prison wardrobe and took my spot in the riot scene. But during a break in the action, I got Phil to the side and asked him if he could spare me to go to another show. I didn't need to explain to him that I thought that my head was going to explode if I stayed there another day, just that a good opportunity had been presented to me.

He gave me a hard look then mumbled something like, "Yeah, go ahead. That sounds great for you." I don't believe that's what he was thinking, but he did let me go, and I appreciated it. So I finished my day and flew out to DC the following afternoon.

Phil has gone on to coordinate and second unit direct such films as *Gladiator* and *The Alamo*. He has had great success in the industry and continues to work non-stop.

But I haven't worked for him or with him since that day in Chicago.

In hindsight, although I probably should have been smarter, I wouldn't have done anything different. Life. It's all about decisions and consequences.

CHAPTER 32
STALLONE: THE SPECIALIST, TANGO & CASH, LOCK UP

I tend to think of action movies as exuberant morality plays in which good triumphs over evil.

SYLVESTER STALLONE

I n 1993, I got a call from Allan Graf, who was coordinating a Sylvester Stallone picture titled *The Specialist*.

Allan knew I was a trained actor and that I looked enough like what the script was calling for. He also knew I'd done a couple of falls into water, so I was the perfect fit.

He told me I'd be playing a bodyguard for Rod Steiger and his son, who would be played by Eric Roberts. Well just let me say that I'm not ashamed of being slightly star-struck. I mean, I was going to work with Rod Steiger, a screen icon, and Eric, whom I'd worked with a few times already, as well as Stallone, Sharon Stone and James Woods, each of whom I'd worked with more than once or twice.

Could it get any better?

Well, yes. I was put up at the historic Fontainebleau Hotel in Miami Beach. This is one of those places you see on travel shows, and you dream about. The weather was spectacular, and the beach was right downstairs. I was in heaven.

Oh yes, the work.

Playing the part of a thug was nothing new to me, but being able to be in shots with Stallone, Steiger, Roberts and Woods was a real thrill. Each was a seasoned pro with his own way of creating a character.

Sly is, well, Sly. He's Rocky! A working class hero. On set he works hard, doesn't complain and is always up for the action. I had worked with him on *Tango and Cash*, where I played a bad guy in a training segment of the movie. Sly gets the best of me and gives me a nice dropkick to the chest. The bruise on my chest lasted, but the scene didn't; it got edited from the film. Such are the hazards of the job.

I had also worked with Stallone on *Lock Up*, which we shot at Rahway State Penitentiary in New Jersey. Stunt Coordinator Frank Orsatti hired me to play both a prisoner and a prison guard—the latter in a now-iconic scene where Stallone's character, Leone, takes some brutal punishment.

Playing tackle football on a frozen field of mud surrounded by convicts who were murderers and rapists was interesting, to say the least. The production used lower-risk inmates as background players, something that never bothered Sly. He would interact with them and seemed to have a genuinely good time playing the football scenes. And he was good!

In between shots, the prisoners would talk to us, all professing their innocence. But I'll tell you, those men had lifeless eyes. It was unnerving.

Some of the inmates huddled around another stuntman, the great Gene LeBell, whose powerful body, craggy face and smashed nose were unmistakable. Gene's reputation as a living wrestling and judo legend had preceded him. The inmates were well aware that Gene is one of the few people in this world who can literally put you to sleep and then wake you with one hand. He uses a move much like Mr. Spock uses in *Star Trek*—but with Gene, it's not an act.

LeBell has mastered the ability to pinch a neck just so, causing you to lose consciousness, then press on your neck again so that you wake up. Although this may sound like a parlor trick, I assure you that it's not. If done incorrectly, the victim may never wake up. Also, although I say you get put to sleep, it's not the lay down and snooze kind of sleep. No, this move will have you twitching, drooling and peeing yourself, and some have been known to even crap themselves. Search it online and read it for yourself. (I believe you'll especially enjoy reading how a certain obnoxious martial artist/movie star we've already discussed was felled by this move.)

Whenever we had time between takes on the football scene, you could find Gene surrounded by inmates just waiting for their turn to have him turn them into one of the dozen or so flopping fish that were at his feet. When the break was over, Gene would wake them all up, and they would stumble into position, googly-eyed and dragging a foot as they wiped the saliva from their face. To a man they were ecstatic that the great Gene LeBell had put the "sleeper" on them.

Things became frightening when one of the inmates tried to escape.

We were on the playing field in the middle of a scene in below-zero weather. We were all dressed like the inmates; the only thing setting us apart from them was a pink tag we wore on a chain around our necks, under our wardrobe.

Suddenly the prison alarm went off. We did as prison officials had instructed us on our arrival: we hit the deck and grabbed for our pink necklaces, holding them high. This let the guards know who we were so we wouldn't be targeted as they aimed their high-powered, semi-automatic rifles down on the field.

As the horns blared, we looked up from our prone positions on the hard frozen ground to see what caused the commotion. There, high on top of the fence that surrounded the prison, stuck in razor wire, was an inmate screaming—and I mean screaming loud. Turns out this desperate man decided this was the perfect time to climb out of the prison over a twenty-foot fence that was monitored by armed guards.

It seemed to us that guards took their time finding a ladder to get this guy off the fence. But at least we had been moved inside until the incident was over— warmth at last.

In the scenes where I played a prison guard, I beat Sly with a nightstick while he was on his hands and knees. And I used a real nightstick.

Here's how we did it.

We put a Yellow Pages phone book on his back, under his wardrobe, and beat the phone book with the truncheon. It was a method we learned from our Technical Advisor, who had once served as a prison guard in a state penitentiary. He said this was how they beat prisoners, explaining that the strikes to the book would make the pain radiate throughout their limbs, rattling their insides until their guts ached. But—and this was the point—it didn't leave a mark on the body.

Sly was a real trooper. When you look at him and then watch his movies, he definitely seems tough. Then you get to work with him, and you discover that he's for real. He insisted that he take the beating, not a stunt double. This was cool for the scene, but a little intimidating for me, the person smacking him with a billy club.

I remember that after the first couple of takes, he stood up and took a moment to look at us and the TA, who came up with this excruciating plan. Then he simply said in that low, growling Stallone voice, "I can see where this would work with prisoners."

And on we went, beating up on one of the toughest guys in town—who also did the majority of his own running and blocking out there with us on the frozen tundra of the film's football field.

Back to *The Specialist*.

As I mentioned, this film was my opportunity to work with Rod Steiger, one of the true method actors of our time. Ever true to his craft, Steiger never seemed to get out of character, even maintaining his Cuban accent between takes.

Eric Roberts, who played Steiger's son, Tomas, had a different, more laid-back style. He had a James Dean quality about him. I've worked with Eric many times, first on *Runaway Train* in 1985, where he was as wild and uncontrollable as the character he played. Later I would work with him on *Best of the Best 2* and again on *National Security*. Eric has become a consummate actor who is in high demand and is truly a pleasure to work with.

As for James Woods, well, he is tough to keep up with. Between his kinetic energy and high IQ, Woods is always at least two steps ahead of the director and the crew. He talks fast, he thinks fast, and if you're in a scene with him you better bring your 'A' game, because he's on his all the time. I would share the screen with Woods a year or so later in *Casino*, although I didn't get to work him there, and then again on *John Carpenter's Vampires* in 1997.

I have learned along the way that I have to keep up with—or slow down for—the actor who stars in the scene. It's their moment, and you're there for them to play off of. You have to let them set the pace, be respectful of their working style and be ready for however they come at you.

My stunt for *The Specialist* signaled the beginning of the end for Woods and the rest of his bad guys. I was to get blown out of a penthouse window perched several floors above the ocean. The scene called for me and two other thugs to search for Stallone in his luxury high-rise apartment. While we're in there, the phone rings, so my character answers it, unaware that Stallone's character had connected it to explosives that would blow the whole apartment into the ocean below.

We shot the first part of the explosion on a set that was built for the scene. Production created the extravagant, glass-walled living room on a hydraulic gimbal suspension. This is a pivoted support that allowed the entire room to tip on its side and eventually turn over as the explosion causes the room to break away from the building and fall into the water.

A twelve-foot ramp was built out of 2x4s on the set's floor. This would serve as my launching ramp as I was blown out of the window. To make the gag work, I needed to run up the ramp to the window and crash through. I would then land—hopefully—on a fall pad waiting about twelve feet blow.

I would complete the shot by falling into the ocean on another day. That plan called for hoisting me up about forty-five feet in the bucket of a crane arm extended over the water, and for me to fall out.

The two pieces of film would be cut together to look like one continuous fall.

The explosion was set off in the room and all three of us reacted. The other two baddies dropped to their knees in hopes of hanging onto the tipping building, but my poor slug of a character was launched through the window to the ocean below.

The window I was to go out of was made of breakaway tempered glass about five feet by four feet and about a quarter-of-an-inch thick. When broken, tempered glass shatters into small, rounded pieces that have less of a chance to cut you.

I'd gone through breakaway windows several times before this shoot. Some were tapped by special effects, meaning they would put a charge on the glass and cause it to break it just before I went through. This was done to make certain the glass would break. But nothing is certain; the glass doesn't always break. I've bounced off of more than one window that didn't get tapped properly. In this case, however, I knew that even without the glass being tapped, my 235-pounds would easily blow it out.

The ramp was up, the glass was in, and we were set. "3-2-1-Action!" Up the ramp I ran, plowing through the tempered window to the pad below.

"*Aha! That was good. That went well. Wait—Ow! Ow! Ow! My ear, my ear!*" That's what was happening in my head. I felt the warmth of my blood running down my neck and face and I experienced a pain on the left side of my head that was new to me and quite excruciating.

Someone stepped in to help me off the pad and hand me a towel to catch the now flowing blood. The set medic sat me down and proceeded to extract a three-inch shard of glass that had found its way through the upper part of my ear. To this day, I can't believe how much it hurt or how much it bled.

As it turned out, the glass company had supplied us with glass that was stamped "Tempered" but was, in fact, not. When glass isn't temper-treated, it breaks into shards. I'm extremely lucky I didn't get it in the eye or chest.

Twelve stitches later I was back at work. I had a day or so before I was to finish the gag, just long enough to get some beach time . . . and show off my ear thread to everyone I could.

When it was time for me to do the fall from the bucket to the water, it was already late in the day. The crew was in a hurry to beat the sunset and the pressure was put on the stunt department to get the shot they needed . . . NOW!

So I threw on my wardrobe and got into the bucket, all the while on the radio with stunt coordinator Allan directing me. The spot where I was to land in the ocean was not far from shore and was surrounded by rocks, providing me a landing target of approximately eight feet by ten feet.

I was ready to go, Allan called action, and I left the forty-five-foot platform. But I didn't get my body turned over far enough during my descent, which made the fall look more like a jump. So back up into the bucket I went for take two. Meanwhile, production was screaming that they were losing the light. They had to get the shot!

Yeah, just what I needed, more pressure. But take two went great. I got myself turned over, hit the water in just the right spot, landed on the back of my neck and upper back and made a huge splash.

It did take me a minute to catch my breath afterwards, but I was happy with the result. My character wasn't so lucky. After he survives the fall and comes up from the water, the building falls on him.

Another bad guy bites the dust, or, in this case, the water.

CHAPTER 33
BONDS.
JAMES BONDS.

Luca Brasi sleeps with the fishes.

CLEMENZA, *THE GODFATHER*

I hit the jackpot in my career by working with *three* James Bonds.

My first Bond was Pierce Brosnan. No, I didn't work on any of his four *Bond* movies, but I did work with him.

I first performed with Pierce on his 1980s hit TV series, *Remington Steele*. This was long before he played the legendary spy, but he was immediately beloved, and fans and industry people alike were always talking about what a great Bond he would make. Producer Albert R. Broccoli wanted him, and when Remington was canceled in 1987, everything seemed locked down. But all the *Bond* publicity served to revive interest in the TV series, so the show was un-canceled, and Brosnan was contractually obligated to return to the role. His turn at *Bond* had to wait until after the Timothy Dalton years.

The second time I worked with Brosnan was after he completed his stint as Bond, on 1994's *After the Sunset*. He was still the same handsome and courteous man he was in the 1980s, but his trailer had become much, much bigger.

Working with Sean Connery, the Bond I grew up with, was a thrill. We worked on *The Presidio* in 1988 with Mark Harmon; I worked with him and Alec Baldwin on 1990's *The Hunt for Red October* playing a Russian submarine sailor; and again in 1996 on *The Rock* with Nicolas Cage, Ed Harris and William Forsythe. That man was as cool as the other side of the pillow.

On *The Presidio*, we shot in a bar that was built on stage. All of the preparations were complete, and the cast and crew were waiting for Mr. Connery to arrive. I couldn't believe what happened next.

The jabber and laughter were at a pretty high level when the door suddenly opened. A shaft of light pierced the darkened set and out of the beam walked Sean Connery. It was like time stopped. A hush came over the crowd, and we all just stared at the man.

It was oddly natural, the deference we all gave him. I have to assume it's like being around royalty—the modern William, Kate and Prince Harry kind of royalty. Because in spite of his legendary status, Connery was pleasant and professional and just a dream to work with.

That work was a bar fight that started with a drunk and Connery's character and ended with about a half-a-dozen stuntmen sprawled in a heap. Connery took out the biggest guy with a couple of *Bond*-like moves, then dumped the 300-pound fool on top of the rest of us. Yes, I was at the bottom.

In 1990s *Hunt for Red October*, I spent several seasick days as a Russian sailor on Connery's submarine. This proved to be a challenge for a lot of us: actors, extras and crewmembers alike.

The studio built their version of a Russian sub complete with a conning tower on top of a barge in Long Beach. Our scene involved a team of about fifteen stuntmen and some seventy-five Russian extras, who were all to pour out of the submarine and load into huge life rafts as the vessel began to sink.

The port authorities wouldn't allow the barge set to leave the breakwater, yet our action was to take place in storm-tossed waters. Production's solution was to arrange for a fleet of smaller boats to continually circle us, creating waves that would rock our vessel. They completed the effect by adding a couple of huge fog machines that were carried on two larger boats.

For each take, all ninety of us would have to cram into this floating carnival ride. It was up to the stuntmen, take after take, to get ourselves and these poor extras—many of whom didn't speak English—out of the sub and into the life rafts before the ship went completely underwater. We also had to make sure the rafts got away from the ship before it went down, so as to not get sucked into its watery vortex.

Not only was everyone wet and cold, but just about everyone, especially the first day of shooting, was heaving up his or her breakfast. On the barge, on the deck of the sub, and especially in the hull of the sub while waiting for the door to open. There were lots of ugly wretching sounds and smells in there.

Connery was involved in these shots, and once again, whenever he joined a group of us, everyone would get quiet—out of respect, but also inspired by the star's potent charisma.

My last Connery film was in *The Rock,* which starred Connery, Ed Harris, Nicolas Cage and William Forsythe. I got to do a fun and cheek-tightening stunt on this film.

I played one of four soldiers who ride the skids of a helicopter that swoops down and hovers over Alcatraz as we rappelled, two at a time, to make our way to the trouble in the prison.

This was a good opportunity for me to do something outside of my comfort zone: flying outside of a military helicopter and then sliding down a rope from said copter to the waiting deck. All four of us readied ourselves for the initial flight around the San Francisco Bay by locking into the hooks just inside of the copter doors standing two on the right skid and two on the left.

As we took off, I got the feeling one gets when the roller coaster is just starting its ascent up the track. My feet were planted squarely on the skid, and just like that we were a hundred feet up in the air. Then two, and then three hundred feet up, flying over the Golden Gate Bridge, looking down on traffic and tiny little people.

We flew over the bridge and across the bay, then we would circle back. On the next pass, the pilot would fly us under the bridge. It was awesome! What an amazing view, and what a ride. I forgot about everything and starting enjoying the wind, the ocean air, the architecture and the . . . *holy crap, my face is cold! Damnit, so is my bbbbutt . . . brrr baby.*

The stunt called for the copter to hover fifty feet above the landing zone on the island; then we were all to rappel at the same time, matching the speed of the man on the opposite skid. When it was 'go time,' the four of us stepped off of the skids and started our fifty-foot descent on our ropes of sixty-plus feet—the ends of which were coiled on the landing spot.

As we started down the ropes, the helicopter caught a bit of an updraft that lifted us several feet. Surprisingly, it didn't register much to us because we were all concentrating on getting down the rope as fast and clean as we could. This went well until we hit the end of the rope, which thanks to the updraft was now several feet off the deck. I remember thinking in that split-second, *"I'm not holding the rope anymore. Why am I not on the ground?"*

And with that I landed on my feet. Surprised as anyone, I ran up the hill like a good soldier.

The last in the trio of Bonds on my hit list is Timothy Dalton. What a cool guy. He's a classically trained actor who knows his work and collaborates with the rest of the cast and crew without difficulty.

Dalton killed me while on location in Mexico City on *License to Kill* where I played an armed security guard in a secret aquarium. He did it by using a gaff hook to yank me off of a perfectly good landing, through a railing and into a glass tank in which a deadly electric eel was swimming. Only in a Bond film would someone be electrocuted by an electric eel.

At about seven feet long and maybe two feet wide, the aquarium I was to land in wasn't the biggest target I'd ever seen. I had to pay close attention to my mark to make sure I'd land square in the middle of the tank and not on the edge. Production created the effect of the eel lighting up by lining the bottom of the tank with small camera flashcubes! (Younger readers might need to do a web search of this obsolete technology.) As I landed in the tank, the special effects department set off the flashes and viola, I'm dead. I died in one take and a few-dozen flashbulbs.

You might be thinking, "Electrocuted by an eel, that's creepy," but there's worse. The other guy playing a security guard was knocked into a drawer, big enough to swallow a grown man, that was filled with flesh-eating maggots.

I was happy to take my chances with the fish.

I had a second chance to work alongside Dalton a couple of years later on *The Rocketeer*, where we shot a movie-within-a-movie in which we played medieval knights, complete with chainmail, armor, and swords. Dalton was completely approachable and real. In between shots, we reminisced about Bond and Mexico. Fun stuff.

CHAPTER 34
MALLRATS

The only thing of value I have in this life is my ability to tell a story.

KEVIN SMITH

T he biggest news in Los Angeles at the end of 1994 was the OJ Simpson trial. Until the announcement that Kevin Smith was going to helm and star in a new movie called *Mallrats*!

OK. Maybe it was only big news for me, but I was glad to get away from all the craziness in L.A.

It was good to be going away for personal reasons as well. You see, I was at a pivotal point in my personal life when I should have been at my happiest, but instead I was facing intense challenges. I had a baby on the way, whom her mother and I wanted more than anything. Sadly, though, my marriage had failed.

Even though I'd already been married twice, despite the tragedy surrounding my first child's formative years, even though I should have known better . . . I married a third time to a woman I didn't know well, and our differences became stronger and more seriously difficult for me with each passing day. I married the last girlfriend to meet my mom; I married her mere months after Mom died (Dad died several years earlier); I married despite only having a long-distance relationship with this person; I married even though I knew at the altar that it was a mistake.

On the one hand, I dearly wish I had been wiser. I sincerely regret causing anyone pain. Yet at the same time, my personal faith tells me that there was a reason for it all—my second daughter needed to be born.

I had definitely reached the point that I knew I couldn't raise a healthy child in an unhappy home. But for the sake of the pregnancy I had to keep everything bottled up.

Bottom line: I was in turmoil and was grateful for the chance to get away and do some thinking.

Director Smith had come into prominence a few years earlier when he produced, directed and starred in the Indie film *Clerks*. As a result, Universal gave him a boatload of money to do *Mallrats*, betting he would become the next Spielberg.

I received the call from Bob Apisa, one-time running back great for Michigan State and now a stuntman and coordinator. He asked if I was available for a few weeks to double Kevin Smith on the show. I said yes, and in March of 1995 I was off to the cold, cold, cold Midwest. Minneapolis, Minnesota to be exact. It was as cold as Chicago with less wind but more snow and lots of lakes.

It was a very eventful shoot for me.

I remember the whole production company was set up in the Eden Prairie Mall just outside of downtown Minneapolis. The mall was partially closed for some remodeling as well as the film shoot.

As usual, upon arriving on location I checked into wardrobe. This time they fitted me in a rather odd outfit. It was kind of a Batman suit, but not quite. It fit pretty well, but not great. It was menacing but also comical.

"So, you're our "Bluntman" stunt double, huh?" said the costumers.

"Yes, I am," I responded.

They chuckled a little, and we got on with the fitting.

I thought their reactions were a little strange until I met Kevin. Who is about five feet eight on a good day. I'm six feet tall. *Ahhh*, I thought, *now it's coming together.*

This explained why the costume didn't fit. But it didn't really matter, because while I'm taller than him, there would be nothing onscreen to allow the audience to compare the two of us, nothing relative that would give it away. Which meant I was a perfect double for him after all.

The first couple of days were spent gathering gear and setting up some rigging for the flying scene. This called for Kevin, as "Bluntman," to fly through the mall, headed for a dressing room wall, while his partner in crime yells out, "Fly Fat-Ass! Fly!" Inside that dressing room was, of course, a semi-nude girl.

One of the locals, Eric D. Howell, was working as the special effects foreman. Eric was an extremely personable young man who wanted to be involved with stunts and action and filmmaking any and every way he could. Eric has gone on to become a talented film professional with credits and awards for writing, stunts, acting and most recently, directing.

One day at lunch, Eric asked all of us stunt guys if he could bring a friend to the set, a writer who loved movies.

"Of course," we chimed.

We were working nights at the mall when he showed up with his friend, a beautiful blonde with soft blue eyes and an infectious smile.

Well, it was on! I watched as Eric's friend was descended upon by the stunt department like a June bug being chased by a flock of geese.

Her name was Theresa Hogue (although when Eric introduced us I called her Tracy . . . tough start.) She was kind and bright and beautiful with an energy you just wanted to be around. I watched as the night finally got to her. The activity on set, the Hollywood boys, the sheer deluge of testosterone from all the attention the stuntmen had given her—it was all too much for her Midwestern soul, and she took off.

That's when it hit me: I wanted to know this woman. I somehow *needed* to know her. Something about this person told me I would at least find an ear for what had become, for me, an impossible situation.

So I spent my break running around this empty mall, a bit frantically, looking for this person so I could . . . well . . . I didn't know why. It didn't make sense. I just needed to talk to her.

I finally found her just as she was just about to exit the mall. Out of breath from my search I gasped at her, "Hey, would you like to go to dinner, maybe a movie . . . ah, tomorrow?"

Well, she said yes—which I later learned was only to help Eric build a stronger connection with me—and the rest, as they say, is history.

We went to a *Pulp Fiction* matinee, got some Chinese food and talked all night. I was right. I was able to express my predicament, and while I was at it, I sparked like never before. The irony didn't escape me; I had been trying to resign myself to an unfulfilled marriage, yet the universe put me in the company of what I wanted but thought I could never have.

On my days off, we spent more time together, sightseeing, talking about life and figuring out how to conquer it.

At work, I was busy playing a cop for a couple of days while we waited to fly across the mall. Between shots, I'd sometimes walk around the big empty mall to stay awake and keep my blood moving. One day I came around a corner and recognized the production office I had entered just a couple of weeks earlier, so I poked my head in.

It looked like a sh*t bomb had gone off! There were full ashtrays with butts all over, empty soda and beer cans, napkins, half-eaten food and a terrible stench in the air. Kind of how you'd picture the aftermath of a frat party. Not like any production office I'd ever been in.

I left with the realization that these "kids" were getting millions of dollars to make a movie that they seemed to have very little clue how to complete. Well, all I could do was hope that they would find their way, which of course they all did. Not surprising, because along with the mega-talented director and star Smith, those "kids" included Jason Lee, Claire Forlani, Ethan Suplee, and a soon-to-be Oscar winner by the name of Ben Affleck.

Back on set I discovered Stan Lee had arrived. He had a cameo in the movie in which he gave Jason Lee's character dating advice. I introduced myself and told him I had been in Roger Corman's production of *The Fantastic Four*. Lee was kind enough to say what a shame it was that the movie was never distributed, then posed for a picture with me before heading off to shoot his scene.

The "Fly Fat-Ass! Fly!" day finally arrived.

I was tucked into my Bluntman outfit with a flying harness underneath it. I climbed to my spot on top of an open-air elevator some forty to fifty feet high. The stunt riggers were waiting for me on a platform they had set up, which was strong and stable. The rig was set, we had tested it, so we were good to go.

I was clipped in, locked off, ready to take flight.

"And Action!" was the call. I flew effortlessly across the mall sky, dipping from my perch to the stage below. This first part of the shot ended with me about ten feet off the ground. The second shot would be the close-up of Kevin's head coming through the wall. (No, I didn't get to see the naked girl. I'm just the stunt guy.)

After riding the wire a few times, Smith, from his director's chair, felt that we had what he needed. So after the last take, there I was dangling about ten feet above the ground, waiting to be let down to the floor, when the cable suddenly slacked and released, sending me hurtling to the stage floor below.

I landed smack on both feet then fell to my knees. It happened so fast that I didn't have time to brace myself for the landing, so I hit pretty hard. Nothing seemed to be broken, so I just got up and walked away.

A couple of days later, Theresa (whom I now knew as Teri) and I were walking through a local park when I felt a sharp twinge in my right hip. It felt like a knife was being jabbed into it and the pain stopped me in my tracks for a moment. I figured I must have jammed myself pretty good on that flying gag and continued on.

Then a little limp started to develop. I fought it, but it was there.

By the end of the shoot both my hips were sore, and I knew that I needed to get some rest to let them get better. I was looking forward to having some time off to recoup. But as it happened, Eric Howell was stunt coordinating two other movies in town, and he asked me if I could stay and double one or two of his actors for him.

Well, hell yes! It not only gave me the opportunity to work, it was also a chance to double Dan Aykroyd in *Feeling Minnesota* and Adam Arkin in *In The Line of Duty*.

And spend even more time with Teri.

Doubling Arkin was fun because I got to do a car chase. But doubling Aykroyd was sublime. I mean, for the simple fact that he's Dan Effing Aykroyd! *Saturday*

Night Live! *The Blues Brothers*! *Ghostbusters*! He is the man! Yes, I'm a fan, so getting my head slammed into the headlight of a Jaguar was an honor to do for a man who had given me so much enjoyable entertainment.

All of my experiences in the Land of 10,000 Lakes were great. But the best thing to happen to me was meeting Teri. I left Minneapolis, resolved to handle my life so I could pack her up and ship her out to California.

I eventually did just that, and twenty years later, everyone involved will tell you things worked out for the best. But it was pretty bad at the time. Bad was to be expected. I deserved bad. But this was epic bad.

I want to respect my daughter and follow my own belief of leaving the past where it belongs . . . yet I've also promised you all a story, so bear with me as I tread lightly over the quicksand that was my Hollywood divorce.

After I got back from location, after the pregnancy was well-established and baby and mother were healthy, my ex and I sat down for "the talk." Although I hadn't shared our problems with any of my friends, she and I were, of course, well aware of them. She hoped the baby would make things better. I was adamant that a baby couldn't and wouldn't fix our problems.

It was sad and it was difficult, but I knew I was doing the right thing. It was that serious. I tried my best to make it clear that even though the marriage was over for me, I didn't hate and wouldn't be horrible and would continue to be there any and every way I could.

Then I made the worst decision ever. I was honest and shared that on top of everything else I had met someone.

I can hear the groans now. Yup. It was a big mistake. The biggest. The worst. Because even though the death of our marriage had nothing to do with anyone else, mentioning another person ended all conversation. Ended any hope of us each taking responsibility for our part in the failed relationship. Instead, I created the perfect scapegoat and a lifelong target. I'm so very sorry for that.

Next up, the news got out to my world. That was a ton of fun.

My friends, including several stunt coordinators who provided a lot of my work, weren't just told that I was a terrible guy who was leaving his pregnant wife.

They were told that I was depressed and suicidal (not something a stunt coordinator wants to hear) and in case that wasn't enough, they were also told that I was a sex addict!

I learned this happy news the afternoon I went to my home to have my "visit" with my daughter (I always hated the term "visitation"—who visits their own child?!) only to discover that I was the guest of honor at a surprise intervention. This little gathering—which we've since dubbed my Tupperware® party—was led by a couple of so-called therapeutic experts (who'd been brought in from Minnesota, no less) who'd never met me, but nonetheless had the stated goal of getting me to enter a treatment program for depression and sex addiction.

I can report that it was one helluva party!

Someone took my car keys, someone else sat me down in the seat of honor, drinks and snacks were distributed, and the whole gathering began taking turns talking. Interestingly, the conversation pretty quickly strayed from me—not surprising, since the "only" thing I was doing was escaping a bad marriage at a very bad time. Instead, one by one, my "guests" began talking about their own issues and histories and dramas.

The whole thing started out as shocking and humiliating, but quickly became just plain ridiculous. I put up with it as long as I could, because I thought it was the right thing to do, but finally stood up, thanked them all for caring, asked for—then demanded and finally received—my car keys, and left.

Interestingly, with only a couple of exceptions, the attendees called me in the following weeks and months full of apologies, saying they'd only wanted to help and believed what they were told. Most also said they now understood much better why I had to do what I did.

I accepted that and never held a grudge.

The other horrible thing about the ordeal was the legal system. It was nothing less than a monster, ravenously feeding on hurt and pain. The terrible irony of this is that Family Law is pretty clear and at heart, rather simple. The California courts have well-established precedent for splitting assets. They have equally strong rules and precedent when it comes to custody, which boil down to putting the child's needs above all else. In a nutshell, absent criminally dangerous behaviors, the court wants children to have equal and peaceful access to both parents.

That bottom line failed to prevent a shitstorm of litigation. Instead, a series of expensive attorneys were set loose on me, continually enabling negative emotions, unfounded accusations, and unreasonable demands that never stood a chance of being supported by the court—all for the sake of billable hours.

I spent a dizzying number of painful, stressful and expensive hours in attorney offices and courtrooms, addressing each attack. This continued throughout our daughter's elementary school years—laying absolute waste, as it turned out, to any future financial security. By the end of it, unable to pay another dollar in attorney fees, Teri and I were handling my case with the help of "freelance" legal advice.

When all was said and done, I spent way more years in court than the marriage itself lasted; the whole thing cost more money than I made in my best years of work; and the result of pretty much every issue was the fundamental 50-50 equality in both custody and assets I've already noted is called for by the law—which was all I ever filed for in the first place.

There's more—a lot more—and if you're interested, let me know and I'll put it in a second book.

Bottom line: I live in the truth that difficult as it was, I did what I believed was best for my daughter. There's no question that divorce affects children hugely and I ache for every bit of pain my decision caused her. But I also celebrate each and every moment in our lives that supports what a good decision it was for us. This beautiful young girl is full of love for all of the parents in her life. She has this amazing old soul with wisdom and insight beyond her years. At the same time, she is a blindingly bright and lively young spirit who continues to take our breath away with each passing day. Just as it is with her sister, I love her beyond all measure.

CHAPTER 35
BATMAN AND ROBIN

Allow me to break the ice. My name is Freeze. Learn it well, for it's the chilling sound of your doom.

MR. FREEZE, *BATMAN AND ROBIN*

Our old friend the ratchet was part of my work as a museum guard on director Joel Schumacher's *Batman and Robin* starring George Clooney and Arnold Schwarzenegger.

I was in the scene where Arnold, who played Mr. Freeze, comes in and uses his giant ice gun to power-freeze everything in the place. The set—inside a huge, multi-level, stair-filled sound stage at Warner Brothers—turned into one enormous blue-hued ice palace. I'm the guy who gets flung backward off those stairs and then shoots about a hundred feet across the floor on his back.

There was something familiar about this gag. That's right. Years earlier I watched stuntman Allan Graf get slammed to the floor and dragged into a counter.

On this show, our stunt coordinator, the great Ronnie Rondell, told me they wanted me to get jerked from behind as I was climbing the steps, which would launch me onto the frozen floor where I would slide across the ice like a curling stone.

"3, 2, 1, Action!" was the call on the set and *fthwanggg!* I heard my cable calling to me. Frap! I was on my back and sliding, sliding, sliding across the floor. They called "cut" and while I was lying there like an upended turtle I heard, "That was great . . . let's do it again."

The second time was more difficult because I knew what was coming. I knew how it was going to feel when my back became one with the floor and how my elbow was going to get dinged, like it did on the first take, no matter how I tried to prevent it.

"And . . . Action!" Here we go again. Fthwangg! "*Uggh. Oh crap, my elbow . . . wow, that was a thump. Okay, I'm done. I don't want to do this again. If the freaking director couldn't get it in the first two, he's never going to be able to get it.*"

Those were some of the thoughts flying through my head as I was lying there waiting to get unbridled from my harness and go home. But instead, Ronnie asked me that famous question, "Got another one in ya?" This means they feel like they need another take. I looked Ronnie in the eye, gathered myself and said, "You bet. Let's do 'em till they get what they want."

And that's what happened. I did it again and again and again until they got what they wanted.

Afterwards, I went home and tucked into bed. This time I slept with my head propped up on a stack of pillows. By now I had learned it wouldn't be easy to get up in the morning, so I figured I'd give myself a little "head start."

CHAPTER 36
JOHN CARPENTER'S
VAMPIRES

Evil hiding among us is an ancient theme.

JOHN CARPENTER

I n 1997, I got a call from my friend and mentor, stunt coordinator and martial arts master Jeff Imada. Jeff is a living legend. He is the action mastermind behind the incredible fighting styles in Matt Damon's *Bourne* movies as well as *The Twilight Saga* movies, *Iron Man*, *The Last Samurai*, *Fight Club*, *Book of Eli* and *The Green Hornet*. He said he was coordinating *John Carpenter's Vampires* and asked me if I wanted to come out and double one of the lead actors.

As I've said, I don't double many guys, so I thought this could be a good way to get onto somebody's "He's my guy" list. If your actor's career takes off, being a double can mean a great boost to your ability to take care of your family—and by then, my family had expanded to include another daughter, my beautiful Tiana. So I said yes, went to a wardrobe fitting, then packed my bags and Teri, who was now my fiancé, for a three-week stay in Santa Fe, New Mexico.

My first day on location—a quirky artist colony south of Santa Fe called Galisteo—was noteworthy. After going through the works (meeting the Assistant Director, going to wardrobe, getting dressed in the stunt double clothes, going through hair and make-up) I was escorted to the set by Jeff. He told me to stay close and when the time was right, to introduce myself to Daniel Baldwin, the actor I was there to double. Then he took off to go take care of something with Mr. Carpenter.

So like a good stunt guy, I stayed in the background, not bothering anybody, about twenty-five or thirty feet away from my actor. Waiting for that right time.

I stood there about an hour.

Finally, he saw me. So I thought, *"This is a good time. He's in between stories, and he's acknowledged my existence."* So I moved toward him as he sat half-turned in his chair, stopped about five feet or so from him and said something like, "Hi, how are you doing today?"

I'll never forget the first words he spoke to me. He said, "What the hell are *you* doing here?"

"What the fuck's it to ya, fat boy!" Was the first thought that came to my quick-tempered mind . . . but that would have been wrong of me to say for a few reasons. It would have made my coordinator, Jeff, look bad—and I'd never do that; I would have been sent home and lost a boat load of money; and since I was a pretty good double for this guy, calling him "fat boy" would have been like calling myself a name!

Instead, I smiled and said, "Just here to help out in any way that I can, sir." He kind of grunted and turned his back on me to continue sharing stories with the others, thus setting the tone for our non-relationship for the rest of the production.

This little blip didn't dampen the enjoyment I felt on the show. Imada and John Carpenter—who had teamed up on Carpenter's previous projects—ran an excellent set and created an endless array of totally compelling action scenes. I got to chase vampires in an armored car and battle my share of ghoulish bloodsuckers to the death. Then there was this one last gag.

The scene called for my actor to prevent Katrina, played by the lovely Sheryl Lee, from escaping. Katrina had been bitten by the powerful vampire Valek, played by the great Thomas Ian Griffith, and was transitioning into a vampire herself. The action called for her to be pulled inside from a window ledge back inside a seedy hotel bedroom.

We got to the shot in the afternoon after the actors did their part of the scene.

"CUT! Bring in the stunt doubles," was the call on the set.

I moved into place along with the actress's stunt double, Cris Thomas Gilbert, a talented stuntwoman and a dear friend.

Carpenter was shooting the scene from the angle of the floor looking up to the window so he could watch our bodies fall back down to the camera. I told Cris I was going to wrap my left arm around her waist and my right around her chest, and that I was going to pull her straight back with me to the floor. No "toe tapping," we agreed. (That's when you try to take the edge off the fall off by dragging your foot or tapping your toe on the ground before you hit.)

We placed a one-inch pad under a throw rug on the floor to give us something forgiving to land on, and we were ready. We both knew this was going to be a chilliwanger.

"And ACTION!" I held on to Cris just like we had planned, and back we went, not unlike a small tree being felled.

Somewhere in midair—after pulling Cris in from the window—in the scant second-and-a-half it took to do this fall—we got a little turned. This caused us to veer off to our left about six or eight inches, which meant we weren't going to hit the pad. Instead, I hit the floor with my left elbow first, then my left side landed on my left elbow with Cris's body weight on top of mine.

I felt a peculiar 'pop' and immediately knew that something wasn't kosher. It felt like a truck was parked on my chest. I couldn't catch my breath for anything. Cris got off of me as soon as she heard me gasp for air . . . and moan . . . and cuss. Well, it hurt!

I told whoever was listening, between gasps for air, that I had broken my rib—a fair assumption since I was the one who heard the internal pop, and I was the one who couldn't breathe.

All they could say was "Lay still. The ambulance is on the way."

It was a long wait. It took the responders about forty-five minutes to get to our location and when "they" did, it was only one guy. One little guy who couldn't move me by himself. So he had to call for backup. Another wait before another paramedic finally showed up. Mind you, all this time I was unable to get a full breath of air.

Laurel and Hardy scooped me up onto the gurney, and I screamed in pain. Then they popped the gurney to a standing position, and I yelped some more. Finally, I was secured in the back of the ambulance, ready for the five- or six-mile ride to the hospital.

Now about that ride. Out of great concern for me, the ambulance driver decided that he had to get me to the ER as soon as possible. To achieve that goal, he decided to drive the first mile of the trip OVER AN OPEN DIRT FIELD!!!

Yep. I howled at every bump, ditch and mound.

By the time I got to the ER, it was midnight. The AD had called Teri to let her know what had happened to me. Production sent someone to pick her up from the hotel and bring her to the hospital where, for the first time in our relationship, she stood by my side in the ER. It wouldn't be her last time doing so.

The ER doc gave me something for my pain and then proceeded to check me out. Poking at me, asking me questions that were difficult to answer because I still couldn't breathe.

Then it was time for the dreaded x-rays.

If you've ever had x-rays, you already know how that went. If you haven't, here's what happens. The x-ray technician asks you to do things like, "Touch your right ear with your left index finger while you reach around your back and place your right hand above your left ass cheek. O.K. Now take a deep breath and hold that position. Don't move. Don't breathe."

The crazy thing was, that after all their efforts, they couldn't find anything wrong with me. I heard the doctor tell the nurses there was nothing wrong, and they should start getting me released. WHAT?!?

"Hey" I gasped from my gurney, "I still can't breathe!"

"We can't find anything wrong with you," is all they said.

In the hours that led up to this moment of quackery, while my Teri was there holding my hand, all I could focus on was that although we had planned to get married while on location, we hadn't yet gotten it done. We had our license and our rings and had spent all of my free time searching, but we just couldn't find a place or person to perform the ceremony that felt right to us.

I remember thinking to myself as my breathing problem got worse and worse, *"If this is something big, if I'm really hurt this time, what will she have for being my constant companion? She's the best partner that I ever had, and my daughters were already devoted to her. If I die tonight, they'll lose each other, and she'll have nothing. No pension, no life insurance—she'd wouldn't even have health insurance for god's sake."*

With all that on my mind, I struggled to speak to her. "I'm so sorry," I said, "I should have married you this week. Please marry me. We can get someone here right now."

I didn't know it, but John Carpenter's wife, Sandy King, was standing right behind the head of my bed and heard everything I'd just said. Sandy was our producer on the movie, as she had been for several of her husband's films, and when she heard I was injured, she immediately came to the hospital. Not only did she make sure I was getting the best care possible, she also stayed close to Teri, reassuring and comforting her.

When the two of them stepped away to let the medical staff work on me again, Sandy asked her what I'd meant. Teri told her about not being able to find the right time or place to get hitched. When she told me about it later, she said that Sandy's face lit up with a smile, she gave Teri a huge hug and said, "Let me handle this." With that, she started in motion a seventy-two-hour whirlwind that is unparalleled to this day.

More on that story in a minute—I've still got to get out of the ER alive.

So as I'm laying there, making it clear I wasn't going to leave until I could breathe again, another doctor walked in. He stopped to look at my x-ray—fortunately it was still clipped up on the light box—and told the duty nurse, "This man has a collapsed lung."

He found what no one else could see. Not only had I fractured a couple of ribs when I landed on the floor, I had collapsed the superior lobe of my left lung. Finally someone understood why I wasn't breathing.

The new doctor called for instruments stat, quickly made a small but deep incision on my left side, and stuck a tube in my chest. This drained the fluid that had built up in my lung and helped it to re-inflate. After several hours of pain and concern and drugs that weren't quite good enough, I finally experienced some relief.

I said goodnight to my love and the nurses checked me into a hospital room where I stayed for the next two days.

Now let's talk about Sandy's whirlwind.

The injury occurred late Wednesday. I made my apologies and asked, told, begged Teri to marry me around midnight. By Saturday afternoon, Sandy put together what I personally believe was the wedding of the century.

I don't mean a hurry-up, get-married-by-Elvis wedding. I mean a full blown, luxury wedding, with no expense spared. Here's how it went down.

Thursday morning, Sandy's staff got my sleepy Teri on the phone, gathering details.

Thursday afternoon the wardrobe mistress took her shopping for a wedding dress. They also picked out slacks, a shirt, shoes and a vest for me to wear. (My darling bride-to-be—who was the most easygoing, down-to-earth bride ever—told me I didn't have to worry about trying to get into a jacket).

By Friday, Sandy had lined up a minister, a flutist, and a pianist. She also created and sent invitations to the entire film company. She rented a beautiful courtyard and conference room for the wedding and reception at the historic La Posada de Santa Fe Resort and Spa, just off the city's famous downtown plaza. Then she arranged for catering, and I don't mean cocktail weenies and mustard. I mean baked salmon, roast beef, shrimp, cases of Dom Perignon, and a cake. A freaking multi-layered, custom wedding cake!

I got out of the hospital on Friday afternoon, returned to our hotel room, swallowed my pain meds and pretty much passed out for the rest of the day, knowing that I was going to get married at five o'clock the next day.

I was up and at 'em Saturday morning, a bit out of it, but happy to be marrying my girl, who had a surprise of her own. A knock on our hotel room door revealed the arrival of several members of our families!

My daughter Carlene had flown in; Teri's sister and best friend Mary Caldarone and her stepson Michael Caldarone came to join us; another sister, Patty Soffer, flew in from Florida with some blonde dude who wore an ascot under a crested blazer;

and Teri's brother, Doctor Michael Hogue, flew in from South Dakota to walk her down the aisle.

Try as we might, we couldn't work out getting our little Tiana to join us, but we each carried her picture so she'd always know she was with us in spirit.

I was and remain grateful and happy that so many family members were able to drop everything to fly in and celebrate with us. Popped lung and all, life was good.

The wedding was perfection. To this day, I remain amazed that Sandy pulled off such a feat in less than three days. Now there's a producer who believes in action.

The outdoor ceremony was loving and special for all of us. It was pretty much an old-fashioned love-in, which was perfect, because my Teri has the soul of a 70s flower child. The weather was gorgeous, the garden was overflowing with flowers, and beautiful music filled the air.

Many of our on-set family joined us as well as random hotel guests who were enjoying the vibe. Jeff Imada stood up with me as my best man; actor Tim Guinee read a poem during the ceremony; and our film's star, Thomas Ian Griffith, graciously smiled in photographs—particularly with my dear sister-in-law Mary, who has crushed on him since his years on the soap opera, *Another World.*

It didn't matter that most of our guests didn't know us or each other. They all seemed to enjoy the day as a celebration of the love they had for their own families.

The reception was more fun than it had a right to be with free food, open bar, family and new friends. We laughed and partied and danced until about 10 p.m. when it was time to take the garter off of Teri's leg. I got down on my knee, reached in and nipped it with my teeth, slid it down her lovely leg, then stood up for the traditional over-the-shoulder toss to the single men.

After that, I turned to Teri and said quietly, "If you don't get me home right now, I'm going die." The drugs and adrenaline had worn off all at once, and I was done for. We gathered up and didn't even make it back to the hotel. My bride rushed me back to the hospital where I spent my wedding night with a morphine drip as my companion.

I recuperated for a couple more days in Santa Fe, then we packed up for the long drive home to L.A. There was no question of us flying, because cabin pressure and my semi-inflated lung wouldn't get along too well. Teri drove and I just kind of held on. We got as far as Flagstaff, Arizona before my strength gave out. We decided to drop down to Sedona where we checked into a beautiful creek-side cabin at the Junipine Resort.

Honeymoon? I couldn't sit up, take a deep breath or cough without crumpling up in pain. Let's just say that getting better took me long enough that Teri could have annulled the marriage. I'm glad she hung in there with me.

CHAPTER 37
FIGHT CLUB

How much can you know about yourself if you've never been in a fight?

TYLER DURDEN, *FIGHT CLUB*

T he first rule of Fight Club is: you do not talk about Fight Club. The second rule of Fight Club is: you DO NOT talk about Fight Club. So I haven't talked about *Fight Club* . . . up until now.

When I got the call, I knew it was going to be a good film based on the attached star-power. Brad Pitt, Edward Norton, Helena Bonham Carter and David Fincher as director. So the success of the film was a lock, but the amount of success was never imagined . . . at least not by me.

Stunt coordinator Mike Runyard was the one who reached out to me. He asked if I was available for three days to play a part in a fight sequence in a Brad Pitt film.

This was 1999, and *Fight Club* would be one of the last shows that I worked before I had my hips replaced stemming from the accident I had on *Mallrats* in 1995. In fact, in the film, you can see me limp down the stairs and up to Pitt behind my boss, Lou, who was played by Peter Iacongelo. I played his bodyguard who was simply named "Lou's guy."

The scene started with Lou and me coming down the basement stairs of his bar to find a slew of sweaty men yelling and cheering on a fight that's taking place.

Lou has some dialog that ends at the bottom of the stairs, which is where Fincher would cut. Then we'd do it again . . . from the beginning . . . from the top of the stairs.

Wouldn't you know, he wanted us to start at the top of the stairs every take. And there were forty steps going down . . . which meant forty more going back up. You'd better believe that by about take ten, my hips were on fire. My joints were screaming and grinding, my back started to tighten up, and my legs ached from my crotch to my knees.

We did that scene at least twenty-five times that day . . . after rehearsing it several times. It was all worth it though, because when we finally got to the floor where the action was to take place, we'd get to work with Brad and Edward, something I'd looked forward to.

From the moment we began rehearsing the fight, I was totally impressed. Fincher knew what he wanted to see from his director's chair, but seemed to be having a hard time figuring out how to get the shot. So he asked Ed Norton how he thought the shot might be set up. In front of the whole crew!

Now you may not think this is unusual, but in Hollywood, with big budgets and even bigger egos, this kind of thing is not done. Or it's handled behind a curtain, so there's no chance for the cast and crew to doubt the leadership of the director . . . the captain of the ship. But Fincher was confident and comfortable in making use of the excellent filmmaking talent that was in the room.

Norton was professional and succinct in his answers and conversations with Fincher. He never even hinted that he might know something that the director didn't. Instead, he acknowledged what Fincher wanted and helped him find a way to get it. Something he did several times when I was on set. The thing that stuck with me was the total lack of ego and the wholehearted desire to be a team player and make the best film possible. I like that a lot.

Stunt coordinator Runyard did a superior job as he worked out the fight and the moves we needed with "Lou" and Brad—as well as handling a crowd of fifty-some background players and actors.

Pitt was as nice as he was handsome, working the fight moves with ease.

The scene called for Brad to start beating on Lou, then for me to grab Brad and drag him off the poor schmuck. Brad was fighting without a shirt, so the only way to hold onto him and pull was to get a really good grip on the back of his pants and belt to lift him. So I spent the better part of two weeks (that's right, my three days turned into a couple of weeks . . . it happens on big budget shows) with my hand down Brad's pants. My girls at home were jealous.

On that note, I will say that between takes I never saw Brad eat anything; all he did was drink diet Coke and smoke cigarettes. Oh, and if you must know, he didn't have a hair on that tight little fanny of his!

CHAPTER 38
THE TAURUS WORLD STUNT AWARDS

We want to thank all of you for watching us congratulate ourselves tonight.

WARREN BEATTY

I f you take a look at my credits on IMDb.com, you'll see only one significant work gap—between 1999's *Fight Club* and my work as stunt coordinator on the *2001 ABC World Stunt Awards*. That gap was the result of my fall on *Mallrats*, a story I told you a few chapters ago.

I ended up having my left hip replaced in June of 1999 and my right one in September of that year. Dr. Herbert Huddleston, then with the Southern California Orthopedic Institute, did a great job. Each surgery took less than two hours. I remember thinking it was like dropping off your car for an oil change, getting a new hip, then picking up your car in time for lunch. Crazy!

Each time, the procedure went well, relieving my intense pain with ease that remains to this day. However not unlike some of my stunts, there was a hitch.

When I went into pre-op for my left hip, the anesthesiologist gave me the shot that preps me for surgery . . . one of my favorite feelings. I was doing just fine floating around in my own little world when I got wheeled into surgery where my buddy, Dr. Feel Good, administered the 'count down' injection. After slurring, "One hunred, ninney-nine, ninney eif, ninney slev. . . ." I was off to la-la land knowing that when I awoke the pain in my left hip was going to be gone.

Well, after surgery, I came out of my daze as I was being wheeled toward the recovery room. My wife and daughter Carlene were there as well as the orderlies who were moving me.

All was good until I felt someone plunge a sword into my hip joint. I let out a scream that woke the guys in the morgue. Our little procession stopped still in the hallway. "Oh my gawd, I'm so sorry," I gasped to Carlene. She hated hospitals as it was, and I knew I had really scared her. Seconds later it happened again, and then a few more times. Each pulse of pain was like nothing I'd ever felt before and each brought on another howl.

The anesthesiologist came running down the hall when he heard me, ah, calling. He quickly grabbed a syringe, filled it with something good and shot it into my IV line. Out I went.

When I finally came around again, I was in my room, the pain was gone, and my hip already felt better. My Teri was there, and I asked her what happened after surgery. As it turned out, just as Dr. Huddleston was about to start my surgery, an emergency demanded his attention in another operating room. He stepped away for just under an hour, then came back and finished me up in about an hour-and-a-half.

Unfortunately for me, Dr. Feel Good neglected to adjust the dosage for that hour Huddleston was gone. So when I woke up on my way to recovery, I felt the full pain of having the top of my femur amputated. Damn that hurt.

During my recovery, I received a call from an acquaintance who was in advertising and product placement for a company here in Los Angeles. She told me she represented Red Bull, and that they were interested in developing an awards show to honor professional stunt people. She said Red Bull thought the global stunt community was a good fit with the professional and extreme athletes they were already promoting.

I had been approached with award show proposals during my SAMP presidency, and this time, like then, I was less than thrilled with the idea.

Why? Because of experience. Years of watching producers rip-off stunt performer footage; years of not being compensated for that footage; experiencing the demise of an awards show put on by the Stunts Unlimited organization in the mid-eighties; and not least, the fact that a huge majority of stunt people wanted nothing to do with awards or notoriety for their work. The long-held belief in the stunt community was "we don't want every yahoo from around the country thinking it's glamorous and coming out here trying to take our jobs."

I expressed my concerns, but my friend and her agency assured me that Red Bull owner Dietrich Mateschitz was fully committed to making this happen.

Furthermore, they weren't asking the stunt community to contribute a dime. Red Bull's reasoning was simple win-win—they believed stunt people deserved acknowledgment for their thrilling and sometimes life-threatening contributions to movies, and they knew that this type of marketing was effective for their product.

This would be a big undertaking.

So while I appreciated all that the Red Bull reps had to say, knowing the stunt community as I did, I was still hesitant. Why oh why would I want to take on this uphill battle with the majority of the stunt world?

Well, at that time, the Internet was only getting started, but it was clear things were changing fast. I figured that if no one made the effort to increase awareness of stunt people, we would continue to be treated as second class citizens on sets and would never be able to highlight our huge contribution to movie-making.

I also saw that this was a way to bridge the gap between the old and established stunt pros with the new and inventive stunt people who were coming into and changing our business with their technology.

Further, I realized this was a way to heighten the awareness of who we are and what we really do to the organization behind the Oscars®. They told stunt people more than once that stunts were neither an art nor a science. Hence, we don't fit into their criteria.

On top of all of that, Red Bull had added an irresistible extra—they planned to establish a fund for stunt people who have been injured or worse, to help aid in their recovery and their families' needs.

Finally, to be brutally honest, I had just had those hip surgeries. I was still between crutches and a walker and wouldn't be able to work for months, yet needed to care for my family.

So it was on.

The first thing I did was tell my wife, Teri, what I had been offered. I trusted her knowledge about the business side of the project since she had been in that realm for years as a writer and event producer.

She agreed it was a wonderful challenge, well worth taking on. In fact, after watching the project stall for a while, she stepped up and put together a proposal that mapped out how to develop the business. We pitched it to Red Bull, got their thumbs up and hit the ground running.

We opened an office near Universal Studios, hired two assistants, and embarked on our plan to get the awards in order and bring the global stunt community on board.

Teri and I researched the structure behind other Hollywood awards shows and developed a version that was right for the stunt world. We laid out the rules and developed timelines and registration and submission processes. We identified award categories such as Best Fight; Best High Work; Best Fire Work, and Outstanding Stunt Coordinator. Our goal was to highlight and honor relevant action disciplines, and I knew that these awards would catch the eyes of producers and filmmakers around the world.

Teri created a myth behind the name Dietrich had given to the program, the Taurus™ World Stunt Awards, that married the immortalized bull symbol to the strength, versatility and determination of stunt performers.

Red Bull's Austrian team arrived around that time, and she coordinated with them and their web developers to create a powerful website featuring all the information and functionality we needed. She also worked the phones, introducing the show to studios and gaining buy-in to use their footage.

Meanwhile, I began the job of introducing the awards to the stunt community and getting them on board.

As I mentioned earlier, this wasn't as easy as you might think. In fact, trying to get the stunt community to listen to our proposal and getting them on board to support the awards was the biggest challenge I faced. I decided to start at SAMP, believing my brothers (I was still in the group at this time) would at least be open to hearing what I had to say.

What the hell was I thinking?

When I brought them our plan for the awards, the televised red-carpet program, and the glamorous after-party, I was met with harsh words, criticisms and naysayers. I have to say, the fact that they didn't trust me after leading them for years was disappointing. But the old guys in the group had been too burned for too long.

I took their comments in the best light possible—as good feedback—and used it to sharpen my talks as I went around the city and spoke to the other organized stunt groups and independents. That feedback proved similar. I heard:

"Well, if you guys have a show that's giving free booze, I'll be there."

"If you can pull this off I might go."

"We've never had any goddamn awards before, never needed them!"

"We are a well-kept secret; that's how it's been, and that's how it should stay."

"You're an ignorant son-of-a-bitch if you think that someone is going to give us something for free."

This was my community, and I respected their opinions. But I had to stay strong to prove to them that this was an honorable enterprise. By then, I completely believed the Taurus World Stunt Awards was going to be the biggest thing that had hit the stunt community since elbow pads.

As we moved closer to the inaugural awards show date of May 20, 2001, Austria-based Red Bull brought us exciting news. They had worked out a deal for fellow Austrian Arnold Schwarzenegger to receive an honorary award and serve as the organization's ambassador. This was the huge news we needed to propel the program forward.

Additionally, we established an advisory panel of well-established and respected stunt people from the United States, Canada and Europe. Not only would this continue to legitimize our efforts, this group would be essential in guiding the core awards work including reviewing the registrations and nominations we hoped would soon come pouring in.

I selected and approached sixteen members of the stunt community who I felt best represented stuntmen and stuntwomen. These men and women represented each stunt organization, independent stunters and stunt professionals from other countries. I'm happy to say that each individual agreed to participate, and that the Blue Ribbon Committee stands strong today. The committee guides the annual Taurus Awards as well as the Taurus Foundation, the organization Red Bull formed to help stunt community members in need.

After almost a year of canvassing the entire stunt community and working to convince them that we had something very special, we reached our moment of truth. It was time for stunt people to register with the awards—a first step that was at the heart of our entire awards concept. Registration would enable stunt people to submit nominations in our awards categories and cast their votes.

We sat in our little Toluca Lake office nervously watching our computers and listening for the phones. We had built it, but would they come?

Needless to say, we were thrilled when stuntmen and stuntwomen signed up in droves. It was official. The Taurus World Stunt Awards was up and running.

While Teri continued to manage the action behind the scenes, I worked with Red Bull as we moved into full production mode. Our generous sponsor added a production team to our little enterprise and I expanded my role to include stunt coordination of the show.

The production was staged at the Barker Hangar at the Santa Monica Airport. It's a huge and unique airplane hangar that's used for all manner of special events— and this was definitely special. It's the same venue that hosts The Independent Spirit Awards, which honor excellence in independent productions.

Our show would feature an impressive roster of A-List stars and would be televised on ABC. Our glamorous Hollywood after-party would take place in a gorgeous tent set up just outside of the Hangar.

I pitched Red Bull on the concept of a live-action stunt sequence designed as an homage to the film, *Crouching Tiger, Hidden Dragon*, which was wildly popular at the time. The stunt scene I put together called for a stuntwoman, swords in hand, to fly across the audience, landing and walking on top of various stunt people I had placed in the audience. This aspect of the project gave me a chance to create a live performance, something that I love to do, as well as hire some twenty-five stunt performers to work the show.

Finally, the night arrived and it was a huge success.

The show was hosted by Alec Baldwin and starred such celebrity presenters as Nicolas Cage, Sandra Bullock, James Cameron, Russell Crowe, Vin Diesel, Michael Keaton, Pam Grier, Jason Biggs, John Travolta and Sharon Stone.

Twenty-seven stunt professionals received the stunning Taurus Awards trophy—a thirty-one-and-a-half inch, twelve pound statue of the mythical bull from which the Taurus Awards take their name. Arnold Schwarzenegger received the inaugural Taurus Honorary Award; director John Woo was given the Action Movie Director Award; and stunt legend Hal Needham, of *Hooper* fame, was recognized with the first annual Lifetime Achievement Award. This honor was presented by his longtime friend and movie-making partner, Burt Reynolds.

As of this writing, the Taurus World Stunt Awards is in its thirteenth year. Although the program is no longer televised, the awards are still going strong under the care of Mitch Gellar, President of GRACE/Red Bull North America, producer Jennifer Webster, and associate producer Teresa Prindle. Today the Taurus World Stunt Academy consists of over 1,500 stunt professionals, and the Taurus World Stunt Awards Foundation continues to assist stunt performers in need. The entire organization continues to be fully supported by Red Bull, which has never asked the stunt community for a dime in financial assistance. The Taurus Foundation does accept contributions and can be reached at office@taurusworldstuntawards.com.

I continue to serve the awards organization as a member of the Taurus World Stunt Awards Blue Ribbon Committee. I couldn't be prouder of being able to help create and then contribute to the ongoing success of the Taurus World Stunt Awards.

C H A P T E R   3 9

THE WHOLE
TEN YARDS

I've been dead once already; it's very liberating. You might think of it as . . . therapy.

THE JOKER, *BATMAN AND ROBIN*

n December of 2002 I had just started a job working for stunt coordinator Rick
Avery on *The Whole Ten Yards* when I became involved in a nearly lethal stunt.
One that wasn't in a script, wasn't filmed, and didn't qualify for a damn dime in
stunt adjustments.

Stuntman, stunt coordinator, second unit director, actor and helicopter pilot
Rick Avery is a top-notch film professional. You've seen his work in such films as
Frost/Nixon, Charlie Wilson's War, The Prestige, Meet the Fockers and *Anchorman:
The Legend of Ron Burgundy*. Rick is one of the classiest and most talented individu-
als I've ever had the pleasure of working with. He offered me three weeks of work on
location in San Pedro, California, about an hour and a half—or six hours—from my

home, depending on L.A. traffic. I gladly accepted and showed up for my first day at about 7 a.m.

We worked a long twelve-hour day, so afterwards, I called my wife and told her I was going to stay for the night at a Holiday Inn near location. That way I could get a few extra hours of rest before the next morning's early call.

The idea was a good one. I woke up refreshed, grabbed my backpack and headed down to the street-level parking garage around 6:30 a.m., ready for another day in the movies.

As I approached my car, I noticed an old Ford truck in the narrow garage, facing me with its engine running. It didn't look right to me. I took a few more steps and realized there was a man in the garage smashing car windows and stealing everything he could. Almost unconsciously, I called out something like, "Hey! What do you think you're doing?"

With that, he ran to his truck, threw his booty in the cab, and dropped it in gear.

Unfortunately, the only exit from the garage was now behind me. The truck was about thirty or so feet away, aimed right at me, and I was trapped by a twenty-foot wall to my right. He gunned the engine and headed right at me. I had no place to go. And without Hollywood magic, there was no way I could make a *Six Million Dollar Man* leap to escape the oncoming assault.

I flattened myself up against the wall, hoping I could at least minimize damage from the hit, but this guy had a different plan. On his approach to the exit, he swung open his driver's side door and slammed it into me as he passed by. The impact knocked me to my back some fifteen or twenty feet into the garage driveway. Dazed and thinking it was over, I rolled myself to my stomach to get up when I heard him put the truck in reverse, back up, and drop into gear once again. I heard the engine race as he barreled toward me.

I remember screaming at the top of my lungs "NOOOOO!"

A moment later, I was plastered to the pavement thinking, "*I can't believe this S.O.B. just ran me over!*" The front wheels of his beat-to-shit, two-ton truck had traversed my left calf and thigh, then crossed over my pelvis as he squealed his way out of there.

I don't think I passed out at first. I don't remember if I did my typical stuntman body check. What I do remember is realizing it was still early and would likely be a long wait before anybody would show up. So I used my lungs and started screaming.

It seemed to take forever, but finally a very nice woman walking on a nearby sidewalk heard me, ran into the hotel, and called for help. By that time I was in shock; I knew enough to recognize it. I began sweating profusely. I got the chills. My head started to spin. The pain, fortunately, was non-existent at that point.

So what did I do next? Well, I noticed that my backpack had landed next to me. It came to me at this point that I was wearing the coolest pair of sunglasses I'd ever owned. I'd never spent more than twenty bucks on shades because they usually found a way to break or get lost when I needed them the most. But my Teri had given me a pair of Maui Jim's and I loved them.

So there I was, laying there in the driveway of the Holiday Inn of San Pedro, California, facing Gaffey Street, with tire marks running across my legs and my ass, unable to move because my pelvis had been broken—carefully taking off my Maui Jim's and putting them in their case in the backpack. I then dragged the pack up under my chest so no one could take it from me.

What can I say? I was in shock!

I must have finally lost consciousness because the next thing I remember is somebody trying to take my pack away from me. It was the paramedics. I recall joking with them as they cut off my favorite Adidas warm-up pants, and then my SpongeBob SquarePants boxers, a Father's Day gift from my sweet daughter, Tiana, or Schmoe, as I like to call her.

They took me to the Trauma Center at Harbor-UCLA Medical Center where I spent what seemed like an endless day laying in an Emergency Room filled with patients even more seriously hurt than me. Every time the attendants came to take me to surgery, someone would come in with a knife wound or a bleeding gunshot wound. So I waited. Early that evening, I was finally taken to surgery and put back together with an assortment of screws and a titanium plate.

The next thing I remember is waking up with my Teri by my side in a hospital room filled with seven other male patients—each handcuffed to his bed, some muttering, others screaming.

As my eyes focused on this surreal situation I asked Teri, "What the hell happened to me?" Once she was confident I was ok, she did some screaming of her own *a la* Shirley McLaine in *Terms of Endearment*. She cornered a nurse and literally marched her around the floor until they found an empty room, then forced them to move me out of the criminal ward.

After a week or so in the hospital, my good friend Steve Hart, a loyal friend as well as a strong stuntman and stunt coordinator, helped get me back home by picking me up in his big SUV, which was easy to climb in and out of.

I recuperated for quite a while, with visits from a few loyal stunt friends who had me laughing till I hurt. Another great laugh came from actor Kevin Pollack, who starred in *The Whole Ten Yards*. He sent a smart-ass get well note and a huge bouquet of flowers in a beautiful yellow vase that we still have. Funny guy. Classy move.

It was several weeks before I was able to work—and walk—again. Obviously I couldn't finish my commitment to Rick for *The Whole Ten Yards* and had to be replaced. But talk about classy, when I later informed Rick that I was cleared to go back to work on a limited basis, he brought me back for a couple of days to finish out the film. As I said before, Rick Avery is a great guy.

C H A P T E R 4 0
MISSION: IMPOSSIBLE III

The Force is strong with this one.

DARTH VADER

I n 2006, I once again got the opportunity to work with Tom Cruise.

I got the call from James Armstrong (son of Andy, nephew of Vic) asking if I was available for a couple of weeks to do some driving around explosions on a little film that they (the Armstrongs collectively) were doing called, *MI3*.

I was happy to accept for a few reasons. First, I'm always thrilled to get work, especially something that might run for a couple of weeks, if not more. This is good for my family.

Second, the Armstrong film dynasty is really something special to be a part of. There's Vic, his wife Wendy, their son Scott and daughters Georgina and Nina; Vic's brother Andy and his son James. They are all extremely talented and you've enjoyed their work over the years in mega-hits like *Raiders of the Lost Ark*, *The Amazing Spider-Man*, *Thor*, *MI3* and *Pirates of the Caribbean*.

Third, I was going to get to work with my old punching-bag buddy, Tom.

Tom Cruise . . . dramatic, huh?

After *Far and Away*, it was a long shot that I'd ever work with him again, but here it was happening. I was excited to work alongside him, because like I said before, he's a great professional. His work ethic is totally inspiring.

We were shooting at the base of the Santa Monica Mountain range on a fully-crewed second unit that included about twenty stunt drivers and a dozen or so stuntmen playing soldiers and stunt doubles for the leads. We had a helicopter and a WWII fighter plane and exploding cars. In the scene, we were traveling along a bridge that Paramount Studios built out in the middle of nowhere. Cruise's character, Ethan Hunt, gets attacked by bad guys on a rescue mission for their boss, played beautifully by the late, great Philip Seymour Hoffman.

I reported to wardrobe on my first day where they gave me my ice cream man's uniform.

Oh boy. I knew that if I was dressed like an ice cream man, chances are I'd be driving an ice cream truck; an old, un-air-conditioned, hard-to-steer, sticky-clutched ice cream truck. Sure enough, James confirmed that's what I would be driving. But it was ok. Driving is one of my favorite stunt jobs. So despite the lack of conveniences, I knew I would enjoy maneuvering that beast around.

The shoot promised to be exciting and very challenging at the same time. That's a lot of people and machinery to coordinate into a movie scene and the Armstrong Action Team did a superb job bringing it all together. It's pretty cool to be part of such a great scene, even if I was dodging bullets and bombs while dressed as an ice cream man.

After I was dressed, I waited, noticing that the production's honey wagons were stationed in the emptiness, with nothing else around them.

This meant that our cast and crew would have to be shuttled from the wagons to the actual set—which turned out to be about a half-a-mile down a barren dirt road.

Actors, stunt people, crewmembers, various make-up chairs and bags, director chairs, stunt bags, backpacks and other equipment would all be driven back and forth in nondescript nine-passenger vans.

This separation of camp and location was arranged because the scenes we were doing included aerial shots, explosions, fire and lots of dust, debris and smoke that would embed into any unprotected orifice.

The choices here were to either wait for a shuttle van with everyone else on set—knowing that you're gonna' get the last of the eight seats available and that the seat will be in the back row and you'll have to get you and your big-ass stunt bag into a space that was designed for a seven-year-old . . . or avoid the crowd by hoofing it to the set.

I chose to walk. To the set after breakfast, back to base for lunch, back to set after lunch and back to camp at wrap. I wasn't the only one; many of us just gave ourselves time to get from point A to point B and back.

Not surprisingly, the stars were transported separately. In Tom's case, he was driven to and from set in a big, beautiful, black Cadillac SUV.

We were several days into the shoot and had already created the traffic jam on the bridge caused by the explosives attack. We were moving into the part of the scene where a helicopter arrives and drops "Black-Ops" soldiers onto the road. Tom had been on set for a few of those days; the rest of the time he had been working with the first unit of the movie.

On the particular day I want to tell you about, I watched as Tom worked closely with second unit director Vic Armstrong to prepare for the scene. I saw him confer with some of his entourage, then review his blocking, camera angles, and script as he walked the bridge. He moved with that unmistakable Tom Cruise strut of confidence. He would graciously greet those he passed with a "good morning," or a pleasant "hello"—at times flashing that famous sparkling smile of his—before returning his concentration to the action sequence ahead: a desperate race up, under, through and over a succession of burning, mangled vehicles.

Although Tom passed by me as well, I'm the last one who would approach an actor when he is preparing for such a complex scene with a "Hey! Remember me?" So if he happened to look up when he was near me, I simply gave a nod. His head was on business. I get it.

But one day as Tom walked by and he looked up to give the by-now familiar polite hello, we happened to lock eyes. It was just like in *Far and Away* when he says to me, "Come on, lad." He did a double-take, but I could tell he couldn't quite place me. So I struck the bare-knuckle boxing pose.

Tom's eyes grew wide, that amazing smile exploded into view, and he said, "No shit!"

He hustled right over to me, hand extended, shaking my right hand firmly as he slapped and grabbed onto my right shoulder with his left. A familiar greeting, it was the same one he gave me on the red carpet at the premiere of *Far and Away*.

"Hiya Tom, it's Carl."

"Of course!" he yelled. "How are you? You look great!" He was full of energy and sincerity all at the same time.

We made some small talk, but I knew he had to get to his spot down the bridge where the camera crew was waiting for him. So we shook hands and wished each other the best and back to work we went. I was happy I had once again connected with such a talented gentleman.

At wrap that same day, after gathering my things and stuffing them into my stunt-gear bag, I started my trek back to base camp.

I was a hundred yards or so down the dirt road when a big black SUV pulled up next to me, and the passenger's door opened. I looked inside to see Tom, facing backward, in a luxurious interior that had been tricked out like a limousine. He says to me, "Would you like a ride?"

"*Hmm, lemme think about that.*" Ya, right!

So I climbed right into the biggest SUV I'd ever seen.

Tom met me with a big smile and an outstretched hand. He was bookended by a couple of young women, and there was a young man in the passenger's seat as well as another woman seated in the back where I was.

I recognized that these other travelers were from the Church of Scientology; I had seen the tents they had set up on location. They were present to offer help, guidance, healing and information to anyone on the production who was interested in knowing more about their religion. They were silent as Tom and I talked.

So, I'm in this limo-like truck and we're driving down the dirt road and I'm passing by several stunt people who are walking back to base. And all I want to do is roll down the window and wave as if to say, "*Hey! Lookatmeeeeee!*"

I didn't . . . but I admit I wanted to.

Tom asked me how life was going, and how marriage was treating me. He remembered that I had gotten married just before we did *Far and Away*, as had he and Nicole. I told him that I had gotten a divorce but had since met the woman of my dreams and that I was now happier than ever.

He laughed that semi-goofy laugh of his and almost stood up in the car exclaiming, "Oh my gawd, me too! Isn't it great?" This meeting occurred when Tom was newly involved with actress Katie Holmes.

We had a pretty good "man-laugh," the kind where you know you've both gone through a similar life-changing experience.

Then I said to him, "You know, Tom, I've gotten quite a lot of mileage out of *Far and Away*. In thirty years, it's the only movie where I've won a fight."

Without hesitation he shot back, "It's the only one I've lost!"

The SUV erupted in laughter just as we arrived at base, then it was handshakes, smiles and goodbyes all around.

The next day at work, Tom and I had a quick hello on his way to his spot on the bridge. After that, we spent several more days on the bridge finishing up the shoot. I never got another ride, but the experience gave me a fun and lasting memory.

CHAPTER 41

THE BOOK OF ELI

You must do the thing you think you cannot do.

ELEANOR ROOSEVELT

D enzel Washington is an actor who marches to his own drum—with amazing success. I've worked with him on three pictures—*The Pelican Brief, Glory* and most recently *The Book of Eli*—and each time, he was the ultimate professional.

On the set of *Pelican Brief*, with Julia Roberts, he was quiet and reserved—and, it must be said, as handsome as could be. On *Glory*, for which Denzel won an Oscar for Best Supporting Actor, he was full of life and quite gregarious on set. On *The Book of Eli*, Denzel was once again quiet and removed, but he was clearly doing what he had to do to best portray his character—a blind Messiah navigating a post-apocalyptic world to complete a divinely-inspired mission.

I doubled Joe Pingue, a Canadian actor and writer who played a henchman for bad guys Gary Oldman and Ray Stevenson. I got to drive an armored truck that towed an ice cream truck loaded with explosives that was ready to go up as soon as I hit my mark in the New Mexico desert.

My passenger for some of the ride was Oldman. I so much wanted to talk to him about his roles and choices he made in his many movies . . . but it was work time. In between scenes, we did chat a bit about our kids, but mostly there was no time for small talk. We had trucks to crash, bad guys to kill and shit to blow up!

Mila Kunis was a salty spitfire with a great sense of humor who held her own amidst all the testosterone and chaos of this shoot. But she did admit that the carnage got to her. She was talking about it in the makeup trailer one morning, and mentioned other movies that scared her, one of which was *Casino*. When I told her I had played Tony Dogs, her eyes grew wide, and she told me how much the vise scene had scared her. I reassured her that even my own girls covered their eyes when watching it.

We moved on to other topics, but as I left the trailer, I gave a quick look back at her, squashed my face with my two hands like I was still in the vise and said, "Hey Mila, squeeze ya' later!"

CHAPTER 42
CHANNELING

The key to life is accepting challenges.

BETTE DAVIS

I n 2012, I was able to participate in something special when I was asked to coordinate a groundbreaking film called *Channeling*.

My friend Gerry Santos, who was serving as the film's producer and UPM, hired me onto the production as the stunt coordinator. (A UPM, or Unit Production Manager, oversees the budget.) The project was the brainchild of writer-director Drew Thomas, who wrote the film and produced it with his business partner, Laila Ansari.

Channeling tells the story of a group of characters who are obsessed with—and make their living by—stealing cars and recording their thefts for their audiences, who follow them every step of the way through social media. How? These high-tech thieves wear contact lenses fitted with cameras that transmit to satellites, thus broadcasting their deeds to the world. The more followers, the more sponsors, the higher the payoff.

In the film, the wrong car gets stolen, kicking off an action bonanza of car crashes, near misses, motorcycle wrecks and intense fights.

Not only was the story cutting-edge, Drew chose to shoot it with a Red Camera®, about which director Steven Soderbergh said, *"this is the camera I've been waiting for my whole career: jaw-dropping imagery recorded on board a camera light enough to hold with one hand."*

We also used several Go-Pro® cameras, billed as "The World's Most Versatile Camera." We mounted them in and on cars and motorcycles and fitted them on the actor's heads so that viewers could see what the characters saw from their perspective.

I'm always a little leery of working with writer/directors because it can be difficult for them to accept that live action doesn't always match the vision they've had throughout the development process. Drew, however, had no such problem. He did an outstanding job collaborating to create the action. We were greatly assisted by first AD Lynette Myers, a multi-talented pro I've had the pleasure of working with on several occasions.

Drew is a speed freak and actually used his own brand new Dodge Challenger in a drag race scene on the 6th Street Bridge in L.A. The other cars and motorcycles that we chose had to be muscled-up and able to take some abuse. We landed a Mustang GT with the full power package of four-hundred-plus horsepower that would take quite a good hand to drive and make it do the things we wanted it to do.

The gifted Cole McKay was my choice to drive the car, doubling the lead actor being chased by a motorcycle gang. We used the roads at Griffith Park and weaved in and out of stunt drivers as we sped—and I mean sped—through the park streets.

That chase comes to an end when the Mustang hits the brakes, and the lead biker slams into the back of the car. The impact causes him to fly over the length of the vehicle, landing on the street in front of it. We created this in cuts. First we slammed on the brakes, sliding the bike up to the camera lens. Then we parked the car in the middle of the street and had second-generation stuntman Jimmy Hart leap from a platform we'd built, over the car to pads waiting in front of the car. Then we captured a shot of the car driving off. The sequence ended with a view from the car's rear view mirror showing the biker crushed and broken in the street.

Under director Drew Thomas's watchful eye, I also created fights that were exciting and brutal for the camera, but made certain to minimize risk to the actors. Part of that was accomplished by bringing in talented stunt doubles; the other was to design action in a way that made the actors' movements as natural as possible. This made them confident they wouldn't look awkward on film.

Actors Dominic DeVore and Johnny Pacar invested themselves in learning their portions of the fight. They were fully open to constructive input regarding their movements and reactions and truly seemed to enjoy getting punched in the jaw and slammed to the ground, punched in the jaw.

We cast two young stuntmen that I call as often as I can. Jeff Groff, a driving and fighting fiend, doubled DeVore. Billy Bussey, who is a terrific fighter, took some big thumps on this one (like getting yanked off a barstool to his back) while doubling for Parcar. Groff and Bussey were patient and generous, taking direction and helping their actor as needed. They understand that being a stunt double doesn't just mean taking the hard knocks, it also means taking care of your actor on set.

Does he need pads?

Is he left or right-handed?

How was he positioned in the last scene so I can match him?

Does he have a certain movement or walk that I need to copy?

How does he take his coffee? (Thankfully, not on this set.)

We got the fight dialed in with a couple hours of rehearsal time and were ready to shoot.

First we captured the wide master shot. This is where the majority of the scene's participants are in the camera's view. A wide master covers the complete scene (in this case, the fight) with cameras positioned far enough away from the action that we were able to use stunt doubles to perform the fight from first punch to last.

Next we moved in closer to film the fight from various angles, replacing one of the actors with a double. Then we repeated the process, this time replacing the other actor with his double. When the film is edited together, you get a great fight, seeing close-ups of the actors and only back of the heads of stunt guys.

For me, being able to hire the stunt people I did on this movie, basically ensured my success as coordinator of the show. I surrounded myself with talented professionals on a low-budget show who gave 110% every day they were on set.

No complaints, just pure performance. That's the only real "payback" that coordinators are looking for.

Drew has taken *Channeling* on a worldwide Film Festival tour, where it has won just about every category it's been entered in. This production has been a big win for everyone involved.

C H A P T E R 4 3
OUT OF
THE FURNACE

Ever notice how you come across somebody once in a while you shouldn't have messed with? That's me.

WALT KOWALSKI, *GRAN TORINO*

I n 2012, I received a call from Ben Bray; the stunt coordinator on a movie shooting in Pittsburgh, Pennsylvania titled *Out of the Furnace*.

Ben told me that director Scott Cooper, who wrote and then directed Academy Award™ winner Jeff Bridges in *Crazy Heart*, took a look at my acting reel on my website, and with Ben's support, wanted to hire me for a role in his movie. I would be playing the part of a drive-in patron who has a fight with Woody Harrelson. He told me the scene would open the film.

I was thrilled that someone had taken a look at my website, and hired me . . . sight unseen . . . without needing to jump through the hoops of auditions and callbacks and the time and traffic and hassle that they entail. I was honored.

I arrived at our location about a week later—an old grass-field, drive-in theater on the outskirts of Pittsburgh, Pennsylvania, that had seen better days. It looked as if it was built in the 50s, closed in the 80s, and had remained untouched ever since. It was a perfect film setting.

I went to the makeup trailer and met Scott, who was getting a haircut. He introduced himself, gave me a very kind and manly handshake and said, "Oh yeah, you look great. You're perfect for this."

What a great way to start my work day!

Once I was done with makeup, I headed to the location where I was immediately impressed by Scott's work. He was managing some one hundred extras as well as camera crews, sound crews, wardrobe, stars, and stuntmen. This was a big production, and there was a lot going on.

Scott set camera and directed the rest of the department heads as to how the scene was going to play out. He was very detailed as well as passionate, but it was obvious that he trusted his department heads to do their jobs because there was no micro-managing involved.

Scott then turned his attention to the actors. There was Dendrie Taylor, playing Woody's date (she tore it up!); Nancy Moser, the local casting director actor who was playing my wife (terrific actress!); and me. Woody hadn't shown up to set yet, and there was some concern he'd be there at all because he had walked off the set a week earlier over . . . well, it doesn't really matter.

The first AD told the second AD to get on the radio and check to see where Woody was. He in turn radioed the second-second AD and asked the question. Who then radioed all the production assistance people . . . and they all confirmed the request by repeating the question with an affirmative response that they received the transmission.

Basically, there were a fuck-load of radios going off for the next several minutes!

Finally, someone broke through to let the second-second AD know that Woody was in a van on his way to set. He then relayed the notice to the second AD, who told the first AD, who told the director, who then told the crew that Woody was in fact on the way.

Whew!

Woody got to set and went straight to Scott's side to catch up on what was going on. He wore his famously boyish smile, looking just like he'd snuck a cookie from the jar and hadn't gotten caught.

Ben and I had already gone through the basics of what the fight should look like, but he reminded me to stay aware. He noted that some actors are prone to adlib during a fight scene because they have so much more to think about than just throwing punches. I was ready for a left instead of a right as well as whatever else might happen. That's part of the excitement.

Scott brought Woody around to the back of the car where we would rehearse the fight and introduced us. Woody stuck out his hand and said, "nice to meet you." I got to say, "nice to meet you . . . again." And then I reminded him that I worked with him on *After the Sunset* with Pierce Brosnan and then again on *Natural Born Killers* inside Mallory's cell where he'd killed me with a shotgun.

He looked at me, broke into a smile and said, "Wow, that was some sick shit going on in that movie." I agreed with him wholeheartedly and then we went to work.

Woody was a complete pro, ready to listen to the director, the stunt coordinator and his fellow-combatant, me. He had some good ideas that worked for his character and kept the fight tight and intense.

We walked and talked through the fight a few times and then did a take at about three-quarter speed. Scott approved, as did Ben and Woody himself. Me? I was very happy. I felt the excitement that comes from working with a good and generous actor.

Before we got started, we got a little sidetracked by the fact that Woody is the ultimate vegan, so he wouldn't touch the hot dog that the scene called for. He didn't have to eat it, just hold it. But he refused to touch the pork stick and told Scott that if he wanted the scene done as written, production would need to go out and find a soy dog to use.

That set off the radios once again. Everybody on set was in search of a vegan hot dog. The prop man ended up running to the market and buying several packages of soy dogs to get us through the night.

While that was happening, we kept working, rehearsing the opening of the scene.

Here's how it goes.

Woody is at the drive-in, in his car with his date. They are snacking, and Woody is drinking gin straight from the bottle. She is about to eat a hot dog when she makes a comment about him being drunk. This sets him off big time, and he takes the hot dog from her and shoves it down her throat. She shrieks and fights him off the best she can, which attracts my attention in the next car. My wife pleads for me not to get involved, but of course I do because, well, that's the way it's written!

I get out of my car and lean into the passenger window of Woody's car and things calm down some. I ask if everything is all right and Woody delivers his line to me. "Why don't you mind your own business?" And I say, "Well when you're slapping a woman around, it is my business!" What a setup for a fight!

He then ad-libbed something like, "Why don't you just get lost, motherfucker?" My acting instincts kicked in and I came back with my own ad-lib line, "That's Mr. Motherfucker to you!"

As soon as I heard it come out of my mouth I knew something was going to happen, and it did. Scott stopped the rehearsal and said, "What did you say to him?"

Damn it. I was going to get reamed because I changed a line—the writer/director's line—and in front of everybody, too!

I answered him, "That's Mr. Motherfucker to you!"

"I LOVE IT! Keep it! Use it!" Scott said. "Okay, let's keep going."

I was relieved, happy and proud of myself that I had made the right choice as an actor . . . and that I didn't get my ass chewed out by the director.

The scene continues with Woody getting out of his car. He walks around to me with both of his hands raised and says, "Hey look, man, I don't want any trouble . . ." and then proceeds to punch me in the throat.

As I buckle to my knees, he grabs the back of my head and knees me in the face sending me flying to my back on the ground. He then straddles me, one knee on my chest, and begins to pummel me with wicked right-fisted punches to the face.

All right! Good rehearsal! We're ready to shoot this.

Woody, Ben and I had a final talk about the angles of the punches and how best to work them for camera. Ben gave me a wink, and I knew that it meant for me to keep my eyes open for any changes that might come up in the middle of the fight.

Take one was good, but Woody felt that he could do better. This is typical. In a scene like this, it's going to take a few times to get exactly what they are looking for, and we had two nights scheduled to make sure we got it right.

Take two was better, tighter, and Woody was right on with all of his hits. We could even feel the dialog getting better between us.

Take three was even better . . . and so was four, five, six and seven.

Next it was time to shoot Woody's close-ups, then Dendrie's close-ups, and then mine. When that was done, production spent a couple of hours moving the cameras around to the other side of the car. Then we started over.

Things were even better from this angle. Sometimes it takes a few minutes to get the intensity back after time away from it, but by around take five or so from this angle, Woody was in his element. He was on top of me punching furiously and growling, "So, how do you like that, Mr. Motherfucker?"

I hope they use that take.

At the end of the fight, as I'm moaning in a big heap, Woody grabs his date by the arm, yanks her out of the car and flings her on top of me. Nancy comes from our car, cradles what's left of my head and screams for help.

Scott was pleased with the outcome of the scene, as were Woody, Dendrie, the producers, and the camera department. I felt that it had gone just about as well as it could have gone.

It was now about three-thirty in the morning. I watched as the director, the assistant director, and the producers all huddled about twenty yards from the rest of us to talk about the next scene . . . we thought.

But it turned out that the scene went so well that Scott and his team decided to use it as the opening. They decided to cancel the originally-planned lead-up, in which Woody enters the drive-in and buys the food.

This trimmed a whole day off of the schedule, and we were wrapped at 3:45 a.m. It's almost unheard of that a movie would cut a day of shooting, but they got the story they wanted, and it was nice to be a part of that.

Scott took the time to pull me aside after the shoot. He was very complimentary saying he was impressed that a stuntman could carry his weight in the scene by doing the dialog, knowing the character and delivering a fight with an actor.

Well, you almost don't have to pay me if you think I delivered like that. Almost.

I stayed in town for a wrap party that production hosted for the cast and crew at Olive or Twist, a very cool bar in downtown Pittsburgh. I hung out for a while, shook a couple of hands and made some good acquaintances. Before I left that night for L.A., I made it my business to talk to Scott Cooper one more time. Yes, politicking is important, but what was more important to me was to tell Scott how it felt to work for him.

I've been given the opportunity to work with some of the biggest directors and names in the industry. Some are great at what they do, and will tell you about it. Some think that they're great at what they do, and will tell you about it. Some don't know their ass from their elbow and never admit it.

Then are the directors I wish would call me to work on all their projects. Great creative geniuses who are also great leaders. Scott Cooper is that type of director; that type of man. I was glad for the opportunity to let him know that in my opinion he was in the category of Ron Howard, Clint Eastwood, Walter Hill, and Martin Scorsese.

CHAPTER 44
MENTORS, MANIACS AND ME

When given an opportunity, deliver excellence and never quit.

ROBERT RODRIGUEZ

men·tor (měn′tôr′, -tər)

n.

1. A wise and trusted counselor or teacher.

ma·ni·ac (mā′nē-ăk′)

n.

1. A psychotic or otherwise mentally ill person who exhibits violent or bizarre behavior.

2. A person who has an excessive enthusiasm or desire for something.

3. A person who acts in a wildly irresponsible way.

From the beginning of my career, I have had the privilege of working alongside some of the most talented stunt coordinators, stuntmen and stuntwomen in the business. I've also worked alongside more than a few maniacs, which is where

I learned what not to do. I'm so grateful that now, in this chapter—of my book and my life—I get to pay tribute to those who showed me the way.

My mentoring began with my folks.

Straight out of the Midwest, Nick and Lu epitomized The Greatest Generation—so aptly coined by Tom Brokaw in his book of the same name. These Depression-era individuals lived through deprivation, fought for our nation and our democratic ideals in World War II, and then came home to build a newer, stronger America. My folks were hard-working, no-nonsense, put up or shut up, take care of your family, and lend a hand to a friend kind of people. They instilled in me a powerful work ethic and a fundamental belief in goodness and loyalty—for which I am profoundly grateful.

My experience with maniacs also dates to my formative years.

I had a high school football coach who was more drill sergeant than teacher. He barked and grabbed face masks while he spit and sputtered in your face and made you the butt of a joke if it suited him. Humiliation has never worked for me. Some of his hurtful words and actions have never left me. I forgave, but never forgot. I resolved to do better than that in my life.

Now my wrestling coaches were a different story. They fell squarely in the mentor category.

In high school, it was the tough and funny John Hammond, who could make you laugh and have fun while you were working hard enough to puke. Paul Breit later stepped in for Hammond and was a coach who learned right along with the team. Who got the fact that we were kids, and most of us were working as hard as we could. Knowledgeable and caring is what I got from him. He was a big influence for me wanting to become a coach. Then I was off to Mt. SAC and Coach Fred Burri, who was like Paul Breit's older, blonder brother. It seemed as if the two of them graduated from the same "Great School of Coaching." Burri and I were a good fit, winning a championship together. He, too, was able to clue into the needs of individual athletes.

In my career, a common mentoring path was to become an influential coordinator's "guy" at work and at play. In turn, the coordinator would bring "his guys" along with him on his shows. That wasn't my path. Instead, I was a bag-carrying ground-pounder who took all calls, which allowed me to learn in the company of a variety of industry professionals.

Yes, some of them were maniacs. I remember the screamers, the shady person-alities and the dirty guys who put lining their pockets above safety and professional-ism. I remember a guy who put his contractor friend in a stunt spot in exchange for a deal on painting his house. And one who put his dentist in a 'crash-car' because of a lost golf bet. And a guy who filled a passenger stunt spot with a twenty-two-year-old he'd met at a club the night before because she thought it would be "super excit-ing" to go "really, really fast." I know of successful guys whose entrée into the inner circle of highly-paid stunt coordinators came from running drugs for actors back in Hollywood's cocaine heyday. There are still guys out there who pushed the boundar-ies, making unsafe decisions that caused injury and even death.

These maniacs make for crazy stories and memories—but it was the mentors who truly made my career.

The first was Gary Salisbury, who hired me to be a member of the first Wild West Stunt Show ever performed at Knott's Berry Farm. Gary somehow saw a per-former inside me and believed he could bring it out. And even though I gave him reason to fire me . . . more than once . . . he stuck with me. The passion he had for people and for every show that he's ever been involved with has stayed with me throughout my career.

Enter Doyle Baker, an unassuming everyman who played one of the students in the 1955 classic film, *The Blackboard Jungle*. John Casino and I attended Doyle's acting class, and it was both love and fear at first sight. In addition to being a gener-ous teacher, Doyle produced and directed plays, casting his students including John and me. We did *Mister Roberts* and *Stalag 17* at the La Mirada Theater, and I loved every minute of it. What a thrill to have a live audience react to your performance.

One of my earliest stunt mentors was Frank Orsatti—handsome, hard as a rock and tough as they come. Frank was the epitome of a stuntman—someone who did it all back when big stunts were in their infancy. He made his name by jumping off the Golden Gate Bridge on 1971's otherwise forgotten *B.S. I Love You.* He also did a fully-engulfed fire burn on 1974's *The Longest Yard.* The burn happened while Frank was locked inside a prison cell, so there was no way to get away from the deadly flames. Among Frank's many other notable credits are the original *Planet of the Apes*, *Bullitt*, *The Poseidon Adventure*, *Towering Inferno* and the original *The Terminator*.

Frank called me in to work a bar fight on the television series *The Hulk* which he coordinated and served as the stunt double for star Bill Bixby. In the scene, a wheelchair-bound Bixby (Frank) gets knocked backward down a flight of stairs. Backward! Chair and all! After watching Frank tumble and crash down those stairs and then pop up to do it again and again, I got the message: butch up and don't whine. Fortunate timing, since I got hit in the face with a breakaway table during my portion of the fight, and a loose screw happened to shoot through my chin.

I also watched and learned as Frank haggled with the UPM and directors to get what he needed to create a successful shot. His style was smooth and charming. After he'd get his way, he'd turn to me and give me a wink as if to say, "And that's how it's done."

Frank gave me so many opportunities to grow and learn. When I expressed concerns about being able to properly thank him and pay him back somehow, a wise Mic Rodgers told me, "The only thing that you owe Frank is a hundred percent of your attention and talent." That's a maxim that I've tried to uphold throughout my career.

Frank passed away in December of 2004. He is missed.

I met stuntman Tommy Huff through working for Frank on *The Hulk*. Tommy was tough and wiry with the twisted nose and jacked-up knuckles you would expect from the prizefighter he once was. He was known for his driving, for hitting the ground like a dead man and especially for his fights. What an artist he was! He did so much! *Little Big Man*, *Earthquake*, *Logan's Run*, *Smokey and the Bandit* and *Hooper*, *The Rockford Files*, *The Wild, Wild West* where he doubled star Robert Conrad, *The Blues Brothers*, doubling Dan Akroyd (whom I would double sixteen years later). Tommy worked right up until his death in 2006 and was a real hero to me. He is missed.

Early on I was at Tommy's house training—learning how to picture fight as a matter of fact. He talked to me non-stop as I bobbed, weaved, blocked and parried in a desperate attempt to avoid contact with his lethal fists. He was generous in sharing the wisdom he'd gained through experience.

"If you train hard"—jab-cross combination—"keep your eyes open"—intense flurry to my midsection—"and your mouth shut"—right uppercut, left hook, and bam! he's looking down at my prone body—"you'll go a long ways, kid."

He was so right.

On one of my earliest jobs, on the TV show *Galactica 1980*, I worked for the first time with the great Gene LeBell, aka *"Judo" Gene LeBell*, aka *"The Godfather of Grappling,"* aka *"The toughest man alive."* Gene is a champion martial artist, professional wrestler, MMA pioneer, venerated instructor, and prolific stuntman. He is beloved by the entire stunt community, and I am so proud to consider him a mentor and a friend.

On that first project, we played members of a motorcycle gang, something Gene and I would do several times throughout our careers. After a day of crashing more than a few motorcycles, Gene invited me to come to his dojo. I was surprised and honored to be invited by the master himself.

Entering the dojo, which was the wrestling gym at LA City College, I immediately felt at home, I soaked in the smell of the rubber mats, the humidity caused by perspiring grapplers, the thumps of bodies landing, and the grunts of guys getting stretched beyond their means. I headed over to Gene, who was dressed in what I soon learned was his trademark pink gi—something only the toughest fucking man alive can pull off.

I took my shoes off and bowed my respects to the dojo and Sensei LeBell. Gene told me that he was happy to see me there and that he always took to people who had a wrestling background. Then he said, "See that guy over there?" He indicated a black-belted gentleman who was folding some poor devil into an extremely tight pretzel. I said, "Yessir." Gene said, "Don't work with him, he'll break your arm. Come on out here and roll around with me." Then he proceeded to throw me around like I was his new plaything.

Gene recommended me for wrestling jobs he couldn't take, he was one of my biggest supporters when we were both members of SAMP, and he was first out the door behind me when I left the organization. And he still calls me Prez.

Gene has always been as hard-hitting with his advice as with his judo throws. "Everyone's a competitor." "The harder you work, the luckier you'll get." "Take care of yourself and your family first." "Prepare for your old age! Even if you only make $500 today, that's $5,000 in residuals down the road."

It all stuck. Thanks, Uncle Gene.

Gary Davis, of course, gave my career a "push-start" on *Against All Odds* in the jungles of Mexico. That experience was the first time I saw a stunt coordinator refuse to go to set if a particular piece of equipment was not present. In that case, it was a rescue helicopter. Gary got his way, as he should have. A valuable lesson learned.

Sandy Gimpel was the first female stunt coordinator I met when I started hustling in the late 1970s. Sandy is an extremely talented stuntwoman who helped to open up the male-only "good old boy" network of stunt coordinators. She opened my eyes, as she did for so many others, to the importance of filling roles with capable stunt women.

Not too long ago, on an Olympia Dukakis film called *Montana Amazon*, Sandy dressed me up in a pink tuxedo and put me through my paces. She ran into me with an old Ford Falcon as I crossed a street, strapped me to its hood, then drove me through a Las Vegas wedding reception. Damn, I love that woman.

Fred Lerner, who thought that even at the tender age of thirty-two I was worthy of being inducted into the Stuntmen's Association, where I became a twenty-year member and a two-term president, was another trusted and valued mentor. The SAMP president himself when I met him, Fred's credits include movies I loved when I was young including *Butch Cassidy and the Sundance Kid*, *Dirty Harry* and *The Towering Inferno*.

Around this same time, the always-working, ever-youthful Al Jones offered me a membership in the International Stunt Association, or ISA, formed by stunt great Alan Gibbs. I admit I spent some portion of the last half of my twenty-year SAMP tenure wondering if I'd made the right choice as a younger, less wise man.

Andy Armstrong and his brother, Vic Armstrong—it's virtually impossible to mention one without the other—are two immensely talented stuntmen who have been immensely influential to me. They are the creative powerhouses behind legendary action franchises including *Mission: Impossible*, *Bond*, *Spiderman*, *Charlie's Angels*, *The Green Hornet*, and these days, *Thor*. They are founding members of Armstrong Action, the largest and most comprehensive, privately-owned stunt and action facilities company in the world, which is operated by three generations of their most talented families.

I've worked with both Vic and Andy over the years, and am continually inspired and motivated by their guts, creativity, innovation, their diplomacy and passion, and their utter dedication to the stunt community and the film industry as a whole. Back in 2000, I invited each gentleman to serve on the Blue Ribbon Committee of the Taurus World Stunt Awards, giving me a closer and even more inspiring view of their talent, commitment and accomplishments.

Known around the world for his masterful work with weapons—and the world's leading expert on the Balisong butterfly knife—Sensei Jeff Imada has coordinated, designed and choreographed some of filmdom's most famous fight sequences including the *Bourne* films, the *Total Recall* reboot, *The Green Hornet*, *Iron Man 2*, and Parts 1 and 2 of the *Twilight* saga. An alum of the cult fave, *Big Trouble in Little China*, where he played the part of Needles, Jeff has gone on to become a trusted collaborator on John Carpenter's subsequent films.

Jeff exudes calm and thoughtfulness, bringing a rightness to almost every situation and solution. And he's a ninja on set! One minute he's nowhere in sight, and the next he's standing next to you—it's unnerving and totally cool. Over the years, Jeff has trusted me with numerous opportunities as a stunt performer. These days, he recommends me as a coordinator when he's booked, recently taking me on as his co-coordinator on *Tooken*, a hilarious spoof of the popular *Taken* franchise. From Jeff I learned focus and the importance of making certain sure that all my angles are covered when creating a shot A most wonderful best man, friend and stunt coordinator, Jeff is now weighing scripts to direct.

Another famous alum from Carpenter's *Big Trouble*, Master James Lew's credits go back to the original 1970s *Kung Fu* series starring David Carradine. He's a superb actor, stunning stunter, and incomparable fight and stunt coordinator. He has also written, produced, directed and starred in a hilarious action movie titled *Eighteen Fingers of Death*. James has a deep knowledge of the martial arts, action rigging, stunt coordinating and at this writing has created a unique action style for the new *Rush Hour* television series.

James and I became fast friends when we were both members of SAMP. We're like-minded in our professional endeavors and do not hesitate to recommend or counsel each other. I would say without hesitation that James has taught—and continues to (try to) teach—me collaboration, humility, joy, kindness and the deepest meaning of loyalty and patience. James is beloved and admired by fans, friends, and colleagues alike. His personal motto explains why: "I aspire to inspire."

Peewee Piemonte and Julie Michaels are today's quintessential stunt couple. They are both Greek God-like in looks and extremely talented. Julie started in the biz as an actress—if you haven't already seen it, catch her as the seductress in Patrick Swayze's *Roadhouse*. Peewee—Google™ him right now to understand the brilliance of that name—has been around since before I lent him my "Lou Ferrigno lifts" so he could double Tony Longo on *Rapid Fire*. That's when we really became friends, so many years ago.

Julie and Peewee have built a following from some of the top producers around the country, as well as a deep following of the entire stunt community. They personify what it's like to work as a team. And every time they move forward, they bring the stunt industry with them . . . always learning, always giving back, always paying forward. I thank them for their loyalty and friendship.

I'd be remiss if I didn't also mention friends and mentors like stuntman Randy Fife, who is a cross between a rocket scientist and MacGyver, with the added gift of patience in teaching the intricacies of a stunt. My best friend from the country of Texas!

Another great mentor is my acting teacher Deke Anderson, a fine actor himself, who has helped guide my talents and support me in my endeavors.

I miss my good friend, Mike Adams, whose guidance was so influential in my career. His constant trust in me as an actor, a stuntman and then a coordinator helped to instill the confidence I needed to move my career forward.

I've said much already about fellow stuntman, Allan Graf. I just want to add that his influence on me has been as huge and enjoyable as the many laughs we've shared over the years.

These good people, and the ones I'm about to introduce you to, are some of the great friends I've made from this life in the movies. True friends who not only work with you, but will tell you when your breath is bad or there's spinach in your teeth or when you're fucking up your life.

JP Romano is an extremely talented stuntman, and one-time ice show head-liner. JP is as honest as anyone I know, and he's taught me how to keep a good atti-tude in a business that can chew you up and spit you out.

I met Steve Hart years ago and we became instant friends. Steve has not only come through for me and my family in an emergency, but has always supported me professionally as well. Steve was the first one who actually showed me how to break down and budget a script. A technique taught to him by stunt legend, Ronnie Rondell. Something that I still share with others today.

Another irreplaceable friend is second-generation stuntman George Richard Sawaya. Coach, as I call him. Although we knew each other before, it was while working on the Steven Seagal film *Above the Law* that we became fast friends. Rick is a multi-talented stuntman who is also a top-notch general contractor. He per-forms both with forethought and professionalism and when something isn't work-ing, he can "MacGyver" it with ease.

Rick is like my "brother from a different mother" and has shown me how important it is to enjoy life outside of the movie business every once in a while. He has shared with me his favorite fishing spots up in the Eastern Sierras—a place he's been visiting since he was a kid. It's the perfect place to leave phones and computers behind and relax, reflect and enjoy nature.

My life has also been enriched by the newer generations of stunt professionals.

I was approached by a gentleman at an Academy function a few years ago who introduced himself and explained to me that he was a stuntman from Israel who had followed my career. He said that one of his missions, when he came to this country, was to meet me. This most talented man, who wanted to meet me and learn from me, has become a friend, confidant and inspiration himself, a great guy who can rig and perform any gag that you can think up. I've hired him several times since we met, and hope to do so many times moving forward. I'm so glad that I met Koby Azarly; he is a most talented man and great friend.

In recent years, I coordinated a teaser reel for a TV project produced by Jamie Foxx and directed by Jamie and Deon Taylor. Titled *Tommy's Little Girl* the project starred Paul Sorvino, Tony Sirico, and Selma Blair. Jamie's music director, Ainz "Brainz" Prasad, asked me to meet his girlfriend who was a champion prize fighter from Canada. He said she had done some work up there but moved to Hollywood to make it as a stuntwoman. I told him to bring her by and had the great pleasant surprise of meeting one Vaia Zaganas, a wonderful young woman who exudes both confidence and humility. She's a beautiful professional who can truly kick some serious butt in the ring.

I saw something in Vaia that told me she was going to be a winner, so the first chance I had, I hired her. It happened to be in a fight scene in a nightclub on the movie, *Channeling*. She did an outstanding job. The film gave Vaia her SAG-AFTRA card, and she has quickly made a name for herself in the industry as she continues to train and learn her craft.

I have also had the pleasure of hiring second-generation stunt performer Jennifer Elizabeth, who just happens to be Gary Davis's daughter and the mother of my sweet godchild, Aurora Joy Caradonna.

Jenn Davis is a lovely combination of her mother's grace and her dad's fortitude. She's a beauty who has the ability and guts to perform stunts. That's a goldmine for a coordinator as well as production. Another young talent that we'll be hearing about for years.

Jenn's husband, Michael Caradonna, is a multitalented film professional and loyal friend. He works as an actor, writer, and director and is an able stuntman I've hired more than once. Michael's greatest talent and passion is operating camera. He is my go-to guy for questions about shooting action scenes. Michael is experienced, thoughtful, and generous with his knowledge, which makes my work as a stunt coordinator more effective.

When you do stunts, when you make movies, you are part of a community of like-minded artists and professionals who understand the science, the art and the magic of our calling. I am proud and humbled to say that these individuals—and so many, many others from throughout my career—are truly my brothers and sisters.

I PLAYED A CHARACTER NAMED
"TACKLE" IN MY FIRST STUDIO PICTURE,
MGM'S *CANNERY ROW*. *COURTESY:*
CARL CIARFALIO PRIVATE COLLECTION.

I HAD THE GREAT PLEASURE OF PLAYING
A NEFARIOUS CLOWN IN *REAL MEN*,
STARRING TWO OF MY FAVORITES, JOHN
RITTER AND JIM BELUSHI. *COURTESY:*
CARL CIARFALIO PRIVATE COLLECTION.

ABOUT TO GET LIT UP BY ELECTRIC EELS IN *LICENSE TO KILL. COURTESY: CARL CIARFALIO PRIVATE COLLECTION.*

PROGRESSION OF A BACK FALL THROUGH A RAILING TO THE GROUND BELOW ON *EXTREME PREJUDICE. COURTESY: CARL CIARFALIO PRIVATE COLLECTION.*

SOME OF THE STUNT CREW FROM *LOCK UP*. FRONT ROW: GENE LEBELL, MATT JOHNSTON, TOM LUPO, BENNIE MOORE, DOC DUHAME, TOMMY HUFF AND PETER BUCOSSI. BACK ROW: JEFF O'HACO, PHIL NEILSON, DANNY EPPER, JEFF WARD, JAY BORYEA, DANNY AIELLO III, MANNY PERRY, REX PIERSON, SYLVESTER STALLONE, REGGIE MCELROY, ANDY DUPPIN, FRANK ORSATTI AND SONNY LANDHAM. *COURTESY: CARL CIARFALIO PRIVATE COLLECTION.*

REHEARSING WITH SYLVESTER STALLONE FOR OUR FIGHT ON *TANGO & CASH*. *COURTESY: CARL CIARFALIO PRIVATE COLLECTION.*

TRYING TO SAVE MYSELF IN *ROBOCOP 2*—IT DIDN'T
WORK. *COURTESY: CARL CIARFALIO PRIVATE COLLECTION.*

A MORTAR EXPLOSION IN *GLORY* SENDS THE UNION SOLDIERS
DROPPING IN ALL DIRECTIONS. I'M FRONT RIGHT IN THIS
SHOT. *COURTESY: CARL CIARFALIO PRIVATE COLLECTION.*

THIS IS HAROLD "HB" BURNS JUST BEFORE HE ATE HIS RIFLE BUTT DURING AN AIR RAM STUNT. *COURTESY: CARL CIARFALIO PRIVATE COLLECTION.*

ON SET WITH SCOTT L. SCHWARTZ, ADAM "BATMAN" WEST, ME, ANTHONY G. SCHMIDT AND IN THE FRONT, BOBBY PORTER. *COURTESY: CARL CIARFALIO PRIVATE COLLECTION.*

JOE PESCI BETWEEN SCENES ON *PUBLIC EYE* SURROUNDED BY ACTOR NAME AND STUNTMEN GEORGE COLLUCI, PETER BUCOSI, ME AND GEORGE FISHER. *COURTESY: CARL CIARFALIO PRIVATE COLLECTION.*

DYING WITH MY EYES OPEN AFTER A MASSACRE ON *PUBLIC EYE*. *COURTESY: CARL CIARFALIO PRIVATE COLLECTION.*

THIS IS WHAT IT LOOKS LIKE WHEN A CAR COMES CRASHING THROUGH A WINDOW AT YOU. THE STUNTMAN ON THE LEFT DIDN'T GET OUT IN TIME. *COURTESY: CARL CIARFALIO PRIVATE COLLECTION.*

BLOWING THROUGH THE WINDOW TO THE WAITING BOXES 12 FEET DOWN. THEN OFF TO THE HOSPITAL TO REPAIR MY GASHED EAR SO I COULD COME BACK AND DO THE 45 FOOT FALL INTO THE WATER FROM A CRANE. *COURTESY: CARL CIARFALIO PRIVATE COLLECTION.*

255

"IT'S CLOBBERIN' TIME" ON THE SET OF *THE FANTASTIC FOUR*. COURTESY: CARL CIARFALIO PRIVATE COLLECTION.

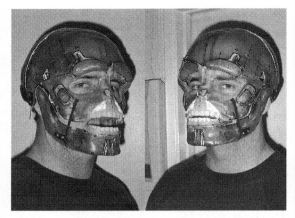

HERE ARE TWO VIEWS OF THE REMOTE CONTROL HEADPIECE I WORE UNDER THE THING MASK. *COURTESY: CARL CIARFALIO PRIVATE COLLECTION.*

MICHAEL BAILEY SMITH (BEN GRIMM) FLEXES HIS MUSCLES. DAMNED IF HIS DON'T OVERSHADOW THE THING'S! *COURTESY: CARL CIARFALIO PRIVATE COLLECTION.*

THIS IS HOW I PICTURE MYSELF MOST OF THE TIME. WHAT, YOU DON'T? *COURTESY: CARL CIARFALIO PRIVATE COLLECTION.*

BEING DRAGGED TO THE 'TABLE OF DEATH' . . . THE BEST IS
YET TO COME. *COURTESY: CARL CIARFALIO PRIVATE COLLECTION.*

HERE IS MY CLASSIC HEAD-
IN-THE-VISE SHOT FROM
*CASINO. COURTESY: CARL
CIARFALIO PRIVATE COLLECTION.*

THIS IS THE SHOT, WITH THE EYEBALL
HANGING ON MY CHEEK, THAT
PROMPTED THE MPAA TO GIVE CASINO
AN NC-17 RATING. THE FOOTAGE WAS
SUBSEQUENTLY DELETED. *COURTESY:
CARL CIARFALIO PRIVATE COLLECTION.*

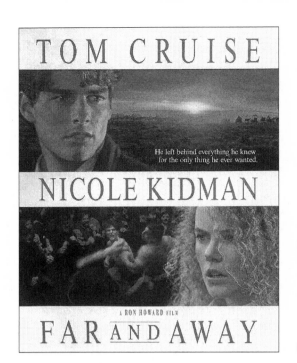

TOM WAS AS GRACIOUS AS HE WAS PROFESSIONAL WITH
EVERYONE ON SET. I WAS VERY FORTUNATE TO HAVE WORKED
WITH HIM. *COURTESY: CARL CIARFALIO PRIVATE COLLECTION.*

CARLO, THE ITALIAN BOXER IN
*FAR AND AWAY. COURTESY: CARL
CIARFALIO PRIVATE COLLECTION.*

WITH TOM AND THE BOXERS FROM *FAR AND AWAY*: JAMES JUDE COURTNEY, ME, CLAY LILLEY, JEFF RAMSEY, TOM, COLE MCKAY, COREY EUBANKS, GARY LEE DAVIS, JOHN CLAY SCOTT (KNEELING). *COURTESY: CARL CIARFALIO PRIVATE COLLECTION.* ©*UNIVERSAL PICTURES.*

WITH FRIENDS, MENTORS AND AT THE TIME, BROTHER SAMP MEMBERS, AT A BOWLING TOURNEY: RANDY FIFE, ALLAN GRAF AND MIKE ADAMS. *COURTESY: CARL CIARFALIO PRIVATE COLLECTION.*

TESTING THE RIGGING WITH COORDINATOR BOB APISA ABOUT 30 FEET ABOVE THE MALL FLOOR. SO GLAD IT HELD! *COURTESY: CARL CIARFALIO PRIVATE COLLECTION.*

ON *MALLRATS*, KEVIN SMITH LIKED TO LAUGH AT HOW MUCH BIGGER I WAS THAN HIM, AND IT WAS A REAL THRILL TO MEET THE LEGEND STAN LEE, A CHARMING AND FUNNY MAN. *COURTESY: CARL CIARFALIO PRIVATE COLLECTION.*

WHAT A GREAT DAY! (FROM WHAT I REMEMBER).
20 YEARS LATER I CAN TELL YOU THAT MARRYING
MY TERI WAS THE SMARTEST THING I HAVE DONE.
COURTESY: CARL CIARFALIO PRIVATE COLLECTION.

SHARING SOME PASTA WITH MY LITTLE ITALIAN GIRL.
COURTESY: CARL CIARFALIO PRIVATE COLLECTION.

AT TIANA'S FIRST BIRTHDAY WITH MY BEAUTIFUL GIRLS!
COURTESY: CARL CIARFALIO PRIVATE COLLECTION.

18 YEARS LATER, TIANA IS READY TO TAKE ON THE
WORLD! *COURTESY: CARL CIARFALIO PRIVATE COLLECTION.*

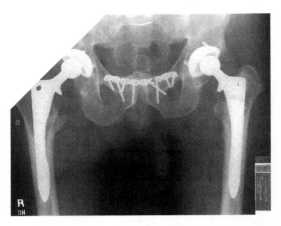

AIRPORT SECURITY CAN BE A CHALLENGE FOR ME. *COURTESY: CARL CIARFALIO PRIVATE COLLECTION.*

THE LEGENDARY HAL NEEDHAM (1931–2013) WITH HIS LIFETIME ACHIEVEMENT AWARD AT THE INAUGURAL TAURUS WORLD STUNT AWARDS. *COURTESY: CARL CIARFALIO PRIVATE COLLECTION. ©TAURUS WORLD STUNT AWARDS.*

ON THE SET OF *BOOK OF ELI* WITH FRIEND AND MENTOR, JEFF IMADA. *COURTESY: CARL CIARFALIO PRIVATE COLLECTION.*

WITH ONE OF MY FAVORITE ACTORS, WOODY HARRELSON, AFTER HE BEAT THE HOLY CRAP OUT OF ME IN *OUT OF THE FURNACE. COURTESY: CARL CIARFALIO PRIVATE COLLECTION.*

EPILOGUE

What I do for a living, this unexpected, exciting, fun and sometimes life-endangering career has given me so much happiness.

In the beginning, I didn't look at the big picture. I wasn't focused on building a career; I just enjoyed myself.

Along the way, even though there were struggles, the job continued to be fun.

Looking back on all of it now, I see a through-line.

Each crash, each fight, and each fall has been part of a journey, leading to the next opportunity to move farther ahead, to rise even higher.

The men and women I've mentioned in this book are just a few of the extraordinary stunt people out there who have done it all. I did a lot, but not all of it. I'm certainly not "stunt legend" status. I'm also aware I'm not famous (outside of my family, that is, and they only think I'm famous when I'm on set with a really big star.) Yes, the title of this book says otherwise, but that's only because "Stars, Stunts and Stories by This Guy" didn't have much of a ring to it.

Who I am is a guy who gives it my all and does every job to the best of his ability. I'm a guy who got involved with his industry and tried to make it better for his brothers and sisters. And an extremely fortunate guy who has been able to take care of his family by bringing unforgettable characters to life, performing memorable stunts and being part of exceptional teams that craft unique stories.

Making movies continues to be a fun and challenging ride for me. As of this writing, I'm dividing my time between stunt coordinating, acting, producing and doing stunts. That's right, stunts. No, I don't do some of the gags I might once have done. But I still love getting in there and making movie magic, whether in front of or behind the camera. I'm still learning today as I work with young directors on independent films and help film students learn to put their vision up on the screen.

Here's the truth. I still enjoy being a face on the screen that causes people to say, "hey, there's that guy." I still enjoy being the guy who creates action that's so entertaining people stay for the credits just to see who did the stunts. I love being part of a team of specialists on a film set. My talent, my art, my soul and my being are what I have to offer to this industry.

So with the continued grace of the universe, and the ongoing support of my family, friends, beloved brothers and sisters in the stunt community and moviemakers not yet met . . . this *Fall to Fame* I am so very grateful for will go on.

Next Setup!

APPENDIX

KICKSTARTER CONTRIBUTORS

You would not be reading this book right now were it not for the generous assistance of old friends and new who supported my endeavor on Kickstarter.com. For their interest and faith and patience and kindness, I am forever indebted to the following individuals—amazing human beings one and all.

Leland Smith

Rick Sawaya

David Morizot

Mary Caldarone

Peewee Piemonte & Julie Michaels

Patty Hogue Soffer

Randy Fife

Kathy Berger

Clint Sunderland

Scott L. Holmes

Janece Grossman

Peggy Kedzior

Nicholas Rheinwald

Pat Moloney

Christine Johnson

Andy Armstrong

Lawrence L. Michel

Pat Millicano

Mike & Tina Hogue

Kevin D'Errico

Deke Anderson & Elsa Ward

Nancy Mosser Casting

Juliette Owens

Michael & Jennifer Caradonna

Gary Schmidt

Ron Sarchian

Janet Embree Art

Steve Cubine

Orna & Koby Azarly

Nancy Thurston

Thom Williams

Myra MacKay

Joel Kramer

Oley Sassone

Mary Karcz

Michael Berger

Linda Cohn

Joni Griess

Jason Benjamin

Dawn Bahr

Allan Karl

Stan Winston School of Character Arts

Viviana Zarragoitia

Mike Tristano

Mark Riccardi

Spice Williams-Crosby

Philip Dido

Marc Shaffer

Clay Van Sickle

Michael Beucler

Missy O'Malley-Reynolds

Ron Lewis

Stepka Li

Jan Cranston

Kerry Carr

Ronda Berkeley

James Harper

Zoli Dora

Denis Yuen

Diana Kelly

Courtney Schwartz

Barbara Rice

Denise (Treon) Findlay

Paul Costanzo

Jonathan Salemi

Cord Walker

Steven Kedzior

Harvey & Linda Walker

Debbie FitzSimmons

Joette Orman

Tracy Smith

Jimmy Lui

Jim Poslof

Diane Waida & Dan Cohen

Brady Romberg

Mark A Wagner

R. Marcos Taylor

Nick Hermz

Cris Thomas Gilbert

Jeff Crawford

Stefan Rollins

Trish December

Brandon Loeser

Keenen Bray

Matt Creeks

Theresa Glenn

Suzanne Sherman

Tara Karsian

Shoshana Michel

Dominick Cancilla

Cheryl Englehart

Brett Miller

Erik Bakken

Steve Bralver

Jean Pierre Romano

Marian Green Hofstein

Marty Langford

Richard Lee Warren

Sheila N. Daniel

Dana Stamos

Ray Sharp

Stephen Hart

Chris Disario

Scotty Richards

Robert Chapin

Birdee Golden

Martin Valinsky

Casey Hendershot

Debbie Guerra

Drew Thomas

INDEX

Adam Arkin 194

Adam West 156

Ainz "Brainz" Prasad 247

Alec Baldwin 186, 217

Alex Daniels 120

Alex Karras 2, 3, 44

Alfie Wise 68

Al Jones 244

Alan Gibbs 17, 244

Allan Graf iv, 34, 56–59, 131, 134, 178, 183, 198, 246, 261

Andy Armstrong ii, 244, 245

Andy Dupin 252

Angelina Jolie 15

Anthony G. Schmidt 253

Anthony Spilotro 159

Arnold Schwarzenegger 108, 130–131, 198, 215, 217

Aurora Joy Caradonna 248

Ben Affleck 193

Ben Bray 233

Bennie Dobbins 130, 132, 133–135, 139

Bennie Moore 252

Ben Vereen 110

Bette Davis 229

Bill Bixby 242

Bill Oliver 24

Bill Murray 142

Billy McCarthy 159

Bing Crosby 107

Black Stuntmen's Association 93

Bob Apisa 262

Bobby Porter 253

Bob Elmore 21

Bob Eubanks 165

Bob Minor 142

Bobo Brazil 12

Brad Pitt xx, 208–210

Brian Munce vi

Brian Williams 135

Brooke Dillman 120

Bruce Boxleitner 54

Bruce Weitz 62

Buck McDancer 30–32

Bud Davis 126, 129

Buddha 11

Burt Reynolds 16, 68, 217

Burt Ward 156

Carlene Ciarfalio Colvin 26–29, 205, 264

Carroll O'Connor 79, 80

Charlie Chaplin 123

Christy Brinkley 95

Christopher Walken 104

Chuck Hicks 82

Chuck Norris xx, 92, 94–96, 117

Claire Forlani 193

Clancy Brown 131, 133

Clarence Gilyard Jr. 93

Clay Lilly 261

Clemenza 185

Clifford Happy 127

Clint Eastwood xx, 238

Cole McKay 167, 261

Conrad Bachmann 95, 107

Conrad Palmisano 85–88

Corey Eubanks 165–168, 261

Cris Thomas Gilbert 202

Dan Aykroyd 194–195

Dane Farwell 154

Daniel Baldwin 201

Danny Aiello 94

Danny Aiello III 94, 252

Danny Epper 252

Darby Hinton 124

Darth Vader 222

Dave Cadiente 70–72, 131

David Ellis 59

David Fincher 208–209

David Hasselhoff 33

Debbie Evans 139–140

Deke Anderson vi, 246

Dendrie Taylor 234

Denzel Washington 142, 176, 227

Deon Taylor 156, 247

Dick Durock 139

Dick Warlock 139

Dietrich Mateschitz 213

Doc Duhame 252

Don Pulford 127

Donald Pleasence 138

Dorian Harewood 69

Doug Coleman 157–159, 163, 176

Douglas Crosby 175–176

Doyle Baker 241

Dr. Herbert Huddleston 211

Dr. Michael Hogue 206

Drew Thomas 229, 231

Ed Harris 186

Ed Zwick 142

Eddie Matthews 90

Eddie Murphy 131

Eddy Donno 102–103

Edward Norton 208–209

Eileen Heckart 69

Eleanor Roosevelt 227

Eliza Coleman 158

Ellie Cornell 138

Eric D. Howell 192

Eric Norris 92–93, 95–96

Eric Roberts 178, 181

Errol Flynn 148

Ethan Suplee 193

Evel Knievel 85

Frank Orsatti 37, 179, 241–242, 252

Frank Sinatra Jr. 124

Frank Vincent 94, 159, 162

Fred Burri 14, 240

Fred Dryer 110

Fred Lerner 67, 138, 244

Gary Davis iii, 2, 44, 53, 63, 244, 248

Gary Jensen 51

Gary Lee Davis 261

Gary Oldman 228

Gary Salisbury v, 20, 241

Gena Norris 96

Gene LeBell i, 179–180, 243–244, 252

Gene Roddenberry 97

George Clooney 198

George P. Wilbur 138

George Willig 77

Georgina Armstrong 222

Gerry Santos 229

Giuseppe "Joe" Menotti 11

Glory Fiormonte 74–76

Gorilla Monsoon 12

Greg Elam 93

Greg Evigan 51

Groucho Marx 49

Hal Needham 68, 108, 217, 265

Harold "H.B." Burns 144–147, 254

Harold E. Rollins Jr. 82–84

Haystacks Calhoun 12

Helena Bonham Carter 208

Homer Simpson 56

Hubie Kerns Jr. 3, 139

Hulk Hogan 253

Ian Quinn 104

Jack Bauer 102

Jack Dempsey 165, 170

Jack Gill 108

Jack Nicholson 16

Jack Verboise 158

James Armstrong 222

James Cameron 108, 217

James Jude Courtney 261

James Naughton 69

James Lew ii, 245, 246

James Woods 178, 181

Jamie Foxx 247

Jared Leto 53

Jason Biggs 217

Jason Lee 193

Jason Statham 108

Jay Borea 252

Jeff Bridges xix, 6, 7, 138, 233

Jeff Imada iii, 200–201, 206, 245, 266

Jeff O'Haco 252

Jeff Ramsey 261

Jeff Ward 252

Jennifer Elizabeth 248

Jennifer Garner xx

Jennifer O'Neill 138

Jennifer Webster 217

Jessica Lange 108

Jim Wilkey 158

Jimmy Haltey 60

Jimmy Ortega 131

Joe Mascolo 99, 119

Joe Pesci 157–162

Joe Pingue 228

Joel Schumacher 198

John Belushi 65

John Candy 21

John Carpenter 182, 200, 202, 204

John Casino v, 21, 23–25, 43, 51, 241

John Clay Scott 165–166, 261

John Cleese 98

John Hammond 240

John Travolta 217

John Wayne … vii, 1, 15

John Wesley Shipp 154

John Woo 217

John-Erik Hexum 138

Jon Auty iii

Jon Cassar 102

Jon Vulage 153

Jonathan Winters 15

JP Romano 247

Julia Roberts 176, 227

Julie Michaels iii, 246

Julie Newmar 156

Juliette Lewis 129, 176

Kate Jackson 54

Katharine Hepburn 23

Katie Holmes 226

KICKSTARTER Contributors 269

Kiefer Sutherland 102–103

Keith David 156

Keenan Wynn 126

Kenny Bates 109

Kevin Pollack 221

Kevin Smith 190–194, 262

Koby Azarly 247

Kurt Russell 21

Laila Ansari 229

Lance Rimmer 23

Lane Leavitt v, 95, 107, 120

Larry Holt 36

Lee Pulford 127

Leonard Nimoy 33

Linda Hamilton 126

Lloyd Bridges 33

Lorenzo Lamas i, 171

Lou Ferrigno i, 37, 68–69, 246, 114

Lucille Menotti Ciarfalio xi, 11–12, 14, 27, 28, 41, 191, 240

Lynette Myers 230

Mr. Freeze 198

Madonna (Davis) Zellitti 53–55

Manny Perry 252

Maria Conchita Alonzo 131

Marian Green-Hofstein 66, 131

Mark Harmon 186

Mark Sikes 154

Martin Scorsese xx, 108, 157, 159, 160–163

Marty Langford 154

Mary Caldarone xviii, 205

Matt Johnston 252

Mic Rodgers 14–16, 18, 19, 252

Michael Bailey Smith 155, 257

Michael Berger 143

Michael Caldarone 205

Michael Caradonna 248

Michael Ironside 131, 133

Michael Keaton 217

Mickey Rooney 35

Mike Adams 99–101, 246, 261

Mike Hill 170

Mike Norris 94

Mike Runyard 208

Mila Kunis 228

Mitch Gellar 217

Monty Cox 74, 75

Nancy Moser 234

"Nature Boy" Buddy Rogers 13

Nick Ciarfalio xi, 28, 41, 69, 71, 79 191, 240

Nick Nolte 130–131

Nicolas Cage 217

Nicole Kidman 164

Nikki Reed 155

Nina Armstrong 222

OJ Simpson 190

Oley Sassone 155

Oliver Stone 176

Olympia Dukakis 244

Optic Nerve 152

Pam Grier 217

Paul Breit 240

Paul Sorvino 247

Paul Stader 32

Peewee Piemonte ii, 246

Peter Bucosi 252

Peter Iacongelo 209

Phil Neilson 175, 177, 252

Philip Seymour Hoffman 223

Pierce Brosnan 185, 235

Powers Boothe 131

Randy Fife vii, 93, 246, 261

Ray Stevenson 228

Rebecca Staab 155

Red Skelton 23

Reggie McElroy 252

Rex Pierson 252

Richard D, Anderson 111

Richard Hancock 90, 158

Rick Aiello 94

Rick Avery 218, 221

Rick Sawaya 65, 90, 131, 158, 247

Rick Springfield 67

Ridley Scott 131

Robert Conrad 242

Robert De Niro 157

Robert Downey Jr. 176

Robert Rodriguez 239

Rod Steiger 178

Roger Corman 193

Roger E. Mosely 142

Ron Howard 168, 238, 259

Ron Kelly 24

Ron Stein 37, 69, 71, 77

Russell Crowe 217

Russell Towery 93

Sandra Bullock 217

Sandy Gimpel iv, 244

Sandy King 204–205

Scott Armstrong 222

Scott Cooper 233–238

Scott Leva 109

Scott L. Schwartz 253

Sean Connery 30, 186

Selma Blair 247

Sendhil Ramamurthy 105

Shane Dixon 2

Sharon Stone 157, 178, 217

Sheryl Lee 202

Sonny Landham 252

Spencer Tracy 99

Spice Williams-Crosby v, 106–108

Stan Lee 193, 262

Steve Hart 221, 247

Steve Urkel 172

Steven Seagal xx, 86, 87

Steven Soderbergh 230

Steven Spielberg 108

Stuntman's Association of Motion
      Pictures ii, 125, 139, 151, 164, 166,
      213, 215, 243–244, 246

Susan Lucci 106

Sylvester Stallone 178–181, 252

Taurus World Stunt Awards 106, 211,
      217, 245, 265

Taylor Hackford 6

Teresa Prindle 217

Teri Ryan Ciarfalio 192, 194–195, 197,
      201, 263, 264

Terry Bradshaw 62

The Beaumont Bear 20

The Joker 218

Thomas Carter 71

Thomas Ian Griffith 202, 206

Tiana Ciarfalio 200, 206, 220, 263–264

Tigger 74, 115

Tim Guinee 206

Timothy Dalton 185, 188–189

Tobey Maguire 94

Todd Hallowell 165

Tom Cruise xx, 164–174, 222–226,
      259–261

Tom Morga 33

Tommy Huff 242, 252

Tom Lupo 252

Tom Selleck 142

Tom Sizemore 175

Tony Sirico 247

Tommy Lee Jones 126–129

Tommy Rosales 131

Treat Williams 170

Tyler Durden 208

Vaia Zaganas vi, 248

Vic Armstrong 109, 222, 224, 244

Vin Diesel 217

Vivian Komari 18

W. C. Fields 51

Walter Hill 130–131, 135–137

Walter Scott 164–166

Walt Kowalski 233

Warren Beatty 211

Wendie Malick 69

Wendy Armstrong 222

Will Smith 129

William Forsythe 148, 186–187

William Shatner 85

Woody Harrelson 129, 175–176, 233,
      234–237, 266

Yakima Canutt vii, 108

WANT MORE CARL?

WWW.STUNTMANBOOK.COM

WWW.CARLCIARFALIO.COM

WWW.IMDB.COM

SPEAKING ENGAGEMENTS | BOOK SIGNINGS | SCRIPT CONSULTING